TRIBE
OF **HACKERS**

TRIBE
OF HACKERS

CYBERSECURITY ADVICE FROM THE
BEST HACKERS IN THE WORLD

MARCUS J. CAREY & JENNIFER JIN

WILEY

Contents

Acknowledgments

Tribe of Hackers would not exist without the awesome cybersecurity community and the contributors in it. I owe them tremendously for allowing me to share their perspective on our industry.

I'd like to give a special shout-out to my wife, Mandy, for allowing me to do whatever the heck I want as far as building a business and being crazy enough to do this stuff. To Erran, Kaley, Chris, Chaya, Justin, Annie, Davian, Kai: I love you all more than the whole world!

I also want to thank Jennifer Jin for helping build the Tribe of Hackers book series and summit. She would like to thank her parents for not thinking that she's crazy for quitting pre-med.

Thanks also goes to Jennifer Aldoretta for helping me build a company that is true to our values. Shout-out to every one of the people I've worked with over the past few years.

Thanks to Dan Mandel, Jim Minatel, and the Wiley team for believing in the whole vision.

—Marcus J. Carey

Introduction

My mind is in a peaceful and reflective mood. I'm nearing the end of my first time away from work in at least three years, most of which has been a blur as I founded my own cybersecurity firm.

I've learned a lot about venture capital, investors, and mentors—as well as what it takes to build a company from just an idea. It's been an amazing journey. My reputation as a white-hat hacker gave me the credibility to get this far, and we're just getting started.

I believe in giving as I go. In other words, instead of waiting until I "make it" to give back to others, I have been trying to mentor everyone I come across along the way. I have always been the type to want to help others, so I mean it when I say you're welcome to email or meet me for guidance about anything. I will always try my best to help.

Over the last year, I've listened to hundreds of hours of audiobooks while going to and from work and while walking my dogs. One of the books that really impressed me was *Tribe of Mentors* by Timothy Ferriss, and it stands as the inspiration for this book's concept. I highly recommend this thought-provoking read on life and business, especially if you're a fan of self-help books or entrepreneurship.

For his book, Ferriss asked famous people from his impressive network 11 questions, and then the magic just happened. For me, this immediately sparked the idea that there should be a cybersecurity version of the book. So, I compiled the most common questions people ask me about cybersecurity and then narrowed it down to the list you are about to see.

In total, I ended up with 14 questions. The questions start with views of cybersecurity at large and then become more personal. I have noticed that when I have conversations at conferences, this is the normal flow. We call these types of conversations "hallway-con," because some of the best learning happens between the scheduled talks and events.

After compiling the questions, I started reaching out to my network of friends and colleagues in the industry and asked them to be part of this book. I was humbled by the response. In total, we ended up with 70 inspiring and thought-provoking interviews with notable hackers—including such luminaries as Lesley Carhart, David Kennedy, and Bruce Potter.

But before we launch into the interviews, let's take a quick look at the questions:

1. If there is one myth that you could debunk in cybersecurity, what would it be?
2. What is one of the biggest bang-for-the-buck actions that an organization can take to improve its cybersecurity posture?
3. How is it that cybersecurity spending is increasing but breaches are still happening?
4. Do you need a college degree or certification to be a cybersecurity professional?

5. How did you get started in the cybersecurity field, and what advice would you give to a beginner pursuing a career in cybersecurity?

6. What is your specialty in cybersecurity, and how can others gain expertise in your specialty?

7. What is your advice for career success when it comes to getting hired, climbing the corporate ladder, or starting a company in cybersecurity?

8. What qualities do you believe all highly successful cybersecurity professionals share?

9. What is the best book or movie that can be used to illustrate cybersecurity challenges?

10. What is your favorite hacker movie?

11. What are your favorite books for motivation, personal development, or enjoyment?

12. What is some practical cybersecurity advice you give to people at home in the age of social media and the Internet of Things?

13. What is a life hack that you'd like to share?

14. What is the biggest mistake you've ever made, and how did you recover from it?

Before we wrap up, a quick note about the book: we edited every interview to improve flow and readability, and in some cases, this meant abbreviating answers or deleting non-responses. You'll also notice that we've included contact information at the beginning of each biography indicating where you can find each hacker on the Web, as well as on social media. We're an engaged and tight-knit group, and we hope you'll join us.

Creating this book has been an amazing journey, and I hope the answers to these questions help guide you along your path.

Marcus J. Carey
CEO Threatcare
January 1, 2018

> "Even if an organization is compromised by a zero-day attack, the lateral movement, registry manipulation, network communications, and so on, will be apparent to a mature cybersecurity practitioner and program."

Twitter: @marcusjcarey • **Website:** https://www.linkedin.com/in/marcuscarey/

Marcus J. Carey

1

Marcus J. Carey is a cybersecurity community advocate and startup founder with more than 25 years of protecting government and commercial sensitive data. He started his cybersecurity career in U.S. Navy cryptology with further service in the National Security Agency (NSA).

If there is one myth that you could debunk in cybersecurity, what would it be?

The biggest myth that I hear is how attackers are always changing up their tactics. While it is true that new exploits come out over time, the initial exploit is just the tip of the iceberg when it comes to attacker movement on a system or network.

Even if an organization is compromised by a zero-day attack, the lateral movement, registry manipulation, network communications, and so on, will be apparent to a mature cybersecurity practitioner and program. So, their tactics don't really change a lot.

What is one of the biggest bang-for-the-buck actions that an organization can take to improve its cybersecurity posture?

The easiest thing an organization can do to prevent massive compromise is to limit administrative accounts on systems. In the military, we obeyed the "least privilege principle" when it came to information access. Organizations should do the same when it comes to their own administrative access. If attackers are able to compromise a user with administrative credentials, it's essentially game-over; they now have all the keys to the castle.

How is it that cybersecurity spending is increasing but breaches are still happening?

Unfortunately, I believe that we are spending too much money on cybersecurity products that bill themselves as silver bullets. Another thing is that there will always be breaches. Anything connected to a network can be compromised and the information pilfered. What really matters is can an organization detect and defend the attacks?

I recommend that organizations get the basics down really well before they blow money on a lot of products. Instead, organizations should hire and train people to defend their networks. In most cases, I've found that there isn't enough investment in the personnel responsible for securing networks.

Do you need a college degree or certification to be a cybersecurity professional?

Years ago, the answer would certainly have been "Yes, you need a college degree." When I was growing up, I was told that I needed to go to college. All of the "successful people" I knew had some form of higher education. Luckily, I went to the military and was able to eventually earn a master's in network security. I still believe I needed it back then and surely do not regret anything.

However, this is 2019, and I do not feel this way anymore. My son has been working as a software developer for a cybersecurity company since he was 16 years old. In technology, especially software development, you can prove your knowledge through blogging, podcasting, and working on open source projects. GitHub is the new résumé for software developers.

I understand that college degrees or certifications are still valid because they show minimal mastery of a subject matter. But nowadays, there are so many more ways to show actual experience. So, in short, my answer to this question is yes, no, maybe, and it depends.

How did you get started in the cybersecurity field, and what advice would you give to a beginner pursuing a career in cybersecurity?

I remember being fascinated by computers ever since I saw the movie *WarGames*. I never had a computer growing up, but I did take a few classes on coding in middle school and high school. Since I couldn't afford to go to college and really wanted to, I joined the U.S. Navy for the Montgomery G.I. Bill.

I scored pretty well on my ASVAB (military aptitude test). At the military processing center, I told them that I didn't care what job I got as long as it had to do with computers. I was told I would be training at a school for cryptologic technical communications. It ended up being awesome. It allowed me to work for the Naval Security Group and the National Security Agency for the first eight years of my adulthood. I learned a lot about cryptography, telecommunications, system administration, basic programming, and internetworking.

The military isn't for everyone, but it definitely helped me. I always tell anyone considering the military route to demand from their recruiter a career field and skills that are applicable to the civilian world.

What is your specialty in cybersecurity, and how can others gain expertise in your specialty?

I'd say my specialty is understanding internetworking really well. I gained these skills while working in the Navy and at the NSA. A big part of gaining expertise in that subject was reading a lot of books and taking several Cisco Systems certifications. After getting the certifications, I was in a better position to practice related skills and gain even more experience.

My advice is to try as hard as you can to validate your knowledge so that others will give you a chance. This is extremely important. Every time I acquired a certification, I was given so many more opportunities. Eventually, I was the first military service member to become part of the NSA's global network engineering team. That was a big deal, and I learned a lot from my time there.

What is your advice for career success when it comes to getting hired, climbing the corporate ladder, or starting a company in cybersecurity?

I'll take a swing at a couple of these. First, my advice for getting hired is to look at job postings and reverse engineer them. Create a résumé that mirrors what they are asking for if you already have the skills. If you don't have the skills, I recommend using your free time to learn those missing skills by reading, using open source software, and consuming any free training you can find. I've found that even if you don't have the necessary degree, years of experience, or certifications, there is still hope. Don't limit yourself and think that you aren't good enough for a job based solely on those requirements. If you believe that you have the skills to do a job, you should always apply.

Starting a company in cybersecurity has been one of the most grueling processes I have ever been through. There are typically two types of companies: those that sell products and those that sell services. On the products side, many of us see opportunities for solutions in our day-to-day lives. Your product must be able to save people time or money and ultimately make them more secure. Once you create that amazing product, you have to be able to sell it.

On the services side, you'll find companies that make money by charging people for their time. Once you have a certain expertise, people may be willing to pay you for your services. The hardest thing about any business is getting sales. The best thing you can do for your company is to partner with an experienced salesperson early on.

I am convinced that sales is the most important part of our professional lives. We have to be able to sell ourselves to get jobs. We have to be able to sell our services or products to build a successful business. In short, learn how to sell, and sell well.

What qualities do you believe all highly successful cybersecurity professionals share?

The most successful people I know in cybersecurity are extremely curious and passionate about sharing information. In my life, I've learned that the people who are most willing to help others are the most knowledgeable. I also think that you can't be afraid to look dumb. Remember, there is no such thing as a stupid question. The most successful people ask the most questions.

What is the best book or movie that can be used to illustrate cybersecurity challenges?

My favorite movie that reminds me of cybersecurity challenges is *U-571*. Although the movie is fictitious, it does have an encryption angle in it because the heroes are trying to steal an Enigma machine from the Germans. There is incident after incident, but despite all the obstacles and everything that happens, the small team of experts is able to overcome each challenge. And that is exactly like cybersecurity.

A really good book I always recommend is *How to Stop Worrying and Start Living* by Dale Carnegie. This book should be on every cybersecurity leader's desk. A great takeaway from the book is learning how to plan for the worst. If you are ready for the worst, you can handle anything that comes your way. This book is a must-read.

What is your favorite hacker movie?

Without a doubt, the Swedish version of *The Girl with the Dragon Tattoo*.

What are your favorite books for motivation, personal development, or enjoyment?

I am fascinated by how our brains and minds work. The following are three books that blew my mind:

On Intelligence by Jeff Hawkins

The Four Agreements by Don Miguel Ruiz

The Fifth Agreement by Don Miguel Ruiz and Don Jose Ruiz

What is some practical cybersecurity advice you give to people at home in the age of social media and the Internet of Things?

Keep your systems up to date. Turn on auto-update on all devices. One more thing, if you don't want your nudes on the internet, don't take them.

What is a life hack that you'd like to share?

Something that I used to complete my higher education that a lot of people don't know about is *credit by examination*. There are several types of these exams, including CLEP, DANTES, and Excelsior College Examinations. This life hack will help a lot of people who are pursuing a college education or who have kids in the United States. Anyone's kids can use this to save their parents college tuition expenses.

Here's how it works: instead of taking a Spanish course, a native speaker can take a CLEP exam for Spanish and receive full credit. Many of these exams are good for three, six, or more semester hours of credit. These exams are cheap, certainly when compared to tuition. A lot of people do not know that these exams even exist.

While I was in the military, I was able to take these exams for free. When I lived on post at Fort Meade, I was able to earn 115 semester hours of credit just by taking these tests. Of course, I had to take the right tests to earn the necessary credits for a degree program, but I was able to get my bachelor of science degree conferred from Excelsior College.

I'd like to note that my case is rare. However, most people could still save thousands of dollars by taking some of these exams. It is totally possible for a college student to save a year on tuition, housing, and so on, by using credit by examination.

What is the biggest mistake you've ever made, and how did you recover from it?

I'm going to share two of my mistakes—one is personal, and one is career related. My biggest personal mistake was not getting over how I was raised, which resulted in me carrying a lot of baggage. I grew up pretty dang rough and blamed a lot of that on family. In the end, they did the best they could, and I ended up doing okay with my life. I recovered by forgiving them and moving forward.

One of the biggest technology mistakes I ever made happened when I was troubleshooting a circuit issue while working as a network engineer at an important place. A common thing to do is to toggle a router interface to make the circuit come back up clean. I don't know why, but this worked a lot.

In this particular case, I shut down the router on the remote side, locking myself out of the router and, therefore, the entire site. This meant that the remote site was disconnected, and since it was about 4,000 miles away, I couldn't reboot the router myself. Luckily, I had a colleague who'd just transferred there about a month before. I was able to call him directly and have him reboot the router. This all happened in less than five minutes—the longest five minutes of my life.

There are many more mistakes I could share, but the lesson I've learned is this: if you aren't making mistakes, you aren't really trying. ∎

"No matter how much you train your users to identify a phishing email or some other attempt to steal credentials, there will be at least one user who is having a bad day and makes a mistake."

Twitter: @ian_infosec • **Website:** medium.com/@ian_infosec

Ian Anderson

Ian Anderson is a security manager focusing on the relationships between information technology and operational technology and how those relationships work to defend industrial control systems. He is also interested in risk and governance and identity management within enterprise environments. Ian is a graduate of the University of Oklahoma and maintains GSLC, GCIH, and CISSP certifications.

2

If there is one myth that you could debunk in cybersecurity, what would it be?

Attackers are human, and as humans, you can conjecture that they are not perfect. Some attackers are good, but they are still human. This may seem trivial, but I believe that when you start to view attackers as human with human goals, you begin to unravel the things that make cybersecurity intimidating. Perfection doesn't exist for defense or offense. That is the way the game is set up. There are steps all attacks must progress through to be successful. This means there are a series of steps where an attacker may make a mistake. As defenders, we need to seize upon these opportunities to detect, respond, and build back our controls to prevent the next attempt. I hope this leads people to feel optimistic—optimistic that our task of securing our systems and networks is an achievable one.

What is one of the biggest bang-for-the-buck actions that an organization can take to improve its cybersecurity posture?

I think the instinct here would be to say "user training." But the rate of return on training isn't good. No matter how much you train your users to identify a phishing email or some other attempt to steal credentials, there will be at least one user who is having a bad day and makes a mistake.

The best bang-for-the-buck action a security team can implement is adopting a framework like the Critical Security Controls or the NIST Cybersecurity Framework. A framework will help you understand your organization's cybersecurity maturity as well as help you plan future initiatives. Something that all of us struggle with is where to spend our limited resources. Frameworks take out a lot of the guesswork and show you, often with supporting evidence, where to apply the pressure. Similarly, planning and implementing a framework can help you understand your operational maturity level and provide metrics that'll feed back into your organization. Security isn't simply one team's job—it is all of our jobs. With that said, security teams need to be the ones to lead the effort to improve the overall capabilities of an organization's security deployment.

How is it that cybersecurity spending is increasing but breaches are still happening?

I think organizational cybersecurity maturity is still fairly low across most organizations. We are spending more money now because cybersecurity hasn't always been a priority. Many organizations have security teams that are relatively new. With a new security team, companies are going to do what companies are going to do—throw money at the problem. So, security budgets increase, and we buy millions of dollars' worth of blinking boxes. At issue is our reliance on security products to save us from our own inability to identify, develop, and utilize human capital to defend against human attackers. The adversary is human...so why aren't we making our humans more capable of defending?

Another issue with being overly reliant on our vendor partners is that we think we can skip over the fundamentals of organizational cybersecurity. "No need for an accurate inventory; I'll just buy this fancy new IDS that is really expensive and uses 'machine learning.'" It's not that these products are bad—they're not—we just aren't ready to use them properly.

Do you need a college degree or certification to be a cybersecurity professional?

Nope, but it helps. There are tons of really talented and qualified cybersecurity professionals out there who have no certifications or degrees. What they likely *do* have is some other sort of professional recognition, such as research, GitHub projects, or something that shows they know their stuff and have contributed to the betterment of the security community.

Admittedly, it is aggravating when you see entry-level security positions opening up that require something like a Security+ or a CISSP. When you see that, it generally indicates that HR doesn't quite understand how security differs from other disciplines. But it is important to consider HR's perspective as well. It's common to gripe about HR and their understanding of security, but it happens in nearly every other field as well. Just ask someone in information technology what it's like hiring a developer, or how about someone in research and development? You'll find that the experience in hiring aligns with many other fields. I'm not demonizing HR at all. HR has to show that they're finding appropriate candidates for the open positions. Having base requirements is part of how they perform their due diligence. Security managers need to develop relationships with hiring teams to ensure the appropriate requirements are identified. Having a strong relationship with HR will only help ensure you're hiring the right person for the job.

How did you get started in the cybersecurity field, and what advice would you give to a beginner pursuing a career in cybersecurity?

I got lucky. Security wasn't nearly as popular as it is today. I was in college and got a job as a student tech. Out of pure luck, I got assigned to the security team. It was a watershed moment in my career and in my life. I was always interested in sneaking around and creating mischief with computers, but never did I think I could get *paid* for it. I had the chance to learn how some pros practiced the art of defense. Really, my job was to help track down students causing problems on the university network. Working in a university security shop gave me the opportunity to see some really clever work as well as some not-so-skilled "bad guys." After graduating, I kept my roots in security, but I made sure to round out the rest of my skill set. I spent time as a developer, system administrator, NOC analyst, and internal auditor. All of these experiences blended together to give me a more complete view of not just security and how it works technically but also how security works as a component of an organization. My advice is this: focusing on security is good, but having a well-rounded skill set will make you a better security professional in the long run.

What is your specialty in cybersecurity, and how can others gain expertise in your specialty?

It used to be application security, but now it's management. I used to be cool. The way I developed security management skills hinged on my ability to find a few security managers and convince them to mentor me. My success in this area is directly tied to the relationships I've built with other managers. None of the things I do are solely my own. I am fortunate to have learned a lot from some of my new friends. I've also been fortunate to have managers who truly cared about my success and who were willing to let me take chances.

The best way to gain expertise is to teach others or speak at conferences. I've gotten to speak at a few large conferences on things that I'm certainly not an expert in, and in preparing for my talks, I probably learned more than just the limited knowledge set required to actually perform the work. This exercise bore much fruit because of the prep time required and the connections it made by forcing me to get up and talk about it. By speaking about a topic, you inevitably talk to people who attended your session, and you'll end up hearing about a unique experience or perspective that furthers your understanding. I highly encourage everyone to go speak (or even blog) once a year about stuff that interests them. It's part of the security community's overall belief that we share our discoveries to make the whole better.

What is your advice for career success when it comes to getting hired, climbing the corporate ladder, or starting a company in cybersecurity?

It all boils down to desire and how hard you are willing to work to put yourself in the right situations. In 2003, during Operation Iraqi Freedom, I was a mechanic in a CH-47 Chinook unit. All I wanted to do was be part of the flight crew. I looked at the group of professionals in the flight suits, and they seemed to have their stuff together. I knew that was the group I belonged with. During the deployment, the mechanics all worked at night, and the missions ran during the day. Almost every day, I would hang around after work and help prep the aircraft for the day's missions. The prep work included cleaning windows, sweeping out the cabin, opening up all the cowlings—all the required work that honestly wasn't a lot of fun. It showed the flight crews that I was serious and was willing to do my part to be a part of the team. From there, I got the chance to fly on some missions when there was a spot open for the day's flight crew. When we got home, a few guys got out, and they were looking for the next generation of flight engineers. Luckily, my number got called, and I got to join the flight platoon. My commitment to my own job, but also the extra effort I put into expanding my role, helped set me apart. And it put me in the position to advance when the opportunity came about. High-performing teams are normally a little selective about who they invite to join the team. If you're in the orbit of one of these teams, there are tons of ways that you can build the relationships that may get you a shot to join them.

For me, success in getting hired and climbing the ranks really depends on two factors. The first factor is to figure out *how to move beyond your work*. What I mean is that managers hire people to help figure out how to solve problems or perform tasks. If you're not working on these two fronts, and doing it in a way that allows the work to be scaled and automated, you may struggle to advance, since you can't really move beyond your work. The second thing is *adaptability*. There's a saying that comes from a great book: "What got you here won't get you there." The lesson is straightforward. To advance, you will have to adjust and adapt. This is the mark of someone who is capable of progressing. Not every organization looks at advancement like this (we've all seen the engineer promoted to management only to struggle), but it's an important concept to grasp.

What qualities do you believe all highly successful cybersecurity professionals share?

Curiosity. Maybe a little bit of a wild streak. Someone foolish enough to think they can when everything in front of them says they can't.

Being a self-starter and having the capability to teach yourself new tricks and techniques are vital skills. A lot of the work going on in tech, and especially cybersecurity, is innovating new ways to meet current and future challenges.

I would also say compassion. Compassion because the things that we help protect people against can have direct and devastating effects on people's lives. How we defend also matters. If you go into an enterprise and just start laying down the "cyber law," you're going to have a bad time. Compassion for how others work and what their goals are helps you craft an effective security posture rather than just the black-and-white security model.

What is the best book or movie that can be used to illustrate cybersecurity challenges?

The gold standard these days has to be *Mr. Robot*. I think it's a little heavy on some of the plot lines, but the hacking they do is dead-on. I knew from the first episode when Elliot was hacking into a guy's social media account that this was a different model. The show portrayed how Elliot called the target, got him to respond to questions because of the urgency that his account was "under attack," and, in doing so, gave Elliot information he needed to compromise other accounts.

What is your favorite hacker movie?

Hackers. The over-the-top antics and nods to counterculture endear it to me. A close second is *WarGames*. I love how the whole movie stems from a kid messing around war dialing and seeing what he can get into.

Believe it or not, this was more realistic than most care to believe. Honorable mentions include *Antitrust* and *Swordfish* for me, although they aren't nearly as good as *Hackers* or *WarGames*. Hack the Planet!

What are your favorite books for motivation, personal development, or enjoyment?

I got a lot out of *The Tipping Point*, *Blink*, and *Outliers* by Malcolm Gladwell. These books helped me understand how to get my ideas to reach critical mass, how decisions are made, and what I can do to improve my chances of success by taking a scientific approach. I'm also a big fan of the *Freakonomics* books because, as an InfoSec professional, I think it's fun to see how things relate to each other even when there is seemingly no logical connection.

What is some practical cybersecurity advice you give to people at home in the age of social media and the Internet of Things?

First things first, desynchronize your passwords! That's the number-one thing you can do. Use a password manager to maintain separate and complex passwords across all your accounts. This is the biggest bang-for-your-buck you can have in terms of home security. If a site offers two-factor authentication, go ahead and activate it. There's a great resource at Twofactorauth.org that can help you find the systems that support two-factor authentication and show you how to activate the service. Just the other day, a loved one told me that they'd received notification that there was a failed login from a different country. They immediately changed their password but didn't know for sure whether the attacker got into their account. In this scenario, the detect and response parts worked great, but what we are really after is *prevention*. Multifactor authentication is a must.

What is a life hack that you'd like to share?

It starts with you. Take care of yourself. Your health and your happiness are force multipliers. If you feel good and are happy, there is no limit to what you can accomplish. Be sure to take the time to pursue passion projects as well. Passion projects keep that fire burning inside of you and lead to professional growth. If all you do is go to work, cruise through incident alerts, and then go home, you are prone to burnout. Take a few hours a week to research or play with a VM lab or something. Whatever it is, do something you *want* to do. Even as a manager, I keep a copy of Kali and other VMs on my laptop to play around with. This isn't a part of my job anymore, but it makes me happy to tool around with attack tools and helps me better relate to our engineering teams.

What is the biggest mistake you've ever made, and how did you recover from it?

The biggest mistake I ever made was believing the mark of success was tied to money. This had a destructive effect on my career as I began pursuing opportunities only because of the potential payoff and not because I believed in the work, the company, or about my own happiness. My recovery began by being laid off.

Coincidentally, I also found out around this time that I was going to be a father. I had much more to care about than just making money or advancing up the career ladder at this point. I had a small person who would soon depend on me to provide food, shelter, protection, and love. I couldn't offer these things by solely focusing on the next promotion or the next raise. Ultimately, I wanted to focus on being happy and creating a happy home for my family, and the funniest thing happened...I began to enjoy an incredible professional renaissance and experience success at a level I never knew was possible. My biggest mistake was not realizing what was really important. The universe helped correct this by offering me a chance out of a dead-end job and a family to focus my attention on. My path isn't for everyone, but it's important that you find what makes you happy and what matters to you. When you're fulfilled, success tends to follow. ■

"The breaches are not a result of higher spending; the higher spending is a result of the breaches. It goes to show that the world is far from ready to handle breaches and most organizations are very likely underspending—increasing their risk in order to reduce cost."

Twitter: @abagrin • **Website:** www.linkedin.com/in/abagrin

Andrew Bagrin

3

Andrew Bagrin is the founder and chief executive officer of OmniNet, a leading provider of firewall as a service (FWaaS) for small businesses. With more than 20 years of experience in the IT security industry, Andrew started OmniNet in 2013 to bring cloud-based, enterprise-level security technology to small businesses at an affordable price. Prior to founding OmniNet, Andrew served as the director of service provider business development at Fortinet, a network security provider. A network security expert, Andrew has been quoted in a variety of media outlets, including the *New York Times*, *Bloomberg Businessweek*, *Small Business Computing*, *Columbia Business Law Review*, and *Business Solutions Magazine*.

If there is one myth that you could debunk in cybersecurity, what would it be?

Focusing on the small and midsize business (SMB) arena for the last five years, my answer is geared toward that world. I often see and hear that people in the IT world believe that "we are secure because we use Product X." In a way, the CySec blue-team vendors are responsible for this dangerous mind-set because they've inflated the scope and capability of their products to make sales. They also minimize the effort it takes to properly set up each system in an organization. The myth of "being secure" has long been debunked in the larger enterprise for the most part. Security is not a red or blue pill, and there is no absolute security. Security is a business decision to reduce or mitigate the risk posed by the cybercrime world at large, and this is accomplished by balancing the different aspects of defending your organization according to the organization's risk tolerance and profile.

The truth is, there is no amount of security, systems, protection, or processes you can put in place to be 100 percent secure. The only way to prevent death is to already be dead; otherwise, there is always a risk of being killed. One hundred percent security is a myth.

What is one of the biggest bang-for-the-buck actions that an organization can take to improve its cybersecurity posture?

This really depends on the type of organization in question, but there are several industry-based frameworks and guidelines to help. Some examples are PCI and HIPAA, which are extensive, but they do have requirements that are specific to each organization. There is also the NIST framework—that's more of a general framework for all business types. If you want to have the best bang for the buck, leverage the systems you already have properly. Don't ignore obvious big problems.

> "If you want to have the best bang for the buck, leverage the systems you already have properly. Don't ignore obvious big problems."

A basic security foundation should include three things:

- *Process/procedure*: Authentication, data management, access control, and so on
- *Network security*: UTM/NGFW
- *Endpoint security*: EDR or at least some protection from downloads/attacks, and so on

Once you have these three items in place, work on tweaking and tuning them so they provide maximum effectiveness and proper information.

How is it that cybersecurity spending is increasing but breaches are still happening?

The breaches are not a result of higher spending; the higher spending is a result of the breaches. It goes to show that the world is far from ready to handle breaches and most organizations are very likely underspending—increasing their risk to reduce cost.

Unfortunately, when that strategy didn't pan out, the organizations started increasing their cybersecurity spending. The other big contributor is the rapid increase in technology. Where there is new technology, there will be vulnerabilities and more security required to protect those new technologies.

Do you need a college degree or certification to be a cybersecurity professional?

I sure hope not.... Some of the best cybersecurity professionals I know don't have any degrees or certificates; however, education is always a good thing and does help. I would never discourage someone from getting a degree or certificate,

> "Some of the best cybersecurity professionals I know don't have any degrees or certificates; however, education is always a good thing and does help."

but I would also not discourage anyone from getting into CySec without a degree or cert.

How did you get started in the cybersecurity field, and what advice would you give to a beginner pursuing a career in cybersecurity?
I got into it from the networking side of things and the firewall world. Later, I became a pentester and then got back to the blue side for most of my career.

At the time, I was the youngest and newest member of a team and got all the stuff no one knew or wanted to work on. Firewalls was one of those.

What is your specialty in cybersecurity, and how can others gain expertise in your specialty?
My specialties are network architecture and network security architecture, as well as how network security is implemented in a managed service environment. To gain experience, you just need to continue to do, learn, and get better. Before trying to get into security, you should understand networking in general. If you don't understand what a packet looks like throughout its life, it will be really hard to fully understand network security.

> "Always continue to learn and stay on top of what's going on. The CySec world advances quickly, and it's easy to be left behind if you don't stay in tune with that world."

What is your advice for career success when it comes to getting hired, climbing the corporate ladder, or starting a company in cybersecurity?
Always continue to learn and stay on top of what's going on. The CySec world advances quickly, and it's easy to be left behind if you don't stay in tune with that world. The rest of the success comes from human interaction, which is sometimes the hardest thing for CySec technical people. Just be a respectful human being; the industry is small, and you don't want to burn bridges.

What qualities do you believe all highly successful cybersecurity professionals share?
Most successful people I know in CySec have a desire to always learn more and discuss what they find or learn. Since the industry changes so quickly, you need to be able to learn what's changing, discuss that with peers, and articulate it to non-CySec people in a way that will make sense to them.

What is the best book or movie that can be used to illustrate cybersecurity challenges?
I can't really think of any movies that excite me on hacking and its challenges; usually they just provoke embarrassment when they try to say something technical. There are lots of great hacking books. One of the first I read was *Hacking Exposed*, which gave a great overview of the basics of hacking and how it all works. Maybe one day we'll make an entertaining movie that is technically correct as well.

What is your favorite hacker movie?
I would have to say *Swordfish*, mainly for its entertainment quality and for portraying a hacker as something other than a geeky little kid. I also like the old *Hackers* movie since it was one of the originals.

What are your favorite books for motivation, personal development, or enjoyment?
I read fewer books since I got hooked on The Great Courses Plus. I try to get through a lecture series in a month (sometimes two months) and gain real knowledge about things that I find fascinating. Learning new, interesting things is something I've always enjoyed doing.

What is some practical cybersecurity advice you give to people at home in the age of social media and the Internet of Things?
Don't use the same login in multiple places. Always change your password, even if by one character. Add the letters *PP* to your PayPal password or *BoA* to your Bank of America password. It will at least change the hash; this way, if your LinkedIn or Adobe credentials get compromised, you don't have to change your password in 100 other places.

> "Don't use the same login in multiple places. Always change your password, even if by one character."

What is a life hack that you'd like to share?
To avoid making a bad decision that I would regret in the future, I visualize myself as my future self giving my present self advice. We always say things like, "I shouldn't have eaten the whole tub of ice cream." As your future self, you're more disconnected from the immediate gratification and more in tune with longer-term, higher rewards. The more you practice this, the better you become at it. Successful people have the ability to postpone gratification.

> "To avoid making a bad decision that I would regret in the future, I visualize myself as my future self giving my present self advice."

What is the biggest mistake you've ever made, and how did you recover from it?
I once started an advertising company but knew little about advertising, the industry, or anything about it. I set up the entire system technically and got things working. Luckily, the largest part of my investment was in the technical part, and I was able to sell the majority of it without too big of a loss. It was an important lesson that taught me to do my research before jumping in and spending large amounts of money. ∎

"You have to learn to balance the technical stewardship of "securing all the things" with understanding the motivations and drivers of the business, and you have to figure out how to get everyone to take ownership of the security of their products and systems."

Twitter: @zate • **Website:** blog.zate.org

Zate Berg

4

Currently employed as a security leader, Zate Berg has knowledge in a wide variety of technologies and prides himself on being able to quickly spot security problem areas and recommend corrective action. He is especially interested in application security, vulnerability management, network security monitoring, and penetration testing. Zate enjoys the challenge of pushing the limits of existing technologies, mastering new technologies quickly, and solving the hardest problems. He seeks to challenge himself in everything he does—building relationships through teaming, coaching, and the sharing of ideas—and does so in a manner that builds integrity and trust.

If there is one myth that you could debunk in cybersecurity, what would it be?

That free tools and free software are free. Often, they are not. "Free" means you need expertise (in systems that are often poorly documented), you need more people to manage it, and it will take longer. When working out the cost, factor in the cost of *time to value* (how long it takes before it's doing what you need), the cost to learn it, and the cost in terms of hardware and people to make it work. There's no such thing as "free"; it always costs you something.

What is one of the biggest bang-for-the-buck actions that an organization can take to improve its cybersecurity posture?

Ingest and monitor your DNS logs. Seriously, set up some kind of free repo (repository) for them (ELK, etc.). Route these logs into the repo you've created, and start looking. It's a gold mine of what your systems are doing, who is talking to what, when, and so on. A step above that is something like Bro IDS on egress traffic to allow you to examine metadata about the actual connections. If you're good on those, educate your users; get them using a password manager. All of this is foundational, but it's the foundational things that most places are bad about and that most attacks take advantage of.

How is it that cybersecurity spending is increasing but breaches are still happening?

Most companies still see cybersecurity as something their cybersecurity team does. The people who build things, administer things, and run the business are not making security part of their job, and they're expecting their underfunded, understaffed, overworked security teams to secure everything—but without impacting the business. The business itself needs to take cybersecurity seriously, not just write some policy, give the cybersecurity team a budget for some people and tools, and then let them go. Security needs to be an important part of business decisions, just like any other risk is. If your business leaders are weighing all the risks associated with the business but they're not taking enough interest in the cybersecurity risks, there will be significant gaps.

> "The business itself needs to take cybersecurity seriously, not just write some policy, give the cybersecurity team a budget for some people and tools, and then let them go. Security needs to be an important part of business decisions, just like any other risk is."

Do you need a college degree or certification to be a cybersecurity professional?

No. I have no degree, and I've let my CISSP lapse. Degrees and certs are good for baseline knowledge, but our industry moves very fast, and if you're not constantly learning both inside and outside of work, you will lag behind. When I'm interviewing interns or people right out of college, I look over what field their degrees are in, but I don't really care. What I care about is do they have enough passion for this field to do the real learning outside of their school time? Do they have a home lab, a GitHub? Are they up on the latest things happening in security? I'll take a mechanic with no experience who has taught themselves enough to get their foot in the door over a college grad with no outside passion who's just done the course material.

I don't need people who know the answer; I need people who will recognize the answer when they see it. The answers are always changing, same as the questions, so you have to be able to move and adapt your learning.

How did you get started in the cybersecurity field, and what advice would you give to a beginner pursuing a career in cybersecurity?

I got started in the Australian Army doing basic IT-related things—setting up servers, building networks out in the field, and connecting them over satellites. It wasn't until a few years later, when I was working as a Solaris Unix admin for PwC, that I got the break into cybersecurity. I was always pushing for security on our Unix systems (and the few Linux systems I managed to sneak in).

Throughout my career, since the Army, I have always been security conscious. Whether it was proving why we needed to restrict LotusScript in Lotus Notes emails—by writing a script bomb that was sent to everyone on the email when it was opened/read/deleted—or by pushing hard for getting our Unix systems to be patched quarterly, I was generally the squeaky security wheel. Eventually, I was "encouraged" to interview with the security team at PwC US IT in Tampa and was given a book to study overnight (*The 19 Deadly Sins of Software Security*). I guess I passed because I transitioned to the US IT Security team and did threat and vulnerability management (TVM) and application security (AppSec) on internal applications and systems.

What is your specialty in cybersecurity, and how can others gain expertise in your specialty?

I guess my specialty now is building security programs and security teams for companies that lack one or the other (or both). In the past, it's been either TVM or AppSec, depending on the company, and I did a bit of game security for online games—which it turned out I was good at.

So, getting into security management has been interesting. It's a whole new ball game; you start to realize that all of our issues in security are people problems. Tech isn't hard, process isn't hard; we can do those. It's people that are difficult.

So, learn how to deal with people. Learn what makes the people around you tick, what motivates them, what is important to them. In security leadership, you will be negotiating with either your team, your peers, or your leadership over a great many things. You have to learn to balance the technical stewardship of "securing all the things" with understanding the motivations and drivers of the business, and you have to figure out how to get everyone to take ownership of the security of their products and systems. It's a constant cycle of negotiation and influencing others, often without being in the right place in the organization or having the right resources. So pay attention to the people around you, above you, and below you.

> "Tech isn't hard, process isn't hard; we can do those. It's people that are difficult."

What is your advice for career success when it comes to getting hired, climbing the corporate ladder, or starting a company in cybersecurity?

Be passionate about security and learn everything. Listen to others around you and get invested in what your company does. Understand the business side deeply, and learn how to express security concepts in ways businesspeople understand. It can be hard to translate some things, but businesspeople understand risk, just often not cybersecurity risk. At the end of the day, though, if you can articulate risk in terms of impact to things that are important for the business, you are most of the way toward getting them to understand your world.

What qualities do you believe all highly successful cybersecurity professionals share?

Passion. Curiosity. An ability to learn. A solid grasp of the foundations of technology. That last one is hard for some people, but if you have it, adopting new things is not as difficult because, under the covers, things in the digital world—just like those in the physical world—have a set of "laws" that need to operate in a certain way. And if you can understand those laws, you can understand how new things relate to existing things and then adapt your process and thoughts to new things.

What is the best book or movie that can be used to illustrate cybersecurity challenges?

Probably *The Phoenix Project*, but I'm not that security guy. The security guy in the book learns and changes a great deal, adapting to do better at supporting his business.

What is your favorite hacker movie?

The original *TRON* or *WarGames*. I'm an '80s/'90s child.

> "Be passionate about security and learn everything. Listen to others around you and get invested in what your company does. Understand the business side deeply, and learn how to express security concepts in ways businesspeople understand."

What are your favorite books for motivation, personal development, or enjoyment?

Ready Player One is awesome. I also reread the entire David Eddings series every year (all 16 books of all four series). For personal development, I highly recommend *The Subtle Art of Not Giving a Fuck*, because, in our line of work, accepting too much blame/responsibility causes lots of stress, and that leads to being sick.

What is some practical cybersecurity advice you give to people at home in the age of social media and the Internet of Things?

Use a password manager, patch your devices, and run some kind of basic antivirus—either what the OS has or something you and others trust. In this day and age, if you want to have the benefits of our connected lifestyle, you are going to have to give up some of your information and privacy. That is the currency of "free things." Just make sure you know what, and how much, these free things cost you. ∎

> "Use a password manager, patch your devices, and run some kind of basic antivirus—either what the OS has or something you and others trust. In this day and age, if you want to have the benefits of our connected lifestyle, you are going to have to give up some of your information and privacy."

"Attackers are the problem—as are ignorance, complacency, and convenience. Hackers are problem-solvers, troubleshooters, and among the best people I know."

Twitter: @3ncr1pt3d • **Websites:** whitehatcheryl.wordpress.com and www.linkedin.com/in/cherylbiswas

Cheryl Biswas

5

Cheryl Biswas loves being a threat intel analyst with TD Bank in Canada and assessing threat actors, vulnerabilities, and exploits. She is a political science graduate, is ITIL certified, and took the long way to InfoSec. She actively shares her passion for security online as a speaker, volunteers at conferences, and champions diversity as a founding member of The Diana Initiative.

If there is one myth that you could debunk in cybersecurity, what would it be?

That hackers are the "bad guys." Attackers are the problem—as are ignorance, complacency, and convenience. Hackers are problem-solvers, troubleshooters, and among the best people I know. Their curiosity and determination have often been misunderstood, fabricating a detrimental stereotype. In this community of learning and mentoring, hackers share what they know and encourage others to try, creating a welcoming space for many people who don't feel they belong anywhere. They dare to probe and poke holes in digital frameworks, to ask the questions big corporations want ignored, and to uncover the truth about how secure we really are.

What is one of the biggest bang-for-the-buck actions that an organization can take to improve its cybersecurity posture?

Asset management. Do you know what you have, what you value most and why, and where it is right now? You can't protect it if you can't find it. Likewise, you can't secure what you don't know, and as BYOD has become commonplace, infection by ignorance should not become an unavoidable risk.

How is it that cybersecurity spending is increasing but breaches are still happening?

There are so many more devices that connect. And there is so much data already out there to be reused by criminals for fraud. It's a numbers game, and we are on the losing side. No shiny, blinking boxes are going to protect us from an army of SOHO routers with default passwords that get co-opted into massive botnets. AI can't help us authenticate against the voluminous growth of stolen credentials available from dumps and on the dark web.

Do you need a college degree or certification to be a cybersecurity professional?

I will say no, especially since I do not have a degree in technology or a cybersecurity certification at this time. Rather, my degree in political science has been useful because I do threat intel, and understanding international relations is a key component.

What really matters is a passion for your field, a curiosity that drives you to learn, and the commitment to continue to learn and grow as technology and threats do. Can you communicate effectively, ask questions to get the answers you seek, and collaborate with others to build effective solutions? Because that's what's important.

> "What really matters is a passion for your field, a curiosity that drives you to learn, and the commitment to continue to learn and grow as technology and threats do."

How did you get started in the cybersecurity field, and what advice would you give to a beginner pursuing a career in cybersecurity?

I had returned to work after being away raising my kids for 10 years. I took what I could get—an admin role with a small managed services firm. I remember reading the Kaspersky newsletter, learning about Stuxnet, and falling in love. When I was given the Twitter account to manage, I fell down a rabbit hole of wonder and learning, and I've never left. I read everything, followed links to learn more, and met people who sincerely encouraged my interest and shared their experience. Eventually, I began submitting talks to conferences, writing blog posts, and developing the security role where I worked. A friend asked me for my résumé, and I was hired at a large company in an actual security role. My advice: follow your passion and do not let others tell you what you can't do.

Listen, learn, and find ways to build your opportunities through writing, volunteering, or speaking.

What is your specialty in cybersecurity, and how can others gain expertise in your specialty?

My specialty is threat intelligence. I am fascinated by how nations interact, what lengths they are willing to go to in order to further their agendas, and how tensions influence

> "I am fascinated by how nations interact, what lengths they are willing to go to in order to further their agendas, and how tensions influence economies and our daily lives."

economies and our daily lives. Sunday morning news shows and a pot of coffee are my weekend treat. But threat intelligence is so much more, and I have made a consistent effort to read and learn all I can from experts in our community who share their knowledge and insight. Start by reading. Twitter is a wealth of information with wonderful threads and blogs. Google what you are interested in and see where it takes you. Ask people who do what you are interested in to tell you about it and how they got there. Find something, research it, and then share a blog post or white paper or give a talk; these are all great starting points.

> "My specialty is threat intelligence. I am fascinated by how nations interact, what lengths they are willing to go to in order to further their agendas, and how tensions influence economies and our daily lives."

What is your advice for career success when it comes to getting hired, climbing the corporate ladder, or starting a company in cybersecurity?

Learn from everyone, be humble, and listen with your mouth closed. Have projects to show how you are learning on your own and what you can do: blogs, conferences, mentoring, writing, your own labs, makerspaces, building badges. Confidence is important, so believe in yourself and that you have a contribution to make, because you will be told "no," and that is hard to hear. Don't let that stop you. Believe in your passion and the abilities that led you here, because there are not a lot of people who do what we do.

As your career progresses, treat everyone with respect. Always take the time to say thank you and to remember what someone may have done for you. You'll be glad you did.

> "Confidence is important, so believe in yourself and that you have a contribution to make because you will be told "no," and that is hard to hear."

What qualities do you believe all highly successful cybersecurity professionals share?

The qualities I've seen consistently are curiosity, passion, focus, drive, and determination. These people are also respectful of others, willing to share what they know, and able to communicate what they know and need. They give back and help build the community.

What is the best book or movie that can be used to illustrate cybersecurity challenges?

I really liked *The Cuckoo's Egg* by Clifford Stoll. It's an engaging mystery that introduces many security basics as the tale unfolds. You're drawn into the "everyman" vantage point. I devoured *Countdown to Zero Day* by Kim Zetter. This is the story of Stuxnet, but it reads like a political thriller, presenting countless twists, the lengths to which nation-states will go for control against the backdrop of nuclear weapons. I still reread certain parts.

What is your favorite hacker movie?
Sneakers! It was so ahead of its time, with a terrific cast.

What are your favorite books for motivation, personal development, or enjoyment?
Women in Tech by Tarah Wheeler and all—to be inspired and encouraged by wonderful role models. *Defensive Security Handbook* by Amanda Berlin and Lee Brotherston because a great defensive stance is key. Tom Clancy and Michael Crichton novels (*Jurassic Park* mixed dinos with computers!).

What is some practical cybersecurity advice you give to people at home in the age of social media and the Internet of Things?
Check and change your default sign-ons. Do not feel obligated to have everything connected. Free Wi-Fi comes with hidden costs, so use a VPN. Use Malwarebytes and an antivirus on your personal computer to guard against online threats.

> "Do not feel obligated to have everything connected. Free Wi-Fi comes with hidden costs, so use a VPN."

What is a life hack that you'd like to share?
Smile. It makes you feel better when you do, and it helps people feel welcome and at ease. A smile opens doors and opportunities. It's something that is uniquely ours to give, a simple act that has great meaning. We don't always feel like smiling, but that can be when you need to do it most to create a "mind over matter" moment.

What is the biggest mistake you've ever made, and how did you recover from it?
One of my biggest mistakes was believing I was not capable of learning math or computer science when somebody important told me I was not good enough. I was struggling because I learned differently than everyone else. So, I focused on my strengths: communications and arts. Thankfully, that changed when I was working as an admin/receptionist, and I happily volunteered to take apart and upgrade my boss's computer because that was way more interesting. I also learned all the new software, the database package, all the challenging tech stuff that scared people off. Plus, I taught the people who were afraid of tech how to do stuff and helped them feel confident to do more. That led to a backdoor into a terrific help-desk role. I use this lesson to help people every chance I get. ■

> "One of my biggest mistakes was believing I was not capable of learning math or computer science when somebody important told me I was not good enough."

> "Whatever work was not being done, I always viewed that as opportunities, regardless of role or title."

Twitter: @KeirstenBrager • **Website:** www.keirstenbrager.tech

Keirsten Brager

6

Keirsten Brager is a lead security engineer at a Fortune 500 power utility company and was recently named one of Dark Reading's "Top Women in Security Quietly Changing the Game." She is also the author of *Secure the InfoSec Bag: Six-Figure Career Guide for Women in Security*. She produced this guide to empower women with the strategies needed to maximize their earning potential. Keirsten holds an MS in cybersecurity from UMUC and several industry certifications, including Splunk, CISSP, CASP, and Security+. As an active member of the Houston security community, she has participated in a number of panels and public speaking engagements, promoting strategies for success. In her free time, she loves sharing career advice on her blog, cooking New Orleans food, and convincing women not to quit the industry.

If there is one myth that you could debunk in cybersecurity, what would it be?

The biggest myth is that we are one technical solution away from solving all of the industry's problems.

Every year, vendors are touting next-generation shiny objects that will automate all the things, reduce head count, and keep the hackers at bay. Meanwhile, organizations are understaffed with partially implemented tools while investors cash out and go on to the next hot technology. Brian Krebs reports the next breach; we all Kanye shrug. It's a vicious cycle.

What is one of the biggest bang-for-the-buck actions that an organization can take to improve its cybersecurity posture?
Empower the sysadmin to implement the secure configuration settings available natively via GPO settings, especially around administrative privileges. This limits the actions authorized or unauthorized users can take without additional tools or costs to the business.

How is it that cybersecurity spending is increasing but breaches are still happening?
Is the spending increasing? Or are we witnessing companies that never (or barely) invested in security finally allocating money for this function? That's a conversation no one wants to have.

Many companies are operating in deep technical debt, running legacy applications and systems that cannot be secured. The need to appease stock analysts and shareholders has historically influenced decisions around product time to market, using cheap foreign labor for development, and running "lean" IT shops. As a result, security is an afterthought or not a thought at all. The retail industry is notorious for this.

Moreover, when companies do get money to invest, they want to skip the basics and either go for the shiny toys or perform "reduce the scope to check the compliance box" security programs. All of this leads to gaps in posture. Therefore, the people, process, and technology fail...leading to continued breaches.

Do you need a college degree or certification to be a cybersecurity professional?
There are many people who found success in the industry without degrees or certifications. However, I encourage people, especially members of minority groups, to pursue credentials as a way to open doors to leadership opportunities and multiple sources of income in this industry. Do not disqualify yourself or give anyone an excuse not to give you more money and power.

How did you get started in the cybersecurity field, and what advice would you give to a beginner pursuing a career in cybersecurity?
I did the work no one else would do. Technical people tend to like tools, but they do not always like creating/maintaining documentation, interacting with auditors, and working in cross-functional capacities that involve dealing with people. I happen to be technical and a people person, so I took on projects that required both.

I identified security deficiencies and implemented technical solutions. If policies or procedures did not exist, I wrote them. When awareness training was not being delivered, I researched best practices and created web-based training. If no one wanted to lead audits, I raised my hand. When monitoring was deficient, I deployed an IDS and SIEM. Whatever work was not being done, I always viewed that as opportunities, regardless of role or title.

Here's my advice for newbies:

- Don't be too proud to apply for tech support or sysadmin roles to get your foot in the door.

- If you are a member of a minority group, connect with people in other minority groups in the industry. All experiences are not created equal, so it is important for you to connect with people who can help you navigate certain issues that others will not acknowledge, understand, or care about.

- Relationships are key: give back to the security community before you need a job.

- Publish research, projects, and/or problems you've solved on LinkedIn, established blogs, or your own blog.
- Volunteer at tech user groups, chapter meetings, and conferences.
- Analyze local supply and demand to identify specific talent shortages in your region and "skill up."
- Understand the business side of security.
- Be nice, share knowledge, and send the ladder back down when you succeed.

What is your specialty in cybersecurity, and how can others gain expertise in your specialty?

I specialize in deploying and maintaining advanced monitoring solutions to maintain secure configurations, support incident response efforts, reduce risk, increase automation, and comply with regulatory requirements.

You gain competence and confidence with dedication to your craft. You do not have to wait for invitations to teach yourself anything in the age of the internet. Many companies have free versions of their products on their websites. If you have an opportunity to work for a product company like Splunk or Tripwire, both are inclusive companies that provide pathways into careers in some of the largest organizations in the world. Those are just examples. Working directly for the product companies is one of the best ways to gain the technical skills needed to build expertise in this area.

Working in sysadmin, tech support, and compliance roles can also prepare you for this specialty. It really requires someone well rounded to be successful. The industry loves to glorify tech skills (and they are important), but people skills are a huge asset.

What is your advice for career success when it comes to getting hired, climbing the corporate ladder, or starting a company in cybersecurity?

- Always negotiate total compensation, not just base pay.
- Be so good at what you do that people cannot ignore you.
- Create SMART goals to drive your career.
- Your career plan is not a one-time exercise.
- Have a results-oriented résumé.
- Your network determines your net worth. If you're part of an underestimated group, your journey will likely be filled with obstacles that others may not face. You will also have to put in extra work to gain access to opportunities. Do the work, network, and find mentors.
- Control Google results about yourself with an online portfolio.
- Dress for the job you want, not the one you have.
- Some jobs are just chapters in your career; close them when necessary.

What qualities do you believe all highly successful cybersecurity professionals share?

Being highly successful is subjective. Some people define success by the number of social media followers. Others define it by industry fame. I lean toward defining success by using influence to make a positive social impact. People who do that share a common character trait of wanting to empower others. They also lead with empathy.

We need to elevate these influencers and stop worshiping the people who exhibit toxic behaviors.

What is the best book or movie that can be used to illustrate cybersecurity challenges?

Geostorm is a movie about, network-controlled government satellites built to control the climate, but greed is involved. What could go wrong?

What is your favorite hacker movie?

BlacKkKlansman, a movie based on a true story about the first African American detective to serve in the Colorado Springs Police Department. Soon after joining, he went undercover and infiltrated the KKK.

What are your favorite books for motivation, personal development, or enjoyment?

- *Becoming* by Michelle Obama
- *How Exceptional Black Women Lead by Keirsten Brager*
- *Secure the InfoSec Bag: Six-Figure Career Guide for Women*

What is some practical cybersecurity advice you give to people at home in the age of social media and the Internet of Things?

- Use a password manager.
- Add two-factor authentication to high-risk accounts.
- Review security and privacy settings regularly.
- Communicate securely and privately where possible.
- Talk to your family about digital security and privacy checkups.

I published a 60-Minute Digital Security Checkup on Homeland Security Today. You can check that out here: `https://www.hstoday.us/subject-matter-areas/cybersecurity/cybersecurity-101-five-back-to-school-tips-to-stay-safe-online/`.

What is a life hack that you'd like to share?

In our line of work, we all spend an extraordinary amount of time staring at screens. Therefore, I'm going to propose a self-care hack: follow fewer people on social media.

When you're new to the industry, you'll want to learn all the things and follow all the people in the listicles and #ff lists. Let me warn you: it is not healthy.

Instead, replace some of the time you spend mindlessly scrolling social media with some form of physical activity. You can do this even after you're a parent.

I used to sit on my phone while the kids practiced for sports after school. Now I bring my dumbbells or kettlebell to exercise while they practice. I also started walking, riding my bike, and/or doing Zumba several times a week instead of staring at my phone in disbelief about the current state of world affairs.

My point is that you do not need a gym membership for self-care. All you need to do is decide less social media, more self-care.

What is the biggest mistake you've ever made, and how did you recover from it?

The biggest mistake I made during my career was believing that I had to be 100 percent qualified for roles with a job description that were a college-essay long. I recovered by coming to the realization that I do not want roles that are five positions written as one.

I also decided that I would apply for future roles of interest even if I am not 100 percent qualified. If a reality TV star can be hired to lead national security, I can do anything. ■

"Between the proliferation of information security conferences (many of which are inexpensive or free) and the abundance of online learning resources and challenges/CTFs, it is easier now than ever for someone to learn the skills required to work in the industry."

Twitter: @evanbooth • **Website:** fort.ninja

Evan Booth

7

Evan Booth is a builder, architect, developer, and challenge designer at Counter Hack—a company devoted to building fun and engaging challenges that educate and evaluate information security professionals. When Evan isn't struggling to get his job title to fit in HTML forms, he loves building stuff out of other stuff, spending time with his family, and hitting the character limit on this bio.

If there is one myth that you could debunk in cybersecurity, what would it be?
"Real hackers wear dark hoodies." My theory is that the predominant hacker stereotype cycles between the shadowy, hoodie-clad character and the aggressive silhouette rendered entirely out of 1s and 0s based on some combination of factors that have yet to be determined.

How is it that cybersecurity spending is increasing but breaches are still happening?
Effective marketing is effective. Ooh! Someone should put together high-gloss sales materials for those boring, tried-and-true security practices. "Introoooooducing [insert lasers + lens flare] Not Leaving Default Credentials on Your Network Printer™—version Blockchain. Cloud PLATINUM..."

Do you need a college degree or certification to be a cybersecurity professional?
Man, I sure hope not. Between the proliferation of information security conferences (many of which are inexpensive or free) and the abundance of

online learning resources and challenges/CTFs, it is easier now than ever for someone to learn the skills required to work in the industry. That said, I think it's important to recognize that there's a wide variety of learning styles and that lots of people thrive in structured learning environments like traditional degree and certification programs. That's perfectly okay.

In any case, I would strongly recommend pairing your education—however it may come—with a mentorship with someone currently working in the industry. This should be someone who can help you learn what you don't know and, more importantly, help you identify skills and concepts that you don't know you don't know.

How did you get started in the cybersecurity field, and what advice would you give to a beginner pursuing a career in cybersecurity?
I suppose I technically started as a mischievous kid with a healthy level of curiosity, a shared phone line, and a 14.4K modem. But for the sake of brevity, I'll skip ahead a decade or so and say I started by being an active participant in the "hacker" community. You see, I'd been working for some time as a software engineer when I heard about this "penetration testing" thing where you basically get a pass to be a bad guy, break into places, and compromise their networks. Well, I just thought that sounded fun as hell, and I figured I'd give it a shot. So, I started learning about lock picking and surreptitious entry. A few months and some ski masks later, a colleague and I were slipping through a window in the dead of night, disabling the alarm with a code that had been conveniently provided to us by the alarm company—after having impersonated one of the client's employees using info we'd found on a network share earlier in the engagement. Good times.

If you're expecting me to say, "It's that easy!" at this point in the story, it's important to note that I still wouldn't have considered myself to be a qualified industry practitioner. In fact, outside of some pretty solid findings, a fairly comprehensive report, and a happy client, the most persuasive evidence of competence to that end was that I hadn't managed to find myself on the business end of a police-issued taser. However, the experience was instrumental in validating that I'm most satisfied and firing on all cylinders when I'm building things as opposed to breaking them, even though I find both highly enjoyable. Additionally, it prompted me to attend my first information security conference, CarolinaCon, which is an excellent annual gathering of hackers held in Raleigh, North Carolina. I can still remember the talks, the people, the packed TOOOL lockpick village, and learning about all the cool projects people were working on.

Fast-forward a couple years, and I was presenting my own work, Terminal Cornucopia, at the third annual DerbyCon conference in Louisville, Kentucky. After the talk, a gentleman in a porkpie hat who had attended the talk walked over, introduced himself, and started a conversation that ultimately led to a job offer—one that I, after taking way too long to come to my senses, would eventually accept. The gentleman was Mr. Ed Skoudis, and the job was building security-related challenges for products such as SANS NetWars and Holiday Hack Challenge.

The best advice I could give people who are pursuing a career in cybersecurity is this: don't wait until you have an InfoSec job to get involved in the InfoSec community. If you want to dance, go where the music is playing.

What is your specialty in cybersecurity, and how can others gain expertise in your specialty?

My professional background is in software engineering and information architecture, and I love to build stuff.

There are enough free educational resources out there on those topics to choke a donkey—just pick a topic and dive in!

What is your advice for career success when it comes to getting hired, climbing the corporate ladder, or starting a company in cybersecurity?

There may be a typical career path or whatever, but that doesn't mean it has to be *your* career path. Early and often, try to intentionally put yourself in the way of work that complements your strengths. If you aren't sure what your strengths are, I highly recommend taking the CliftonStrengths assessment.[1]

What qualities do you believe all highly successful cybersecurity professionals share?

They all either teach or write tools at a very high level and, in many cases, do both.

What is the best book or movie that can be used to illustrate cybersecurity challenges?

What's that one movie where Anonymous uses social engineering and open source intelligence (OSINT) to bankrupt a local small business owner while they're offline due to a nasty virus? Oh right, that was Tom Hanks and Meg Ryan in *You've Got Mail*.

What is your favorite hacker movie?

Joe Dante's *Explorers*, circa 1985.

What are your favorite books for motivation, personal development, or enjoyment?

The Complete Calvin and Hobbes by Bill Watterson. It's basically an instruction manual for life.

What is some practical cybersecurity advice you give to people at home in the age of social media and the Internet of Things?

1. Keep your software up to date.
2. Use a password manager.
3. If someone contacts you first, stop and verify the number/email address/ carrier pigeon before relinquishing any information.

What is a life hack that you'd like to share?

Unless you are actively working on something that carries at least a 50 percent chance of complete and utter failure, the odds that Steven Seagal or Chuck Norris will ever portray you in a direct-to-video movie are pretty much zero.

What is the biggest mistake you've ever made, and how did you recover from it?

Early on, I spread my time extremely thin working on tech startups for "sweat equity." Ugh. I didn't have nearly enough time to devote to them, and they ultimately ended in failure. Steven Seagal and Chuck Norris were wildly disappointed. ∎

> "Perhaps I'm just jaded by all the marketing, but I think the biggest myth in security is that risk can be reduced, and security posture can be improved, by purchasing products."

Twitter: @kylebubp • **Website:** kylebubp.com

Kyle Bubp

For more than a decade, Kyle Bubp has worked for enterprises, hosting providers, the FBI, the Department of Energy, and the Department of Defense to analyze and improve their security posture. As co-founder of Savage Security, he focused on cutting through fear, uncertainty, and doubt (FUD) to help make defensive strategies cheaper and easier for customers. His company was later acquired by Threatcare, where Kyle served as the director of strategic services and worked directly with the CEO. Kyle continues to develop practical defensive strategies, research security issues, and publish articles and presentations on improving the security industry. Outside of work, you'll find him hiking, riding motorcycles, hitting the gym, playing music, and exploring the globe.

8

If there is one myth that you could debunk in cybersecurity, what would it be?

Man, this is tough, because I've spent the latter part of my career trying to debunk cybersecurity myths. In fact, I started a company whose number-one goal was to change the industry. The decision to quit my job and start a bootstrapped security consulting company was likely fueled by my displeasure with all the myths in the industry.

Perhaps I'm just jaded by all the marketing, but I think the biggest myth in security is that risk can be reduced, and security posture can be improved, by purchasing products. In my experience, extremely secure networks cannot be built by investing millions in security products but instead require process, procedure, and configuration changes.

"In my experience, extremely secure networks cannot be built by investing millions in security products but instead require process, procedure, and configuration changes."

I liken this to the way we treat personal health as well. It's the reason there are so many fad diets and why the diet industry has to continuously come up with new ways to convince you that they can make you healthier in less time. Less time than it would take you to do the things we *know* make you healthy: eat right, get plenty of rest, stay hydrated, don't smoke, and drink in moderation.

The cybersecurity industry does the same thing. Instead of taking the time to implement proper policies, procedures, training, and configuration, the marketing machine of the industry tries to sell you fad diets for your technical debt. And, just like personal health, even if you do lose the weight/become more secure, statistics show that you're going to put that weight back on (and maybe more) within the year, just as you will reclaim that technical debt that your silver-bullet solution was supposed to solve.

What is one of the biggest bang-for-the-buck actions that an organization can take to improve its cybersecurity posture?

Least privilege—not only least privilege in the user permissions sense but in all areas of technology and business processes. From the technical sense, users should be given the minimum number of permissions they need to do their work. This generally means no local admin, no right to read (or modify) data that they don't absolutely need, and no ability to enter physical areas they don't need access to in order to do their jobs.

The same should apply to your technical assets. If your workstations don't need to talk directly to your servers, then don't let them. Segment your networks and apply firewall rules to explicitly allow only those machines and services that need to "talk." This not only helps to reduce the scope of your risk, but it also limits the amount of damage an attacker could do if he or she were able to get into the network.

How is it that cybersecurity spending is increasing but breaches are still happening?

Just because one is investing money doesn't mean they will see a return on investment. I think this is the case in our industry. Investment in products is going up, up, up, but where's the ROI? It's really no different than the stock market. Buyers have to do their homework and make sure they're making wise investments with their cybersecurity budget. I would also argue that, just as in the financial services industry, it may make sense for organizations to partner with a trusted security advisor (much akin to a fiduciary for investors).

Do you need a college degree or certification to be a cybersecurity professional?

Need? No. But getting a certification not only shows me that you can jump the hurdle, it also shows me that you can apply yourself. I think similarly for a college degree. In addition to showing your ability to stick with something until the end, generally you'll come out of college with above-par written communication skills, which are extremely important in technology.

How did you get started in the cybersecurity field, and what advice would you give to a beginner pursuing a career in cybersecurity?

I got started in the field by going to school for it. I grew up tinkering on PCs but also had an affinity for working on cars (my dad was a mechanic). One day, I told my dad that I wanted to be a mechanic, and his advice was to go into computers instead, so I took the advice. In high school, I took as many computer courses as I could; then I went straight into a technical college to work on my bachelor's in network security and forensics.

During my time in school, I got a full-time job and switched my school schedule to nights. So I worked eight hours a day, then went to school for three to four hours at night until I graduated.

My advice would be to enroll in a program at your local community college, find as many local tech meetups as possible, and start networking. Start a personal blog where you document your tinkering and research. Don't be afraid to jump into things that you think you aren't qualified for. Always apply for the job, give it your best shot, and never sell yourself short.

What is your specialty in cybersecurity, and how can others gain expertise in your specialty?

I'm not sure I have a specialty. I really enjoy analyzing the current security programs of organizations and laying out a blueprint to make things better.

I suppose if I had to pick a specialty, it would be the ability to leverage the technology that organizations already own and greatly increase their security posture. I cut my teeth at the Department of Defense, where the majority of our security came from how we configured our machines and the policies and procedures we wrapped around everything we did.

What is your advice for career success when it comes to getting hired, climbing the corporate ladder, or starting a company in cybersecurity?

Well, I've done all three. First, getting a job is easy, but getting a job you actually *want* is hard. Read some books on negotiation, understand how to pick up on social cues, and understand that interviews are really a conversation, not a deposition.

If you show your curiosity and dedication to learn, as well as being able to subtly move the conversation in the way you want, you should have no issue getting a job.

Second, climbing the corporate ladder takes some finesse. You need to understand how to tell someone they are wrong without telling them they are wrong. You will have to suck it up and take responsibility for issues you didn't cause, and you'll definitely have to pick your battles. Show that you're always willing to help solve the problem, but don't let the organization take advantage of your time either. Finally, but perhaps most importantly, make it clear to your superiors that you want to elevate your career within the company. Make your ambitions known and ask for a plan for how to achieve your goals.

Third, starting a company is not easy, and running a company is even more difficult. Make sure you have enough financial runway to cover your expenses for a full year. Whether you take funding or save it up yourself, this is important. Also, make sure there's a market for what you are going to offer, and make sure the market is not saturated. Finally, understand that you are absolutely going to need someone to do sales and someone to do marketing. If this is you, great! Just make sure you're ready for long days and long nights. If you can handle all that, then go for it! As they say, "It's better to fly and fall than to never fly at all."

What qualities do you believe all highly successful cybersecurity professionals share?
Curiosity. Perseverance. Determination.

What is the best book or movie that can be used to illustrate cybersecurity challenges?
It's gotta be something by M. Night Shyamalan. Once you think you've got it all figured out...bam, you get hit with a twist you never saw coming. Just put that on repeat and that, in a nutshell, is cybersecurity.

What is your favorite hacker movie?
The Imitation Game. Not your traditional "hacker movie," but it's a great film.

What are your favorite books for motivation, personal development, or enjoyment?
I've gotta be honest, I don't read many "personal development" books or books in general. The only time I actually read is when I'm on a plane, and then it's usually whatever Amazon Prime is giving away for free. I've never read a book twice. If I had to name a favorite book, I suppose it would be *Rework*.

What is some practical cybersecurity advice you give to people at home in the age of social media and the Internet of Things?
Be suspicious, seek out your own truth, stay vigilant. Practical advice for the home user in no particular order: don't run as local admin, keep your machines up to date with patches and antivirus definitions, use an ad blocker, set a strong WPA2 password on your Wi-Fi, set your DNS servers to ones that filter malicious domains such as Quad9, and use a password manager such as LastPass.

If you can get away with running Chromebooks for at least some of your family, go with that instead of a full-blown Mac or Windows machine. There's less attack surface, and they are easy to maintain.

What is a life hack that you'd like to share?
Use technology to limit your access to work. Work-life balance is important, so if you can't manage that on your own, use technology to do it. Set do-not-disturb times, don't sync work emails between certain hours, and so on.

Work will always be there, and there will always be more work to do. You will never be done with work, so don't let it stress you out.

What is the biggest mistake you've ever made, and how did you recover from it?
I've made a lot of mistakes in my career, but the one I felt the worst about was when I brought down our production SAN. I was trying to do the right thing and keep all of our machines patched and up to date. I got the firmware from vendor support and confirmed with the vendor that the firmware was the correct one. I applied the patch during the scheduled maintenance time, and it needed to reboot to apply the firmware update. The thing is...it never came back up. Our public-facing websites and web apps were running off of that SAN, and I brought them all down.

I recovered by working with the vendor until it was fixed. That meant a couple of late nights, but I took responsibility and made sure that I saw the issue to resolution. ■

"Take time to understand the risks and threats you face. It may not be beneficial for every organization to know which specific countries or criminal organizations are targeting them, but every organization should know what their "worst possible day" looks like."

Twitter: @hacks4pancakes • **Website:** tisiphone.net

Lesley Carhart

Lesley Carhart (GCIH, GREM, GCFA, GPEN, B.S. Network Technologies, DePaul University) is an 18-year IT industry veteran, including 9 years in information security (specifically, digital forensics and incident response). She speaks and writes about digital forensics and incident response, OSINT, and information security careers. She is highly involved in the Chicagoland information security community and is staff at Circle City Con in Indianapolis. Lesley is currently the principal threat hunter at Dragos, Inc. In her free time, she studies three martial arts, is a competitive pistol marksman, and is generally an all-around huge geek.

9

If there is one myth that you could debunk in cybersecurity, what would it be?

The organizations we work with are rarely in the business of security. We are security professionals providing a service to organizations with their own missions. The sooner we understand that, the sooner we can stop asking counterproductive questions such as "Why don't you just..." regarding IT decisions. A *good* security professional studies the technical minutiae of their niche. A *great* security professional also studies business operations and assists their senior leadership in making pragmatic risk decisions that balance operations and security.

What is one of the biggest bang-for-the-buck actions that an organization can take to improve its cybersecurity posture?

Take time to understand the risks and threats you face. It may not be beneficial for every organization to know which specific countries or criminal organizations are targeting them, but every organization should know what their "worst possible day" looks like. Is it not being able to conduct transactions? Theft of sensitive information? Inability to perform a physical function?

Once an organization identifies and quantifies risks and the assets associated with their key functions, it becomes inherently easier to identify potential causes of a critically impactful incident. Consequently, the organization will be better prepared to appropriately mitigate risk and spend security resources sensibly.

How is it that cybersecurity spending is increasing but breaches are still happening?

Security vendors are great at marketing individual products as panaceas, and the crucial concept of "defense in depth" is not reaching senior leadership. Adversaries will always improve their tactics to compensate for emerging security technologies. The only real defense is a layered approach, combining security products, risk management, sensible policies and procedures, proper disaster recovery planning, and human expertise. There is no single silver bullet.

Do you need a college degree or certification to be a cybersecurity professional?

You don't need a college degree or certification, but it can certainly help boost your career from an HR perspective. There are many possible paths to becoming a successful professional in the cybersecurity field. Studying hard, getting a four-year degree, and then applying for entry-level positions is a fairly common one. Degrees and credible certifications can also help later in one's career while pursuing promotion to management, academic, or senior leadership positions.

Unfortunately, at the time of this writing, I have seen few cybersecurity-specific degree programs that produce well-rounded security professionals. While degrees are a great tool for learning fundamentals, clearing HR hurdles, and increasing promotion potential, I would strongly caution against assuming they will teach all of the skills needed to succeed in the field (or even to clear technical interviews). Self-study and community participation are still crucial to success.

How did you get started in the cybersecurity field, and what advice would you give to a beginner pursuing a career in cybersecurity?

I honestly avoid telling my origin story because I got an unusually early start in security, so I fit a stereotype that's not a realistic representation of most security professionals. I started coding around age 8 and was hired as a developer at 15. I quickly realized that I didn't particularly enjoy professional coding as much as security, and got involved in my local hacking community. I will note that getting into the niche of digital forensics specifically was a much longer and harder battle for me because of the specialized, expensive tools used in the field.

If I could give one piece of advice to every person considering a career in security, it would be this: try to figure out what, in general, you want to do. There are many different roles in cybersecurity—from "red team" penetration testing to "blue team" malware reverse engineering. They require fairly different personalities and skill sets. When you come up to a security professional seeking mentorship, the first question most of us ask is, "What do you want to do?" We aren't asking you to decide your entire future career, or even name a specific role, but it helps us a lot to understand what general areas of security you find interesting. Eventually, you'll need to focus on one or two. Some of this decision will be aided by working in an entry-level role that offers exposure to a variety of hands-on tasks. However, you can glean a lot about various security roles by watching conference talks and trying out "capture the flag"–type exercises at home.

What is your specialty in cybersecurity, and how can others gain expertise in your specialty?

My specialty is digital forensics and incident response, specifically in response to targeted attacks. I investigate incidents of human intrusion into networks—often state-sponsored actors.

This entails collecting system, network, and malware forensic evidence; processing it or routing it to specialist teams; creating detailed timelines of attacker activity; coordinating incident response activity across security and business teams; and then producing a comprehensive report that explains what happened, when, how it happened, and how similar activity can be prevented in the future.

Does this type of detailed detective work appeal to you? I suggest getting your start as an analyst in a security operations center where you'll gain exposure to the many different niches of security we utilize and coordinate during incident response. You'll want to beef up on disk, network, and memory forensics; live and static malware analysis; and trawl gigabytes of logs.

What is your advice for career success when it comes to getting hired, climbing the corporate ladder, or starting a company in cybersecurity?

Get out there, get involved, and network! The broader security community may have its foibles, but most people are willing to help you if you're willing to put forth effort. If you have trouble interacting with people, it's well worth your time to try to improve your interpersonal skills. Take an improv class or join Toastmasters. I've seen numerous intelligent security people repeatedly fail to get hired because of poor interview or résumé-writing skills.

What qualities do you believe all highly successful cybersecurity professionals share?

An intense desire to learn about how all sorts of things work, and a talent for thinking outside the box and seeking out unusual solutions to problems.

What is the best book or movie that can be used to illustrate cybersecurity challenges?

If you really want to delve into the murky world of advanced adversaries, I'd recommend *Countdown to Zero Day: Stuxnet and the Launch of the World's First Digital Weapon* by Kim Zetter, *Dark Territory: The Secret History of Cyber War* by Fred Kaplan, and *21st Century Chinese Cyberwarfare* by Lieutenant Colonel William Hagestad.

What is your favorite hacker movie?

Oh, man. So many fictional movies I love that are ostensibly about hacking really have little to do with hacking at all. If you enjoy documentaries, *The KGB, the*

Computer, and Me is a fascinating story, albeit one told better in the book *The Cuckoo's Egg*. In terms of fiction, I still love the movie *Sneakers*.

There are a number of recent TV shows that have represented hacking and hacking culture far better than films, such as *Mr. Robot* and *Halt and Catch Fire*.

What are your favorite books for motivation, personal development, or enjoyment?

I have a particular fondness for Isaac Asimov, particularly his Susan Calvin stories. Asimov envisioned futures that weren't specifically dystopian or utopian but rather reflected realistic ethical and scientific dilemmas. Artificially intelligent humanoid robots in everyday homes may still be science fiction, but the complex dilemmas and conflicts Asimov posed in his stories are often not far-flung from ones we face in the second decade of the 21st century.

Currently, my top picks for digital forensics and incident response technical reading are *Practical Malware Analysis* by Michael Sikorski and Andrew Honig, *Windows Registry Forensics* by Harlan Carvey, and *The Art of Memory Forensics* by Michael Hale Ligh et al.

What is some practical cybersecurity advice you give to people at home in the age of social media and the Internet of Things?

Consider how badly you need or want these devices and segment them from your computer network as much as possible. Most modern wireless routers allow the simultaneous broadcast of guest and private network SSIDs. Another solution is installing two routers with independent wireless networks and firewalls enabled. Keep those smart light bulbs and media players off the network you do your taxes on, and make sure they remain behind a firewall!

What is a life hack that you'd like to share?

Let's talk about body language! When you're speaking to somebody who is standing up, glance at their feet. If you're engaging them and they want to talk to you, their feet will usually be pointed toward you. If their feet are pointing toward an exit, you're either losing their interest or have already lost it. Time to let them go, or consider why you're losing them! If you want to show interest in a conversation, maintain polite eye contact and make sure your feet are facing toward the person or people you're talking to.

In many Western cultures, standing with legs apart and arms uncrossed comes off as more aggressive, while crossing one's arms, looking down, and keeping the legs close together comes off as more defensive and deferential. Keep these nonverbal cues in mind when having a conversation, and try to balance them to keep the conversation comfortable.

What is the biggest mistake you've ever made, and how did you recover from it?

Many years ago, while working as a telecom tech, I got sent to a mine in the Arctic Circle with a replacement router in the dead of winter. It was a spontaneous, last-minute fix for a critical failure in poor conditions, and I didn't check my gear properly. After a bizarre journey by prop plane, hitchhiking in the dark, and entering the mine with no cell phone service, I realized that my console cable didn't work. I had traveled across an ice sheet in the dark, I was totally alone, and I couldn't connect to and configure the router. I ended up building a server out of parts in the telecom closet of the mine. They never knew. Hopefully, they never read this book. ∎

"There is also a digital transformation occurring, and many of the new jobs will be substantially different from the security jobs we know today."

Twitter: @lcarsten • **Website:** www.linkedin.com/in/leecarsten

Lee Carsten

10

Lee Carsten is a vice president at Aon Cyber Solutions. Based in the firm's Dallas office, he is responsible for developing and growing the firm's relationships with enterprise clients, helping them proactively manage and control their risk and reactively respond to incidents. Lee is also the president of the Alamo Information Systems Security Association and a steering committee member on EC Council's Global CISO Forum. In this capacity, he helps information security leaders build relationships with their peers, get recognition for innovative initiatives they are leading, and give back to their communities. He is active in a number of other security organizations, including the Open Web Application Security Project, InfraGard, CyberPatriot, and the National Collegiate Cyber Defense Competition. Lee is a graduate of the University of Arkansas, where he studied engineering and business, and has a degree in Accounting and Computer Information Systems.

If there is one myth that you could debunk in cybersecurity, what would it be?

That the security profession has a million open jobs, and we just need to attract and train more people to fill all of the open positions. Organizations are adopting more cloud-based infrastructure and services, and tool- and service-specific jobs are moving away from those organizations and into the service provider space. There are examples all over the place of companies getting more done with 35 security people today than they could with 100 a few years ago. There is also a digital transformation occurring, and many of the new jobs will be substantially different from the security jobs we know today. Deep learning and neural networks are going to supplement predictable, repetitive work streams. Security roles will be more aligned with business processes specific to certain industries and organizations, and knowing the business will be as critical as knowing the tech. There will continue to be good jobs in our industry, and we need a diverse group of intelligent, motivated people who are interested in helping us solve hard problems, but we need to ensure that we are training security professionals for the jobs of the future.

What is one of the biggest bang-for-the-buck actions that an organization can take to improve its cybersecurity posture?

Implement trusted DNS and country-specific blacklisting. Learn how to implement and use the tools you have. Sunset end-of-life/unsupported systems and get them off the network.

How is it that cybersecurity spending is increasing but breaches are still happening?

Attacks and attackers are becoming more sophisticated and are increasing in scale. You don't even have to be technical with the exploit-as-a-service models that are popping up. Anyone can do it.

> "The need to compete drives businesses to introduce an ever-increasing number of endpoints, significantly expanding the cyberattack surface—whether through a retail bank's mobile app, a manufacturer of connected cars, or even office equipment like printers or employee devices."

The need to compete drives businesses to introduce an ever-increasing number of endpoints, significantly expanding the cyberattack surface—whether through a retail bank's mobile app, a manufacturer of connected cars, or even office equipment like printers or employee devices.

Organizations are also bringing processes and infrastructure online, for example, through connected grid systems, supervisory control and data acquisition (SCADA), and industrial control systems (ICS). Cyber risk is dynamic: every change in a company—an M&A transaction, working with a contractor, introducing new software, or moving data to the cloud—affects a company's cyber-risk posture. Securing this shifting target is challenging. Legacy systems are also vulnerable to being exploited with modern attacks.

Do you need a college degree or certification to be a cybersecurity professional?

No, but I personally think it helps. It doesn't even need to be in a technical field, but college is a place where you learn how to learn. Internships and associate programs within companies are extremely beneficial if you want to be in the security field. If college isn't an option for you, there are many examples of top security pros who didn't come out of a traditional four-year degree program.

How did you get started in the cybersecurity field, and what advice would you give to a beginner pursuing a career in cybersecurity?

I got started in 2002. I was working for an IT services company and a client of mine needed help managing their firewalls. I went to an Information Systems Security Association (ISSA) meeting and got involved with the local chapter, and that started my move toward security. I liked the people and thought this was an important problem to help solve, and that changed the course of my career.

As for pursuing a career, my advice would be to get involved in your local community. The people you meet will be as important to your career as any degree or certification. Find a meetup, an ISSA or OWASP chapter, attend a Security BSides—whatever seems to have some momentum in your area. Leverage online learning resources.

Don't focus just on the security or hacking tools; learn what you can about systems as well. Learn how to code, or, at a minimum, learn how to script and work with the command line. Podcasts are another way to ease into what people in the industry are working on. Follow 10 security thought leaders on Twitter.

What is your specialty in cybersecurity, and how can others gain expertise in your specialty?

I started in IT and moved toward information security in the early 2000s. I've spent most of my time in my security career on the business side of things.

AppSec (application security) is an area of focus for me. The Open Web Application Security Project (OWASP) is a great place to begin. Having a development background is also important if you want to work in software security.

Right now, I am working in the risk quantification space to help security leaders measure the dollar value of their programs and evaluate how to maximize their investment. There are lots of opportunities in the industry that are people-oriented and don't require years of technical experience.

What is your advice for career success when it comes to getting hired, climbing the corporate ladder, or starting a company in cybersecurity?

You have to understand what you are good at. Know your strengths and weaknesses. Be honest about them. Suit up and show up (dress the part).

Don't let your appearance turn people away so they can't hear what you're saying. You have to be continually learning. Know who you're talking to. Do your research. Add value. Take the tasks nobody else wants and overperform. Then, train your replacement.

What qualities do you believe all highly successful cybersecurity professionals share?

The best security people are inquisitive tinkerers and have a sensitivity around what is right and wrong. They don't take things at face value. They test boundaries and look for evidence. They break things to understand how they work. They don't always follow instructions. Integrity matters.

> "The best security people are inquisitive tinkerers and have a sensitivity around what is right and wrong. They don't take things at face value. They test boundaries and look for evidence."

What is the best book or movie that can be used to illustrate cybersecurity challenges?

The Phoenix Project. This book is a novel that anyone can read and follow, as it highlights one of the important shifts that occurred in the software development industry. It's not solely a security book, but it represents the business environment we are tasked with securing.

What is your favorite hacker movie?

Ocean's Eight. I know the technical advisor for the film, and I'm excited about some of the tech that was used.

What are your favorite books for motivation, personal development, or enjoyment?

Wild at Heart by John Eldredge. *The Purpose Driven Life* by Rick Warren.

What is some practical cybersecurity advice you give to people at home in the age of social media and the Internet of Things?

- There is no such thing as privacy on the internet.
- Don't say or do anything online you wouldn't want your grandmother to see.
- What you say no to is as important as what you say yes to.
- Who you are as a person is more important than what you do.
- Understand what tech does for you. Don't adopt tech just to adopt tech.

What is a life hack that you'd like to share?

When you get to your hotel room, take a picture of the room number with your phone so you won't forget which room you are in.

What is the biggest mistake you've ever made, and how did you recover from it?

Many years ago, I was responsible for an email migration for a professional sports team that went wrong. It was on Lotus Notes if that gives you any indication of the timeframe. I had a subject-matter expert brought in for a weekend to help with the migration. The team had a virtualized environment. We started the upgrade without checking the available disk space, and the upgrade failed halfway through. There were no good backups. All systems on that server went down and were unrecoverable. It was also done during the season, and the league was doing a DNS change at the same time.

> "There is no such thing as privacy on the internet."

I took full responsibility for the error and committed every resource I had to get them back up. Twenty-hour days—with lots of communication with the team, the ownership group, and the league about where we were at—and my team stayed completely engaged and on task till we got all of their systems restored. Even during the 48 hours of DNS propagation changes, where we couldn't do anything but wait to determine whether the fixes would take, we were there. A 12-hour project turned into five days. It was a character-building experience. ∎

> "We spend countless hours securing things from the more obvious outside attacks, but we don't always spend enough time auditing who has permission to do what from within, or disaster recovery."

Twitter: @shortxstack • **Website:** whitneychampion.com

Whitney Champion

11

Whitney Champion is a systems and security architect in South Carolina. She has held numerous roles throughout her career—security engineer, systems engineer, mobile developer, cloud architect, and consulting architect, to name a few. In the last 15 years, she has worked on operations teams, support teams, development teams, and consulting teams in both the private and public sectors, supporting anywhere from a handful of users to hundreds of thousands. No matter the role, security has always been an area of passion and focus.

If there is one myth that you could debunk in cybersecurity, what would it be?

It's not always the hacker in the black hoodie trying to steal your data, and it's not always about someone trying to steal your personal information, credit card numbers, or secrets. Sometimes, it's the teammate who is still getting their feet wet—but has administrative access to all your systems—who accidentally took down or deleted an entire piece of your infrastructure.

We spend countless hours securing things from the more obvious outside attacks, but we don't always spend enough time auditing who has permission to do what from within, or disaster recovery. Both of which are equally important.

What is one of the biggest bang-for-the-buck actions that an organization can take to improve its cybersecurity posture?

You don't need to spend thousands to improve your security posture. There are a lot of fantastic open source tools out there that will secure your infrastructure for free. You should be spending your money on the people you want to use those tools so you can implement them properly. That will get you much further than buying an application that checks a few boxes that no one knows how to maintain.

How is it that cybersecurity spending is increasing but breaches are still happening?

People and organizations seem to think they have to spend a massive amount of money to secure their infrastructure because that's what they're often told by the media, salespeople, or others. People will drop all kinds of money on the fancy security appliance that does all the things, but at the end of the day they probably don't know how to use it properly, and they probably didn't even realize they could have spent all that money on qualified individuals to implement most of these same features on free or open source software. Spend the money on recruiting and training the talent it takes to secure your organization instead of on the fancy box with all the bells and whistles.

> "Spend the money on recruiting and training the talent it takes to secure your organization instead of on the fancy box with all the bells and whistles."

Do you need a college degree or certification to be a cybersecurity professional?

Absolutely not. That's not to say it doesn't help with getting your foot in the door in certain organizations, because it absolutely does in some cases. Requirements are different everywhere. But I think a large part of what has driven me, and many other people in the field, is natural curiosity and a drive to do the things we do.

We are inquisitive as a community, and we question everything we use. How is this system or application put together? How does it work? What can I do to change X feature? What happens when I do this? We learn by tearing things apart and putting them back together again, reconfiguring, and constantly trying to keep up with the technology firehose. There is always something new to learn, break, or demystify, and that never-ending list of ways to improve is what has gotten me to where I am today.

How did you get started in the cybersecurity field, and what advice would you give to a beginner pursuing a career in cybersecurity?

I got started in security specifically in college. I had always been obsessed with computers and development and building my own systems, but I wasn't properly introduced to the security field until about 2005. I had a handful of friends who were minoring in security, and they told me about the security lab and some classes I didn't even know about. I volunteered to be a lab assistant because I had a strong Linux background and it sounded fun. I've been hooked ever since.

Bottom line: get involved. Talk to people. Go to conferences or even volunteer at one. Get your hands dirty. Listen to all the podcasts. Take advantage of free training and knowledge. Jump into a capture-the-flag contest or an open source project, even if it makes you nervous. Always be learning. The more people you meet in this industry, the more you'll realize there are things you don't know. That can be daunting to many people, but take that feeling and turn it into motivation. So many doors open this way, and you will never be bored again a day in your life. This speaks to not only security, but IT in general.

What is your specialty in cybersecurity, and how can others gain expertise in your specialty?

My security focus has always been related to Linux and cloud infrastructure. For years, I have specialized in hardening Linux systems on dev, production, and operations teams, and the infrastructure and networking they run on. My experience has spanned a wide variety of application stacks and platforms, and this has been beneficial in many ways. One way being that I have never been tied to any one language or piece of technology.

Lots of companies need these skills, and the landscape is always changing, so the opportunity is there for the taking. My advice is to dive in head first and get your hands dirty. Build out some systems, or a network. Stand up a server and deploy an application. Try all the cloud platforms, or even deploy your own private cloud. Poke holes and figure out how to fix them. There are even exercises online built specifically for the purpose of exploiting systems and figuring out the flaws.

Internships, shoulder surfing, capture-the-flag contests, building your own lab, and hands-on practical experience are all great ways to get more experience in this area.

What is your advice for career success when it comes to getting hired, climbing the corporate ladder, or starting a company in cybersecurity?

As for getting hired, let your passion speak for you. What drives you? What keeps you up at night? What do you start working on and suddenly four hours have gone by? Chances are, companies will recognize that. Show things you've worked on or written about, and talk about why you loved that project you worked on a year ago, how you built it, and why it was awesome. Companies need to hire people with skills, sure, but they also need to hire people who have the hunger to learn and are teachable.

As for climbing the corporate ladder, the more you learn, the more you can teach others. Start mentoring people with less experience. Share your knowledge. Show that you are capable of leading others. Express interest in taking on more responsibility. Don't be afraid to tell your boss or manager that you want to take the next step. Be vocal about your career goals while working toward them, and make sure they can see you putting forth the effort.

What qualities do you believe all highly successful cybersecurity professionals share?

Motivation to keep learning new things and to continuously get better at what you do. If you're not trying to sharpen your skills, you're falling behind.

What is the best book or movie that can be used to illustrate cybersecurity challenges?

I don't get to read much these days, but I've been reading the book *Daemon* by Daniel Suarez. It might not be the best example, but it sheds light on so many different pieces of the security landscape. It allows you to think outside the box and see other perspectives, which is a huge aspect of cybersecurity.

What is your favorite hacker movie?

Well, this isn't a movie, it's a show, but *Mr. Robot*. So much thought and research are put into it by some of the sharpest minds in the industry. And so good. Also, *Catch Me If You Can* because the social engineering…unbelievable.

What are your favorite books for motivation, personal development, or enjoyment?

Between work, and three kids, and side projects, there is little time left for reading. A few months ago, as I mentioned earlier, I started reading *Daemon* by Daniel Suarez. I needed something to read on flights, and this was recommended to me by several friends in security. It lets you think outside the box and is a really exciting read.

What is some practical cybersecurity advice you give to people at home in the age of social media and the Internet of Things?

Update. Always update. Personal computer, home router. Probably even your refrigerator in this day and age.

What is a life hack that you'd like to share?

I don't know if this counts as a "hack," but it's something my mother has told me since I was little, and I have never found it to be more true than in recent years: exercise. If you take care of yourself, it is a lot easier to take care of everything else in your life. Period. It helps clear my mind from work and the day-to-day. I disconnect, and to be honest, it's probably the only time of the day I *actually* disconnect.

What is the biggest mistake you've ever made, and how did you recover from it?

This one time I restarted a production database (and as a result, the application) in the middle of the day. I "recovered" from it—in that I brought it back online and made sure everything was okay again. I was absolutely embarrassed, for obvious reasons. But I never made that mistake again, and I will never forget that feeling of panic for as long as I live.

> "Never let another person cause you to forget your sense of self."

As far as a broader answer, there were several years in college when I focused on my relationship more than I focused on myself, my education, and my future career. I let a lot of time slip away from me that I could have done so much more with, and I missed out on a lot of opportunities and experiences. I placed more importance on wanting to be elsewhere than I did on living *my own* life. Never let another person cause you to forget your sense of self.

There are plenty of other mistakes, but those in particular have left lasting impressions. ∎

"Having a computer science degree doesn't mean you know anything about cybersecurity—or even how to program, for that matter."

Twitter: @0xmchow • **Website:** www.cs.tufts.edu/~mchow (will redirect you to mchow01.github.io)

Ming Chow

Ming Chow is a senior lecturer at the Tufts University Department of Computer Science. His areas of interest are web and mobile security and computer science education. Ming has spoken at numerous organizations and conferences, including the HTCIA, OWASP, InfoSec World, Design Automation Conference (DAC), DEF CON, Intel, SOURCE, HOPE, and BSides. Since 2014, he has served as a mentor to a BSides Las Vegas Proving Ground track speaker—a track focused on helping new speakers in the information security and hacker communities acclimate to public speaking. Ming was named the 2016 Henry and Madeline Fischer Award recipient at Tufts; the award is given annually to a faculty member of the School of Engineering and judged by graduating seniors of the School of Engineering to be "Engineering's Teacher of the Year." He was named the 2017 recipient of the Lerman-Neubauer Prize for Outstanding Teaching and Advising at Tufts, which is awarded annually to a faculty member who has had a profound intellectual impact on students, both inside and outside the classroom.

12

If there is one myth that you could debunk in cybersecurity, what would it be?
That you need to have a computer science (CS) or a technical degree to be in cybersecurity. Having a computer science degree doesn't mean you know anything about cybersecurity—or even how to program, for that matter. Mudge[2] has a music degree. When I graduated with my bachelor's degree in computer science, the only exposure to cybersecurity I had had was a cryptography course, which is only a piece of cybersecurity. Fast-forward more than a decade later,

and many CS graduates still do not have any exposure to cybersecurity.[3] Recently, I did an interview in which I talked about this in more depth: "Failings in Cybersecurity Education: An Interview with Professor Ming Chow."[4]

What is one of the biggest bang-for-the-buck actions that an organization can take to improve its cybersecurity posture?
Emphasize cybersecurity during the onboarding/orientation process and constantly run exercises, including phishing exercises. Emphasizing cybersecurity early and often will demonstrate how seriously the organization takes cybersecurity and, more importantly, spread knowledge. Many learn the lesson not to touch a hot stove as a child after getting burned by one; it's the same idea for running exercises and drills constantly.

> "Emphasizing cybersecurity early and often will demonstrate how seriously the organization takes cybersecurity, and, more importantly, spread knowledge."

How is it that cybersecurity spending is increasing but breaches are still happening?
There is a range of problems here. First, many think throwing money at the problem will alleviate it. Second, does management even know what cybersecurity is, what they're protecting against, and what the actual threats are? I've seen a number of security products advertised to protect against advanced persistent threats (APTs), but how many organizations really have an APT problem?[5] Third, it is no secret that many cybersecurity products are overly complex and even riddled with vulnerabilities—oh, the irony. Fourth, if you take a look at why many breaches happen, it is because of "low-tech" factors, including social engineering, weak passwords, and failing to patch.[6]

Do you need a college degree or certification to be a cybersecurity professional?
At the moment, no. Cybersecurity is still not emphasized in many colleges. Some certifications have specific goals, such as incident response, malware analysis, offensive security, and so on. But that's a very small part of the bigger cybersecurity picture.

Now, I am not bashing the idea of a college degree or certification—they hold value and demonstrate some baseline knowledge. We may need to revisit this question when the cybersecurity field becomes more mature.

How did you get started in the cybersecurity field, and what advice would you give to a beginner pursuing a career in cybersecurity?
If it wasn't for Gary McGraw—and taking his tutorial on building secure software at the USENIX 2004 Annual Conference—I wouldn't have even known about cybersecurity as a career path. I am also very grateful to the Wall of Sheep for giving me lots of basic knowledge I never received in college (e.g., networking, packet analysis).

One beauty of cybersecurity is that it is a broad, interdisciplinary field that has technical and nontechnical underpinnings—which many fail to comprehend.

Another beauty of cybersecurity is its accessibility: you don't need a college degree to delve in, and you don't need the fanciest computer, either. You can be a political scientist or a psychologist and still relate to some aspects of cybersecurity immediately. And most of the tools and software are free. However, this all poses a problem: there is way too much out there. Thus, my advice:

- This is a field that requires you to work hard. There is too much information, too many incidents, and many new tools and techniques being introduced. To keep up and be relevant, you have to work hard.

- Have intellectual curiosity to understand how something works. Gary McGraw and Greg Morrisett coined the term "The Trinity of Trouble." According to them, complexity, extensibility, and connectivity are the "three trends having a large influence on the growth and evolution of the [security] problem."[7] So much is now being abstracted away from people when it comes to education, software, and hardware products that we now take things for granted without considering the security, privacy, and social ramifications.

- Have the ability to tinker. Hands-on practice is so vital in this field. Cybersecurity professionals are asked to build, break, fix, and explain. For starters, I tell beginners to build a vulnerable web server at home using a Raspberry Pi. That will give you the ability to build a system from scratch and understand the necessary components to install. Then, learn how to poke holes and find weaknesses in the system.

> "Hands-on practice is so vital in this field. Cybersecurity professionals are asked to build, break, fix, and explain."

- There is no substitute for real experience and projects.

What is your specialty in cybersecurity, and how can others gain expertise in your specialty?
My focus is teaching cybersecurity. Take every small opportunity, build credibility, and keep learning from great people. My first time teaching and presenting on cybersecurity was at my job at Harvard more than a decade ago. Then, I took a small gig to teach a cybersecurity module at Middlesex Community College. I also took the SANS course "Hacker Tools, Techniques, Exploits, and Incident Handling," which further developed my skills.

What is your advice for career success when it comes to getting hired, climbing the corporate ladder, or starting a company in cybersecurity?
Personality and emotional intelligence/empathy, hands down. To put it bluntly, no one wants to work with an a—shole. Your academic or engineering prowess may get you the job, but your personality and soft skills will get you the promotion.[8]

What qualities do you believe all highly successful cybersecurity professionals share?
The ability to explain the *what*, the *why*, and the *how*—and the ability to communicate that to a variety of audiences. When you're communicating with

a technical audience, they expect depth and proof. This is why I'm a fan of Rob Graham's work and Tavis Ormandy's security bug postings. When you're communicating with senior management, you need to keep your thoughts concise. That's why we have a policy memo deliverable in our "Cyber Security and Cyber Warfare" course at Tufts. One of my favorite stories is about convincing Tufts to build a joint Cyber Security and Policy program between the School of Engineering and the Fletcher School of Law and Diplomacy, starting with an investment to hire a bridge professor in cybersecurity and policy.[9]

What is the best book or movie that can be used to illustrate cybersecurity challenges?

It's not a movie, but there's a scene from *The Simpsons* I use quite often. In the episode, Mr. Burns and Smithers have to go through an elaborate security system to enter Springfield's nuclear power plant, and an amusing scene unfolds. You can watch the clip on YouTube.[10]

For a movie, *Catch Me If You Can*, because all the old tricks still hold even in the age of technology. In fact, technology has made fraud even easier.

What is your favorite hacker movie?

Minority Report because almost everything in the movie turned out to be true in reality.

What are your favorite books for motivation, personal development, or enjoyment?

Masters of Doom by David Kushner. I love stories of legendary hackers (in this case, John Carmack and John Romero). It's also a good book on starting out at the bottom; work ethics; business, personal, and professional failures; and the good old days of computer/video games.

What is some practical cybersecurity advice you give to people at home in the age of social media and the Internet of Things?

Less is more.

What is a life hack that you'd like to share?

Directly related to my "less is more" comment is the Minimalist Mantra: "Stop buying the unnecessary. Toss half your stuff, learn contentedness. Reduce half again. List four essential things in your life, do these first, stop doing the nonessential. Clear distractions, focus on each moment. Let go of attachment to doing, having more. Fall in love with less."[11]

I've thrown away so much stuff over the last three years that I now have less than I had when I moved into my home. It is liberating. The joke among my family and friends is that the only thing I haven't thrown out of the house is myself.

What is the biggest mistake you've ever made, and how did you recover from it?

Not having a good grasp on systems early. This includes operating systems, pointers, memory, and networking. It goes back to what I said earlier: *to understand how something works.* Most of these topics are fundamental to cybersecurity, especially the technical side. I had to relearn almost everything on my own, and I feel like I'm still paying penance. ■

> "Sometimes you have to go backward or laterally to be in a position to move forward."

Twitter: @Jimchristyusdfc

Jim Christy

Jim Christy is a retired special agent who specialized in cybercrime investigations and digital forensics for more than 32 years with the Air Force Office of Special Investigations and the Department of Defense Cyber Crime Center (DC3). He now works in the private sector and is a cyber lead for the DB Cooper Cold Case Team.

13

If there is one myth that you could debunk in cybersecurity, what would it be?

The one myth I would like to debunk is that the government has your back when it comes to cybersecurity. The government can't take care of its own problems, let alone help its citizens. Plus, it's not the government's mission. The different government agencies are not created equal and certainly don't share information among themselves. State and local governments are, woefully, decades behind the federal agencies in protecting themselves. They certainly can't help you. You're on your own.

In fact, the intelligence community (IC) actually works against the best interests of citizens and other government agencies. The only thing that matters to the IC is offense. If they detect a vulnerability in an operating system, software package, or network, they hold that close to the chest so they can exploit it, no matter how much that vulnerability puts individual citizens, companies, or other government agencies at risk. I personally believe defense needs to come first when we're talking about cybersecurity.

What is one of the biggest bang-for-the-buck actions that an organization can take to improve its cybersecurity posture?

The biggest bang-for-the-buck action an organization can take to improve its cybersecurity posture is a function of where in the organization the cybersecurity office reports. Most organizations place the cybersecurity office under the chief information officer (CIO) because it's technical in nature. That is absolutely the worst place to put it due to the competing priorities and conflict of interest that creates. CIOs report directly to the chief executive officer (CEO), whose mission in the private sector is to make money. As such, the CIO's mission is to provide information systems and technology that make the company more efficient and effective at the lowest cost. The CIO also helps the company stay on the leading edge of technology, which ideally translates into making more money. It is hard to quantify the impact of the cybersecurity function on the company's bottom line until you have a breach.

The security office should also report to the CEO, as their mission is to provide all aspects of security for the organization. This includes the very different security disciplines of physical security, personnel security, and cybersecurity. You don't make personnel security the responsibility of the human resources office (or do you?). You have personnel security within the domain of the security office because it's a security function. Likewise, you don't make physical security the responsibility of the building maintenance/logistics office (or do you?). It also falls under the security office.

I concede that many security offices don't have the technical expertise to provide technical cybersecurity, but resources should be redirected and security personnel educated and trained.

How is it that cybersecurity spending is increasing but breaches are still happening?

Breaches continue to occur despite the spending on cybersecurity due to greed. In today's market, you have to be first with new innovations and products to be successful. Build that new widget or app to help productivity and efficiency. Unfortunately, to build security into the product and completely test that widget before it's put into the marketplace would be costly; plus it would take much longer, giving your competitor the advantage. They will be first in the marketplace and thus able to charge a cheaper price. Most companies let the public beta test their products for them. Consumers pay for the product and then have to perform the beta testing for the company. Unfortunately, consumers are not yet sophisticated enough to demand security in their products up front.

Do you need a college degree or certification to be a cybersecurity professional?

You don't need a college degree to be a cybersecurity professional, but it helps. Many military cybersecurity professionals go to tech schools to learn their trade and are far more competent than folks right out of college. But even the military is emphasizing degrees and certifications now. You can still get a good-paying cybersecurity position with a technical school certificate and practical work experience.

How did you get started in the cybersecurity field, and what advice would you give to a beginner pursuing a career in cybersecurity?

Well, I'm really in the cybersecurity field by default. I was first a systems administrator in the military and then a programmer analyst before becoming a cybercrime investigator. Cybercrime investigators were called in when cybersecurity failed and there was a compromise or an intrusion. You learn a lot about cybersecurity as you investigate what worked and what didn't and what allowed the crime to occur in the first place—as well as the tactics, tools, and procedures (TTPs) used by the bad guys to exploit the system—and also the TTPs that failed for the owner of the compromised system.

What is your specialty in cybersecurity, and how can others gain expertise in your specialty?

My expertise was in cyber investigations and digital forensics. These are not cybersecurity disciplines but are critical to cybersecurity. The cybercrime investigative and digital forensics disciplines are extremely undermanned. This is a great opportunity for readers. There are more than 18,000 different law enforcement agencies in the United States alone. Every city, county, state, campus, tribe, and federal agency has multiple law enforcement agencies. There definitely aren't 18,000 cyber cops and digital forensics examiners in the whole world. That means every agency may not even have a capability at all. Especially at the state and local law enforcement levels, there is a dire need for this capability.

In today's world, digital forensics is not limited to law enforcement. Companies and organizations also require a digital forensics capacity and expertise to conduct internal investigations that they don't want to go public or for investigations that don't reach the threshold for a federal law enforcement agency to even take an interest. State and local law enforcement organizations don't have the capability to help at all, leaving companies and individuals on their own.

Colleges and universities have finally started to create courses in digital forensics, but not many criminal justice programs have cybercrime investigations as more than a footnote yet. Great opportunities in cyber investigations and digital forensics abound.

What is your advice for career success when it comes to getting hired, climbing the corporate ladder, or starting a company in cybersecurity?

Progression in life isn't necessarily linear. It's more like a spring. Sometimes you have to go backward or laterally to be in a position to move forward. In my career, I always looked at every promotion as my last promotion. That gives you a sense of freedom. I could then make decisions and operate with that sense of freedom to do what I thought was right, no matter what my bosses thought. Always do the right thing—what's right for the country, not what will get you promoted. Don't be a political yes man. Smart bosses may not like you, but they will respect you. The others will look foolish in the long run.

What qualities do you believe all highly successful cybersecurity professionals share?

The qualities successful cybersecurity professionals share are a deep technical knowledge, continued education and training (because it's a moving target), and a tenacious attitude. You must also be an educator. You must enlighten your co-workers, friends, and customers about the growing and ever-changing threat—and do it in English that a non-geek can understand. You can't just be a geek. You have to be able to communicate in a manner that everyone can understand. Educate, communicate, and never give up.

What is the best book or movie that can be used to illustrate cybersecurity challenges?

I'm a bit prejudiced about the best book and movie involving cybersecurity challenges. My first case as a cybercrime investigator was presented in Dr. Cliff Stoll's *The Cuckoo's Egg* from back in 1986. This was the bible for cybersecurity professionals in the '80s and '90s. It's the true and accurate account of how the Soviet Union hired five West German hackers to break into Department of Defense computers for two to three years. All still relevant today.

What is your favorite hacker movie?

The best movie for me was *Live Free or Die Hard* with Bruce Willis, because the writer, David Marconi, asked me to develop and write the infrastructure attacks used by Gabriel to wreak havoc on the critical infrastructure of the United States. The Smithsonian Channel also did documentaries on the real stories behind hit movies like *Saving Private Ryan*, *Braveheart*, and *Live Free or Die Hard*. A British film crew spent a day in my office going over the different infrastructure attacks and whether they could actually occur. The bottom line was that Hollywood made it look much easier than it would be. Each separate attack was possible, but the magnitude and the coordination and speed at which they happened would have been extremely difficult to pull off.

What are your favorite books for motivation or enjoyment?

Motivation: *The Cuckoo's Egg* by Cliff Stoll

Enjoyment: *By Force of Patriots* by Cameron Reddy

What is some practical cybersecurity advice you give to people at home in the age of social media and the Internet of Things?

Like TV judge Marilyn Milan from *The People's Court* always says, "Say it, forget it; write it and regret it." The internet and social media are like your wife. She never forgets!

What is a life hack that you'd like to share?

I spent most of my career in and around the traffic jams of Washington, DC, and Baltimore, MD. The best life hack is to always stay in the lane that is blocked. All the way up to the point where the two lanes finally have to merge. People always bail out of the blocked lane, which allows you to move up faster. Americans are polite and will almost always alternate, letting cars merge at that final point where the two lanes merge. Stay in the blocked lane; you'll get through much quicker.

What is the biggest mistake you've ever made, and how did you recover from it?

I've made so many mistakes in my life that I surely can't remember them all. But recovering from them is a different story. First, you have to recognize and acknowledge your mistake and then apologize for it. Own it. Contrition is key. Real contrition, not just providing lip service. If you need to repair the situation, do it. The sooner the better. You have to have a short memory sometimes, like a Major League pitcher who just gave up a 450-foot home run. Apologize, learn from your mistake, and do better on the next play. ■

> "What hackers do isn't magic;
> it's logic, and it can be taught
> and learned from."

Twitter: @IanColdwater

Ian Coldwater

Ian Coldwater is a DevSecOps engineer turned red teamer who specializes in containers and cloud infrastructure. She has spoken about Kubernetes security at conferences including DerbyCon, O'Reilly Velocity, and SANS SecDevOps Summit. In her spare time, she likes to go on cross-country road trips, participate in capture-the-flag competitions, and eat a lot of pie.

14

If there is one myth that you could debunk in cybersecurity, what would it be?

People think hackers are wizards, and we don't do a lot to debunk that. I like shiny zero-days as much as the next hacker, but the dull truth is that most cybersecurity breaches stem from far less sexy causes, such as misconfigurations, logic failures, and defaults that never got changed.

It's not as much fun to talk about the basics over and over, but scaring people doesn't help them fix problems. What hackers do isn't magic; it's logic, and it can be taught and learned from.

What is one of the biggest bang-for-the-buck actions that an organization can take to improve its cybersecurity posture?

I think one of the biggest bang-for-the-buck actions an organization can undertake is to threat model well. Organizations that know what they're trying to protect and whom they're trying to protect it from are more likely to think strategically about their cybersecurity posture and be able to make better decisions from there.

Without a threat model, organizations can't build an appropriate security road map. They might throw resources at problems they won't realistically face, while failing to deal with issues that could actually impact the assets they care about.

How is it that cybersecurity spending is increasing but breaches are still happening?

Cybersecurity spending may be increasing, but the base problems causing breaches remain. On the technical end, everything is broken. Everyone who has ever worked as a programmer has horror stories about their code base. The internet is held together with popsicle sticks and Elmer's Glue, patched with duct tape for good measure.

On the human end, most people mean well, but they're tired, on deadline, and wanting to get on with their days. Humans tend to be imperfect, complicated, and prone to error. Combine this with the state of technology today, and disaster is bound to happen somewhere.

No amount of money spent on vendor solutions and blinky lights is going to fix these issues. They're systemic and probably not entirely solvable. To the extent that these problems can be solved, they're going to require people getting together to radically rethink the way we do things and doing them differently from the ground up.

Do you need a college degree or certification to be a cybersecurity professional?

I sure hope not, because I don't have one! I do think you need to understand how things work to be a cybersecurity professional, but there are lots of ways to get to that point. Formal education is certainly one way, but self-teaching and on-the-job experience can also help give you the knowledge you need. The InfoSec community is helpful, and there are a ton of free resources for motivated people to learn from. You don't need to spend thousands of dollars on tuition and textbooks for that.

How did you get started in the cybersecurity field, and what advice would you give to a beginner pursuing a career in cybersecurity?

I started hacking when I was 11. I was kind of a bad kid who had always liked computers but never liked rules. When I found out that you could do interesting things with computers that could break rules, I knew that was exactly what I wanted to do with my life.

I took a fairly circuitous path to get there. I dropped out of high school, had kids very young, and spent most of my adult life raising my family in poverty, making it work by a combination of resourcefulness, hustle, and sheer force of will. I never did lose my love for computers, and when the kids got older I dedicated myself to getting a career in tech. I started out in web development, moved into DevOps from there, and combined that with my interest in security to do what I do now.

I would advise beginners who are interested in pursuing a career in cybersecurity to first figure out exactly what they want to do. It's a broad field with a lot of choices, a lot of acronyms, and a lot going on. Once you figure that out, go play! There's so much to do and learn. Getting a Twitter account and following people you admire in your chosen discipline probably doesn't hurt either; a lot of them will post resources, and you can learn from them too.

What is your specialty in cybersecurity, and how can others gain expertise in your specialty?

I specialize in DevSecOps, specifically cloud, container, and Kubernetes security. There's an order of operations for gaining expertise in this stuff. If you're interested in DevSecOps as a cultural concept, I recommend reading about DevOps principles first and then moving on to DevSecOps from there. If you're interested in container security, I recommend learning about Linux administration in general, then learning about containers (they aren't tiny virtual machines!), and then learning container orchestration frameworks like Kubernetes after that. It's helpful to know what a container is and what you might want to use one for to be able to understand the process of orchestrating a lot of them, and it's helpful to know how all the moving parts work in order to be able to secure the whole thing well.

What is your advice for career success when it comes to getting hired, climbing the corporate ladder, or starting a company in cybersecurity?

Network like crazy. Get involved in the community, and make sure to give back. Going to meetups and cons is great, but organizing and volunteering are better. You'll meet good people that way, and if you're friendly, dedicated, and willing to put in the work, people will notice. It may not happen right away, but over time, you'll more than get out what you put in.

Never stop learning, and show people what you know! This can look like speaking or writing, teaching or mentoring, creating or sharing tools or resources. You don't need to be an expert to do these things. Every single one of us has something to teach and something to learn.

Basically, demonstrate that you care and go above and beyond. This isn't an industry where you can coast, but it is one in which there's a lot of good to be done. Being part of that will do good things for both you and others.

> "This isn't an industry where you can coast, but it is one in which there's a lot of good to be done. Being a part of that will do good things for both you and others."

What qualities do you believe all highly successful cybersecurity professionals share?

Curiosity, a high frustration tolerance, and a refusal to give up when things are hard. A healthy dash of paranoia probably doesn't hurt either.

What is the best book or movie that can be used to illustrate cybersecurity challenges?

The Cuckoo's Egg was written in 1989, but it holds up amazingly well with time.

What is your favorite hacker movie?

It's cliché to say, but *Hackers* stands out, both for the relatively accurate depiction of hacker culture by Hollywood standards and for its characters' amazing fashion choices.

What are your favorite books for motivation, personal development, or enjoyment?
How to Win Friends and Influence People isn't just for social engineers! The writing may be old-fashioned, but the advice it contains is timeless, and putting it into practice will enrich both your personal and professional lives.

I also really enjoy magical realist fiction because there's so much beauty in the world, and thinking about it in new ways can help you see what's in front of you.

> "Be careful what you post on social media, especially on public accounts. Small, seemingly innocuous pieces of information can be put together to paint much larger pictures than you might think."

What is some practical cybersecurity advice you give to people at home in the age of social media and the Internet of Things?
Be careful what you post on social media, especially on public accounts. Small, seemingly innocuous pieces of information can be put together to paint much larger pictures than you might think. What you put online is out there forever, and not everyone is as friendly as you may be. Being thoughtful can make a real difference in protecting yourself and your loved ones from potential attackers.

What is a life hack that you'd like to share?
If you want something to happen, you don't need to wait for permission. Amazing things can be accomplished by determined people in small groups. Get a few friends together and go make it happen.

What is the biggest mistake you've ever made, and how did you recover from it?
I've done a lot of things with my life that I think people would consider mistakes. I've lived my script out of order, had kids too young, dropped out of school, became homeless, went on welfare. When I was younger, I used to tell people I made a good cautionary tale.

But I also think I've made a damn good tale of resilience. I've worked my ass off to get where I am today, and I've brought those experiences with me, using everything that they've taught me. I wouldn't be who or where I am without them, and I'm grateful for that.

> "Girls like me weren't supposed to make it, and I'm glad that I can show people that it can be done."

Girls like me weren't supposed to make it, and I'm glad that I can show people that it can be done. If you've ever worried that it's too late or that you're too weird or that you don't belong...I promise, it's not, you aren't, and you do. ■

> "There is no perfect security, and making perfection your goal results in a brittle security strategy."

Twitter: @danielcornell • **Website:** denimgroup.com/resources/blog/author/dancornell

Dan Cornell

A globally recognized application security expert, Dan Cornell has more than 15 years of experience architecting, developing, and securing web-based software systems. As chief technology officer and principal at Denim Group, Ltd., he leads the technology team to help Fortune 500 companies and government organizations integrate security throughout the development process.

15

If there is one myth that you could debunk in cybersecurity, what would it be?

That it is possible to prevent breaches. Obviously, you need to protect yourself, but also make plans to detect issues and recover from them. There is no perfect security, and making perfection your goal results in a brittle security strategy.

What is one of the biggest bang-for-the-buck actions that an organization can take to improve its cybersecurity posture?

This depends on the organization. For smaller organizations, get the basics right via a managed IT services provider. Automate updates and patching, install antivirus and anti-malware, and back up your data. (Also, don't forget to test your backups. You've tested your backups, right?) Unless you have a really nonstandard threat model, smaller organizations aren't going to be able to do this in house, and it's going to be cheaper and better to get it from an organization that specializes in IT outsourcing for smaller firms.

For larger organizations, use the crap you already bought. I see far too much shelfware in large organizations—software packages that either haven't been installed or are being minimally used and network appliances that either aren't installed or are in "logging" mode only. Instead of spending a bunch of money looking to purchase more stuff (that probably won't be used either), focus on what you *already have* and try to maximize its value.

How is it that cybersecurity spending is increasing but breaches are still happening?

This is a dynamic space with human adversaries who are always evolving. If you look at the value of commerce that has moved online—and continues to move online—you'll see that it is always increasing. As value moves online, that creates an incentive for criminals and other adversaries to move online as well. Most organizations have historically underinvested in cybersecurity spending, so that has left them with a lot of security debt that needs to be addressed to decrease future breaches.

That said, to me, the important thing is that the world still works. You flip the switch, and the lights come on. You can buy stuff with your credit card. Maybe your card number is compromised, but your bank sorts it out, and everyone goes about their business. Breaches are going to happen. Spend in a deliberate manner both to decrease the risk of future breaches and to maximize your agility and ability to respond to the breaches that will inevitably occur.

Do you need a college degree or certification to be a cybersecurity professional?

Well, I do have a college degree, so I'm speaking somewhat from a position of ignorance of all the challenges that someone without one might face. That said, I don't think you need to have a college degree or any professional certifications in order to be a cybersecurity professional. They certainly help—especially if you want to move into management and executive roles—but there are so many free resources available and such a need for more people in the industry that I don't see it as an absolute requirement to get started.

I've seen a lot of people get into systems administration work without degrees or certifications, and I've seen these people transition into pentesting and other roles in information security. In fact, some of the most effective security professionals I've met were so effective in part *because* they had a background where they used to have to keep systems working from a pure IT standpoint.

How did you get started in the cybersecurity field, and what advice would you give to a beginner pursuing a career in cybersecurity?

I've always been interested in how systems work and especially how they can be broken or made to do things they weren't supposed to do. When I started my career as a programmer, I didn't have security as a direct responsibility, but I would always keep an eye on the stuff that the guys at the L0pht were releasing—L0phtCrack, Back Orifice—thinking that they were doing really interesting work. I also remember keeping track of what the folks at NFR Security/Network Flight Recorder were doing. I had an interest, but it wasn't part of my day job.

Fast-forward to a couple of years after Sheridan Chambers and I had started the Denim Group, originally doing custom software development. We got linked up with John Dickson, who essentially said, "I'm a former Air Force officer, and I have a traditional security-guy background. I think the interesting problems in security are going to be centered around software development going forward, and me and all the other traditional security folks don't understand anything about that yet." This led me to start looking at web application security—how do web applications fail, and how can they be made to fail in interesting and useful ways? What are common programming idioms that lead to poor security behaviors in web applications? From there, we built out our application-testing practice, and a big advantage we had was that we had experience building systems, so we could think about breaking systems in general. This helped us expand our practice to look at nonweb applications and more complicated systems.

After that, I started looking at how organizations develop software and how those practices lead to security issues in applications, as well as how those practices could be evolved and augmented to help organizations more reliably create secure software. Finally, from there, I started looking at how to make those changes scale across programs for large organizations. It's been an exciting journey.

What is your specialty in cybersecurity, and how can others gain expertise in your specialty?

My specialty is application and software security—working with organizations to help them create and maintain secure applications. I'm a software developer by background, so I have experience both writing software and working with teams of people who are writing and maintaining software.

If you want to be great at application security, I think you need to have a development background. Obviously, people with other backgrounds can contribute, but the biggest impact comes from those with experience working with teams developing large-scale software systems.

The Open Web Application Security Project (OWASP.org) is a great starting place for anyone interested in getting into application security. They have awareness documents like the *OWASP Top 10 Security Risks* as well as tools like OWASP ZAP that are free and available for people who want to learn more.

What is your advice for career success when it comes to getting hired, climbing the corporate ladder, or starting a company in cybersecurity?

Getting hired:

- Find a place where you're a culture fit.
- Do your research before the interview.

Climbing the corporate ladder:

- Focus on solving problems.
- Do what you say you're going to do.
- Keep learning.

Starting a company in cybersecurity:

- Do something that your customers are truly going to value—not just something you've convinced yourself they'll pay for.

What qualities do you believe all highly successful cybersecurity professionals share?

One key thing I've noticed is that highly successful folks focus on *solving* problems, not just pointing them out. That's a common mistake—especially among too many folks in the attack-side crowd. "Look at how stupid this company is—they have all these vulnerabilities" isn't a super-helpful attitude.

"Highly successful folks focus on solving problems, not just pointing them out."

"I found these issues. Let's talk about how they came about and how you might fix them" is a helpful attitude. Decisions that impact security get made for a variety of reasons. Default-assuming that someone did something because they're dumb is usually wrong, and further investigation will reveal that there was a perfectly logical set of steps that led up to the outcome. The outcome might not be ideal from a security standpoint, but at least there are reasons.

What is the best book or movie that can be used to illustrate cybersecurity challenges?
The Cuckoo's Egg.

What is your favorite hacker movie?
Sneakers.

What are your favorite books for motivation, personal development, or enjoyment?
Rogue Warrior by Richard Marcinko and *Zen and the Art of Motorcycle Maintenance* by Robert M. Pirsig.

What is some practical cybersecurity advice you give to people at home in the age of social media and the Internet of Things?
For the consumer-based Internet of Things, take at least a quick look at the default settings to look for stuff that you might want to lock down, and make sure everything is set to automatically patch and update itself.

For social media, take a quick look at the default settings to look for stuff that you might want to lock down, and watch what you post.

Basically, just take a moment to think about what you're doing and you'll probably have better outcomes.

What is a life hack that you'd like to share?
Wake up early to work out because it gives you a great head start on the day. Four days a week, I get up at 4:45 a.m. and start lifting weights by 5:30. Nobody who has the authority to mess up my day is willing to wake up that early to do it, so this gives me great consistency, which is key for making progress. If you have the physical aspects of your life in line—diet and exercise—it makes the mental aspects far better, and other stuff just tends to fall in line.

What is the biggest mistake you've ever made, and how did you recover from it?
I sold my first company in September 1999, and we negotiated a deal that left us completely trapped and totally unprotected against the dot-com crash in 2000. I went from being "retired" at age 23 to needing a job at 24. I recovered from this by starting the Denim Group in 2001.

Or maybe my biggest mistake was that time I typed `rm -fr *` in the root directory of our main server—and we didn't have backups. I recovered from that by apologizing to a lot of people and manually recovering a whole bunch of data. The lesson? Back up your stuff, and make sure you can restore it! ∎

"This is purely anecdotal, but I would say more than half of the cyber threats that corporations face involve social engineering at some level or another."

Twitter: @kim_crawley • **Websites:** threatvector.cylance.com/en_us/contributors/kim-crawley and www.linkedin.com/in/kimcrawley

Kim Crawley

Kim Crawley is a regular contributor to the corporate blogs for Tripwire, Cylance, Venafi, AlienVault, and Comodo. She has previously written for Sophos's *Naked Security* and *CSO* and has also appeared in *2600 Magazine*. She loves JRPGs, black clothing, Swedish Fish candy, her weird boyfriend, and her equally weird platonic friends. Sometimes while researching cybersecurity topics, she can go through three cans of Red Bull in one sitting.

16

If there is one myth that you could debunk in cybersecurity, what would it be?
That it's all highly esoterically technical. Computer programming code and quantum computer science definitely pertain to cybersecurity. But I'm someone with the mind of a sociologist, so I'm really happy to write about topics like social engineering, scams, and cyberattacks that involve deceiving human beings. Or how effective UI design can help users use their software in a more secure way. Both of those areas have a lot to do with psychology and very little, if anything, to do with cryptographic mathematics, you know?

What is one of the biggest bang-for-the-buck actions that an organization can take to improve its cybersecurity posture?
That's an excellent question! This is purely anecdotal, but I would say more than half of the cyber threats that corporations face involve social engineering at some level or another. It would be a great idea to train all of an organization's employees and contractors on how to spot and avoid social engineering attacks.

That includes not only email, social networking, and phishing websites, but also social engineering attempts that could be made in person or through a phone call. Train your employees on how to avoid social engineering at least twice a year. That'd be the absolute best bang-for-the-buck of anything you could do.

How is it that cybersecurity spending is increasing but breaches are still happening?

I think more and more of our data is online than ever before. I'm not just talking 2018 versus 1998—even in the past few years, the amount of our online data has exploded. That's largely due to the growth in the popularity of third-party cloud services like AWS, Google Cloud, and Microsoft Azure. Then, on the consumer end, a lot of us use a few online accounts to authenticate into dozens or even hundreds of online services and apps through vectors like OAuth. I'm as guilty of that as anyone else. So, if my Google account or my Twitter account was breached, it would spell doom for me. The way we, both as individuals and as enterprises, use data through the internet has gotten exponentially more complicated. So, securing our organizations and our lives is inevitably much more complicated too. The added complexity and volume of data have made security more expensive and the attack surface much larger.

So, that's how more money spent doesn't eliminate breaches. Absolutely nothing is completely secure anyway; it's all a matter of risk assessment and mitigation.

Do you need a college degree or certification to be a cybersecurity professional?

I'm living proof that the answer is no! I got my GED when I was 25. I've had a few CompTIA, Cisco, and EC-Council certifications over the years, all of which I self-studied for, and pretty much all of which have since expired. Now mind you, the nature of my job is highly unusual. I study cybersecurity in general, I contribute to the official blogs of several vendors, and I write for computer technology magazines. The majority of people who do what I do have a day job as some sort of technology practitioner. I haven't had a hands-on IT role since I was laid off from my last tech support job in 2011. I work completely in words and theory. Now, if you want to know if it's possible to be a network administrator or malware researcher without formal credentials, you'd have to ask them. I not-so-secretly envy people who have university degrees in computer science. But, I've managed to become someone who's considered knowledgeable without massive, crushing student debt.

How did you get started in the cybersecurity field, and what advice would you give to a beginner pursuing a career in cybersecurity?

I've been fascinated by computers for as long as I can remember. In 1988, 4-year-old me was intrigued by my older half-brother's Commodore 64, an impressive toy for its time. He wouldn't let me touch it, and I was very sad. In 1993, the Crawley household got its very first Windows PC. They were often called IBM compatibles back then. Ours ran an OEM version of brand-spanking-new Windows 3.1. Dad let me play with it when he wasn't doing his work as a novelist. I became adequately adept to provide him with tech support, such as LPT1 issues. By 1995, we had internet access through a Prodigy Online trial offered with our 9600bps modem. I used IRC and Mosaic a lot. After Mosaic, I moved on to Netscape Navigator, and so on, and I watched the Web rapidly evolve from there.

So, I've been online since I was 11. But back then it was unusual to have internet access at home, so I got a head start. I was interested in computing, but I didn't see myself with a related career of any sort. I started to struggle with math, and my teacher told me that I had to be a math whiz to work with computers. I think she thought all computing jobs were like cryptographer roles or programming in assembly. She also probably thought that she was encouraging my math to improve rather than discouraging me from IT and computer science. She was wrong. I didn't start studying IT properly until I was 25 because I was so discouraged by sexism and my nonverbal learning disorder. To make a long story short, I became a tech support agent. I got loads of malware-related tickets, and my curiosity about security grew from there. I was working on a *Toronto Star* political journalism project. One of my colleagues had connections with a cybersecurity blog and highly recommended me. That was back in 2010. Once my foot was in the door, I had tech magazines and vendors asking me to work for them. I've been very fortunate, and I'll never forget the people who helped me along the way. I think my career is my career for life now.

> "I've been very fortunate, and I'll never forget the people who helped me along the way. I think my career is my career for life now."

What is your specialty in cybersecurity, and how can others gain expertise in your specialty?

My job makes me be a generalist in cybersecurity, because the more topics that I can research and write about, the more work I can get, and I'm paid purely for the work that I produce—no wages, no salaries. As a practitioner, you'll probably have to specialize a lot more because being a jack-of-all-trades means you're a master of none. I still have favorite areas, though. Social engineering fascinates me, as does malware in general. Whenever I write about trojans, I get to luxuriate in both! And I just wrote about Fortnite Android trojans for Comodo's corporate blog, so I got to write about video games as well. It was pure bliss.

What is your advice for career success when it comes to getting hired, climbing the corporate ladder, or starting a company in cybersecurity?

Unfortunately, capitalism has made the job market a harsh, cold, dog-eat-dog world. There's nothing you can do to guarantee success; there are only things you can do to improve your odds. People are susceptible to making hiring decisions based on social bullshit. So, network a lot, and be nice to everyone even if you have to fake it. Find events and groups where people in your industry are, both online and offline. This pertains to starting your own cybersecurity firm as well because you'll need investors, clientele, and word of mouth.

What qualities do you believe all highly successful cybersecurity professionals share?

Curiosity, most definitely. You can't learn anything effectively without it. You also need the right mind-set, a very paranoid mind-set. How can people use this technology to do bad stuff?

What is the best book or movie that can be used to illustrate cybersecurity challenges?

I like every Bruce Schneier book that I've read so far. I recommend *Secrets and Lies: Digital Security in a Networked World* for starters.

What is your favorite hacker movie?

I wear black lipstick, and I have a face full of piercings. So, the expectation is that I'll say either *The Girl with the Dragon Tattoo* or the Millennium series to conform to people's expectations—or anything but, to rebel against said expectations. I choose the former. I've read all of the books so far, including the two that have come out after Stieg Larsson's death. I prefer the Swedish movies. Yeah, it's not all technically accurate, though. It's no *Mr. Robot*. But *Mr. Robot* doesn't have a forced tattooing scene!

What are your favorite books for motivation, personal development, or enjoyment?

I'm awfully skeptical of most self-help books, anything that Oprah would endorse, and stuff like the UpliftingNews subreddit. I think everyone should read Karl Marx, William S. Burroughs, and Marilyn vos Savant with an open mind. People should drop acid and watch old George Carlin routines. I'm also very fond of anime and manga, and my taste in that stuff makes me a terrible weeaboo, you know? As far as anything that people think is new-agey woo is concerned, I do genuinely believe in western astrology, which would put me in contention with many in STEM culture.

I also think meditation and mindfulness are good; just don't get your advice in those areas from Lululemon or someone Oprah would endorse.

What is some practical cybersecurity advice you give to people at home in the age of social media and the Internet of Things?

Sure, the data in data storage will physically deteriorate eventually, but you should still have the mind-set of "the internet is forever." I was born the same year as Mark Zuckerberg, and social media and smartphones didn't take off until I was in my mid-20s. I was lucky to become an adult when I did. But now we have probably a couple of billion people worldwide who grew up with all of that. Their impulsive Snapchat posts will come back to haunt them. Snapchat told you that it's private and it will disappear when your session is over. They're lying. Assume that nothing is private and everything is permanent. As far as IoT is concerned, it's promising for both consumers and industries. But think twice before you decide that your kitchen stove needs an internet connection—21st century Teddy Ruxpin could spy on your young children. Anything IoT becomes subject to tremendous internet vulnerabilities that connect the device to everything else that's online.

What is a life hack that you'd like to share?

If you're like me and you wear lots of makeup, buy setting spray and matte lipstick. The right use of those products keeps me looking freshly tacky all day.

Each day, tell the people you love the most what you like about them. It will help your personal life immensely.

What is the biggest mistake you've ever made, and how did you recover from it?

Oh, I've made so many mistakes! It's tough to only choose one! Many of my mistakes have been made by speaking impulsively or by reacting based on my hurt feelings. Try to teach yourself to pause for a few seconds to consider the possible implications of it. As I've gotten older, it has gotten easier, but I still screw up from time to time. Recovery can be done with genuine apologies, forgiving yourself for the mistake, and moving on while trying again. ■

"Know your stuff inside and out. There's a serious dearth of expertise in the basics— and in knowing the simple, easy-to-answer questions about simple topics like the OSI model—which is the bare minimum for both getting started and expanding your career."

Twitter: @hexadecim8 • **Website:** www.hexadecim8.com

Emily Crose

Emily Crose is a network security professional and researcher whose career spans nine years. She has worked in both offensive and defensive security roles, including time spent with both the NSA and the CIA. Currently, she works for IronNet Cybersecurity. When she's not caring for her wife and children, she directs the NEMESIS project and finds threats to the openness and safety of the internet for fun in addition to profit.

17

What is one of the biggest bang-for-the-buck actions that an organization can take to improve its cybersecurity posture?

Cybersecurity doesn't have to be a cash-for-play business. Developing a threat model for your organization and planning out what you'll do if realistic scenarios play out is a cheap and easy way to prepare for issues that could appear later. Maybe you don't know all there is to know about cybersecurity threats. The good news is that learning the basics of cyber defense has never been achievable at a lower cost-to-entry!

How is it that cybersecurity spending is increasing but breaches are still happening?

They say, "Money don't buy happiness." It turns out money don't buy a lot of things, good security practices included. An organization is only as safe as its friendliest individual. When technology fails, humans will always pick up the slack, even when it comes to helping a dangerous individual gain access to their own organization. That doesn't mean that humans are responsible for all security failings.

The nature of innovation necessitates new technology, and with new technology comes new threats. Even old thoughts and concepts being applied in new ways against ever-evolving technology can be threatening in the hands of someone clever enough to exploit it. What you get out of this concoction of human error and ever-changing technology in a world where data is constantly moving is a complex world full of motivations and capabilities trying not to crash into each other. We shouldn't be surprised that collisions occur even with an abundance of stoplights.

How did you get started in the cybersecurity field, and what advice would you give to a beginner pursuing a career in cybersecurity?

Take the time to learn the basics, and learn them well. You'll always return to them, and with a solid grasp of the basics, you will stand out in interviews later in your career. One of the primary complaints I hear from hiring managers is that they can't find anyone who has a solid foundation in networking. Don't be the candidate who can't expand on the seven layers of OSI.

What is your specialty in cybersecurity, and how can others gain expertise in your specialty?

The thing I'm probably best at is hunt methodology. The most valuable advice I have for people trying to improve their skill in this area is to seek tools that will help them pivot information, both internally sourced and externally sourced. Building internal tools like a working and effective passive DNS system will pay huge dividends in the long run once you're able to get them up and running. Open source intelligence (OSINT) skills help greatly in this part of the field, and new tools are always emerging.

What is your advice when it comes to getting hired, climbing the corporate ladder, or starting a company in cybersecurity?

Know your stuff inside and out. There's a serious dearth of expertise in the basics—and in knowing the simple, easy-to-answer questions about simple topics like the OSI model—which is the bare minimum for both getting started and expanding your career.

What qualities do you believe all highly successful cybersecurity professionals share?

Resourcefulness. Using whatever you have at your disposal to get access to a restricted area, fixing a problem on the fly, or getting an answer to something against all odds are all necessary skills to have in InfoSec. Most people acquire that last one by living through IT support.

What is the best book or movie that can be used to illustrate cybersecurity challenges?

Groundhog Day.

What is your favorite hacker movie?

If it counts, I'd say *Ghost in the Shell*. I think it counts.

What are your favorite books for motivation, personal development, or enjoyment?

Black Hat Python is a fun book if you want to learn how to build tools for red-hatting whenever you need them. I'd also recommend *Practical Malware Analysis*. But if you need a truly inspiring book, *If I Was Your Girl* will change your life.

What is some practical cybersecurity advice you give to people at home in the age of social media and the Internet of Things?

In a pinch, a microwave makes an excellent Faraday cage for small, personal electronic devices. Bonus points for turning the microwave on while your phone is in there.

What is the biggest mistake you've ever made, and how did you recover from it?

Taking a management job. Avoid this at all costs. ■

"Free static code analysis tools can be used to find bugs in software, whether it's developed in house or open source. It won't find every bug, but it can help tell you quickly what kinds of risks you're taking on by using that software."

Twitter: @Dan_Crowley

Daniel Crowley

18

Daniel Crowley is the head of research and a penetration tester for X-Force Red. He denies all allegations regarding unicorn smuggling and questions your character for even suggesting it. He is the primary author of both the Magical Code Injection Rainbow, a configurable vulnerability testbed, and FeatherDuster, an automated cryptanalysis tool. Daniel enjoys climbing large rocks and was *TIME Magazine*'s 2006 Person of the Year. He has been working in the information security industry since 2004 and is a frequent speaker at conferences, including Black Hat, DEF CON, ShmooCon, and SOURCE. Daniel does his own charcuterie and brews his own beer. His work has been included in books and college courses. He also holds the noble title of baron in the micronation of Sealand.

If there is one myth that you could debunk in cybersecurity, what would it be?
That we truly are a meritocracy as The Mentor claimed. When he wrote his famous *Hacker's Manifesto*, it was a time when everyone was just a screen name. You couldn't judge someone by their race, nationality, sex, and so on, because you simply didn't know those things. While things are improving, we're still not the magical utopia we're supposed to be, but some people assume we are just because The Mentor said it was so.

What is one of the biggest bang-for-the-buck actions that an organization can take to improve its cybersecurity posture?
Free static code analysis tools can be used to find bugs in software, whether it's developed in house or open source. It won't find every bug, but it can help tell

you quickly what kinds of risks you're taking on by using that software. You can also set up your development pipeline to allow code to be pushed only when no bugs are discovered.

How is it that cybersecurity spending is increasing but breaches are still happening?

We are building on a shaky foundation. Computers and the internet were built without the idea that they would one day be attacked. We still have a long way to go. It sometimes horrifies me to think about just how insecure things are in general. Even if we were to fix all the technological problems tomorrow, you can still just ask people for their passwords and a certain percentage will actually give them to you.

Do you need a college degree or certification to be a cybersecurity professional?

I know a number of very skilled professionals who do not have any degree or certification. One former colleague of mine had a degree in digital art. So, no.

How did you get started in the cybersecurity field, and what advice would you give to a beginner pursuing a career in cybersecurity?

My start was a bit odd. I was doing freelance work while in university for *way* less than it was worth. I was finding bugs and reporting them to get my work in the public record. I ran a computer security education group at my university (unofficially, they were scared about the liability associated with a bunch of students learning to hack). I got to do a cooperative semester. I went to interview with Core Security in Boston for an internship because I knew I wanted to work in computer security. I sat down with a folder of prepared documents showing all my forays into computer security across from a guy named Mike Yaffe. He nodded and smiled as I talked about each one, and said, "Seems like you know a lot about computer security!" to which I responded with a big smile. Then he asked what I knew about marketing, and I realized with slow dread that I had been interviewing for a marketing internship. I explained the mix-up, and Mike offered to let me take the position so long as I was willing to do some marketing work, noting that in the meantime I could do computer security research. I agreed, and soon enough I had scripted away all my marketing work and spent nearly all my time doing security research. They hired me after I graduated, and the rest is history.

My advice to beginners is to get familiar with whatever technology you want to learn to hack. Most of hacking is about understanding how the system works better than the person who put it together.

What is your specialty in cybersecurity, and how can others gain expertise in your specialty?

I specialize in web applications and physical security. Web applications potentially involve a lot of different technologies, so there's a lot of things to learn, but I would first recommend familiarizing yourself with HTTP, HTML, JavaScript, and a server-side language of your choice. No matter what application you're looking at, they all use those things, more or less. Build yourself a basic web application and learn to use Burp Suite, or some other intercepting proxy, and see what it looks like when you post a form or click a link. Once you understand how web applications are built, you can start to understand how they're subverted and why data from the client side can never be trusted.

What is your advice for career success when it comes to getting hired, climbing the corporate ladder, or starting a company in cybersecurity?

For getting hired, do some pro bono public work. Find and release bugs. Write tutorials. Do conference talks. Develop and release free tools. Play capture the flags. You can point to those on your résumé, and it goes a long way when you're getting your first job.

What qualities do you believe all highly successful cybersecurity professionals share?

An eagerness to learn new things. You'll always have to learn about the system you're hacking before you can find most of the interesting vulnerabilities. As a security professional, you're always having to learn. If you stop, you'll become irrelevant in a few years because technology changes so fast.

What is your favorite hacker movie?

For good hacker movies, I'd say *WarGames*. It didn't focus a lot on the hacking, but it didn't need to; it was just a vehicle for the story. For bad hacker movies, I'd say *Blackhat*. They claimed they were making the most accurate hacking movie ever, and then you had Chris Hemsworth phishing the NSA, beating up six guys single-handedly in a bar fight, and going into a nuclear power plant in meltdown to retrieve a hard drive. It's glorious cheese.

What are your favorite books for motivation, personal development, or enjoyment?

The Web Application Hacker's Handbook and *The Tangled Web* are both excellent.

What is some practical cybersecurity advice you give to people at home in the age of social media and the Internet of Things?

Use a password manager. Using weak passwords and reusing passwords are big risks to your personal security. If I really wanted to hack someone, I'd find every dinky website they ever signed up for and every exposed IoT device they have and hack whichever ones I could. Then I'd try every password on all the other accounts—not that I would do that, since I'm too pretty for prison.

What is a life hack that you'd like to share?

However long the package of food tells you to microwave it, microwave it for twice as long at 50 percent power. Your food will be more evenly cooked and less rubbery.

What is the biggest mistake you've ever made, and how did you recover from it?

A long time ago, I put several copies of a rather lewd and disgusting picture that was an early running joke on the internet around a local shop, emulating the rather common practice at the time of getting people to view it accidentally by clicking a link you sent them. I got caught and had a terrifying experience where I almost became a felon over what I saw as a silly prank. Some begging forgiveness to a magistrate, a fee, hours of community service, and two years of keeping out of trouble later, the whole thing was dismissed. I feel lucky that I was given that opportunity to move on with my life, and I realize that if things had been a little different, I may not have gotten that chance. ∎

"In fact, the industry greatly benefits from hiring people of differing backgrounds, precisely because crafting solutions to difficult and nuanced problems in this space requires differing opinions."

Twitter: @__winn • **Website:** www.linkedin.com/in/winnonadesombre

Winnona DeSombre

19

Winnona DeSombre is an Asia-Pacific threat intelligence researcher at Recorded Future, focusing on Chinese underground hacking communities and East Asian cyber-espionage campaigns. Previously, she updated legacy systems in government software at MITRE and MIT Lincoln Laboratory and conducted policy research at the Harvard Belfer Center. In recent years, Winnona spoke at the Forbes Under 30 Summit and TEDxTufts, won the Harvard Belfer Center's D3P Information Operations Technical and Policy Hackathon, and was a semi-finalist in the Atlantic Council's Cyber 9/12 competition.

If there is one myth that you could debunk in cybersecurity, what would it be?
The myth that individuals who work in cybersecurity are all one type of person. Cybersecurity is a wide field with many different types of jobs and consists of individuals from various backgrounds. In fact, the industry greatly benefits from hiring people of differing backgrounds, precisely because crafting solutions to difficult and nuanced problems in this space requires differing opinions. However, because so many people believe they need to fit a certain type of mold to succeed in this industry, many don't even consider it as a possible career option. As a biracial woman who only started coding in college, I want to encourage as many people as possible to consider the field, even if they don't "fit the mold."

What is one of the biggest bang-for-the-buck actions that an organization can take to improve its cybersecurity posture?

Signs around the office that stress proper OPSEC/baseline security awareness for employees. Hanging up a poster on the ramifications of clicking a phishing link, not backing up their data, or even allowing someone to piggyback their way into a restricted area. This allows individuals to remind themselves of these issues every day. At a past internship of mine, I noticed that when many of these posters contained simple messaging, such as "Trust but verify," even employees quoting the poster in jest became far more mindful about clicking phishing links. Super simple, really cheap, and pretty effective.

How is it that cybersecurity spending is increasing but breaches are still happening?

Legacy systems, unpatched systems, and human error. Unless money is being spent on good training or system updates, no amount of cybersecurity spending can fix an unpatched system running Windows XP or an easily guessable password. For attackers, there are free tools available for download in multiple places on the internet that exploit both of these issues. (There's even an entire operating system that comes with these tools for free—Kali Linux.)

Do you need a college degree or certification to be a cybersecurity professional?

This really depends on the work environment, who the hiring managers are, and what type of work the organization does. When I worked at a federally funded R&D center, I was reading PhD-level papers to apply certain concepts to projects and (personally) would not have been able to do so without my college degree. While working there, I was told by a women's mentoring group that not only did I need a college degree but I needed to have one more degree than most men to be taken seriously. I believe this is an extreme perspective—and is not necessarily an accurate representation of most cybersecurity roles—but it's important to know that it does exist. This is especially relevant if you're hoping to work for a government organization.

In contrast, the startup I work at currently has individuals from incredibly varied backgrounds, and my education often does not directly impact my ability to get a project done. I firmly believe that college degrees and certifications display a conventional knowledge of the field that may not be necessary if you can prove your expertise in other ways (jobs, projects, etc.). Degrees and certifications are an easy thing to point to when someone doubts your credentials (and this is likely to happen, especially if you're a woman), but it's nearly impossible to beat the real-life training that you get through experience.

How did you get started in the cybersecurity field, and what advice would you give to a beginner pursuing a career in cybersecurity?

I was studying international relations when I took an "Introduction to Computer Science" class. As I explored the intersection of these two fields, I realized that cyber-threat intelligence was a natural fit. I found state-sponsored cyber campaigns fascinating, and I enjoyed explaining technical concepts to nontechnical people—and it felt like I was making a positive impact. However, before finding this niche, I spent a good chunk of my college career figuring out paths in cybersecurity that I didn't want to take. I had some technical internships, competed in capture-the-flag competitions, and did compliance research for pro bono projects. At some points, it felt like I was randomly choosing career paths, only to be disappointed by each one. I assumed that I was narrowing down my career path by choosing cybersecurity, but I was totally wrong.

This field contains careers with a range of technical and nontechnical flavors, each with its own industry-specific jargon. If I could give advice to someone starting out in this field, I would tell them to explore as many options as possible and to not be discouraged by ones that don't appear to be a good fit. It took me a few tries, but I'm incredibly happy with the path I've ended up on.

What is your specialty in cybersecurity, and how can others gain expertise in your specialty?

I am an Asia-Pacific threat intelligence researcher. Aside from conducting research that fills knowledge gaps for customers and the public about cyber threats originating from or occurring in East Asia, I'm also responsible for tracking, maintaining, curating, and improving coverage of these threats for my company. I'm able to combine my technical skills with a wider geopolitical and cultural understanding of the Asia-Pacific region when researching cyberattacks originating from that area.

I find technical resources in multiple languages for my analysis and occasionally interact directly with threat actors within the region. It's a really fun job and definitely a specialized part of security. It's really about honing nontechnical skills as much as the technical skills. I read the news as often as I read technical reports, practice my language skills, and try to be involved in both the foreign policy and cybersecurity communities.

What is your advice for career success when it comes to getting hired, climbing the corporate ladder, or starting a company in cybersecurity?

While studying computer science in college, I found that most individuals would frantically submit résumés to tens, if not hundreds, of job portals while studying obscure coding questions for possible technical interviews. While this approach worked for a number of fellow students, it is also an incredibly exhausting and disheartening process.

Instead of adding my résumé to the pile, I started attending security meetups and conferences in my city. (I would highly recommend the Boston Security Meetup, BSides Boston, and Women in Tech conferences in general.) I cannot overstate how rewarding this experience was for me. I recognize that going out and meeting new people—especially when you're just getting into a field—can be both intimidating and overwhelming, but it's highly effective and often gets easier over time.

Many conferences have career fairs, and I would get to meet the same company recruiters throughout the events. By attending talks at these conferences, I developed a better understanding of what skills allowed individuals to succeed in the field I wanted to go into, and I picked up some valuable technical skills along the way. Most importantly, I got to meet people who were already in the industry at these events, talk to them about their jobs, and hear some incredible stories about our industry. Another common misconception for students is that, to get a job out of college, they have to demonstrate their knowledge outside of the classroom with multiple personal projects to supplement their résumés. Some of these projects, like developing a mobile application or contributing to an open source security tool, are definitely crucial to displaying passion and technical prowess. However, many also believed that these personal projects had to be one-person projects, and they'd spend hours by themselves developing large-scale programs for the sake of résumé building. I want to stress that there are many other ways to put personal projects on a résumé. Hackathons are great opportunities to build a cool, fun project with friends. Offering your technical services to an organization you care about makes an individual project so much more meaningful and fun (it also technically counts as a job!). Personally, I love group projects and competition, and I sought out high-pressure competitions throughout college that I could coerce my friends into. Most recently, I roped some of my co-workers into participating in the DEFCON threat intel capture the flag with me (personal technical development shouldn't stop once you get a job!). Essentially, focus on finding part of this field that you love and can work on instead of trying to find things that make you "employable."

What qualities do you believe all highly successful cybersecurity professionals share?
A love of learning, a passion for the field, and a desire to help others. It's as simple as that. Our field evolves at a rapid rate to keep up with (or keep abreast of) new technologies, and I believe these three traits keep a person motivated and successful regardless of how quickly or dramatically the industry changes.

What is the best book or movie that can be used to illustrate cybersecurity challenges?
Catch Me If You Can is based on the true story of Frank Abagnale, Jr. (now a security consultant), who successfully performed cons worth millions of dollars using social engineering tactics and by finding weak points within a series of systems. Simply by purchasing a pilot's uniform at a Pan American World Airways retailer (third-party supply chain risk, anyone?), he was able to trick his way into impersonating a Pan Am pilot.

Abagnale also eventually started to use his fraud skills to assist the FBI, which shows that individuals with skills in fraud can use their gifts for the common good.

When it comes to high-level overviews on issues in cybersecurity in literature, Bruce Schneier's *Click Here to Kill Everybody* and Joel Brenner's *Glass Houses* are two of my favorites.

What is your favorite hacker movie?
I know it's a TV series and not a movie, but I'm a huge fan of *Black Mirror*. So many of the technological components the series revolves around exist (hacked web cameras, social credit scores, even robot bees), and the show does an excellent job of warning about how individuals and societies can exploit this technology.

What are your favorite books for motivation, personal development, or enjoyment?
Most of my reading material is for professional development or enjoyment. When I'm not reading science fiction or short stories, I'm reading policy reports, DoJ indictments, or news articles. I highly recommend *Can't and Won't* by Lydia Davis, and I've currently been poring over the Foundation series by Isaac Asimov, which has been on my list for a while. When it comes to motivation or personal development, I usually listen to podcasts instead. I follow quite a few, and I listen to them as I'm getting ready in the morning. I would recommend *The CyberWire* for cybersecurity, *TechBuzz China* and *Reply All* for technology-related news, and *Intelligence Matters* for national security analysis. These podcasts offer deeper

dives into really interesting topics, and it's motivating to hear accomplished individuals talking about their experiences in the industries I care about.

What is some practical cybersecurity advice you give to people at home in the age of social media and the Internet of Things?
For Internet of Things devices, I recommend doing the prerequisite security research and weighing your choices prior to buying. While it has become incredibly convenient to use an internet-enabled house thermostat or alarm system, there are many devices that have well-disclosed vulnerabilities that, upon Googling, can be alarming to an average consumer. Here's a helpful level set: if a company is prompt in responding to new vulnerabilities, practices coordinated disclosure, and has a robust system for patching, it's a good sign they're on top of things. When you see companies dodging the issue, denying, or refusing to provide a timeline for patching, it's right to worry, and you'll want to steer clear.

> "As for social media, "checking into" locations or sharing location data indefinitely is a bad idea."

As for social media, "checking into" locations or sharing location data indefinitely is a bad idea. Short term, depending on your security settings, sharing location data can enable any of your social media contacts—some of whom are definitely not close friends—to show up at your exact location. Long term, it allows anyone with access to your geolocation data (not necessarily just your contacts) to figure out your habits and routines, which can be great for illicit activities ranging from social engineering to burglary and kidnapping.

What is a life hack that you'd like to share?
Reading before bed. I realize that this is incredibly simple, but it's one of the few times I can sit uninterrupted to read anything from cybersecurity research to a good science fiction book, and I get better sleep than I would have had I been watching Netflix.

What is the biggest mistake you've ever made, and how did you recover from it?
During college, I submitted a poster to the Women in CyberSecurity conference (WiCyS). The research I had done was my own analysis of Chinese military cyber-espionage campaigns based on multiple threat intelligence reports and news articles. The poster was accepted, and it was then that I realized my poster was going to be judged against a rubric and compared against other posters in the session. I decided that the rubric was going to judge me poorly because my poster was not a traditional technical paper, and I withdrew my poster from the conference—completely out of fear. I walked into the conference a few months later and realized how much of a mistake I had made. Because I was scared of being judged as an imposter, I missed an incredible opportunity to discuss my research with women in security from various backgrounds.

I work in an industry where it is incredibly easy to feel unqualified. It's really hard to shake "imposter syndrome"—it's honestly something I still struggle with regularly. However, I remind myself constantly that I love this field precisely because there is so much to learn and so much room to grow—and there always will be, for everyone, regardless of how long you've been in it.

And here's the thing: if this field didn't scare the hell out of me and challenge me daily, would I really want to be in it? ■

"Take a look at the biggest companies around today— Apple, Facebook, and Google. They all use bug bounty programs with security in mind and dedicate a lot of resources to them— even after their software has been developed. That's because bug bounties work."

Twitter: @ethicalhack3r • **Website:** dewhurstsecurity.com

Ryan Dewhurst

Ryan Dewhurst has been professionally testing web applications for security issues since 2009. He has a BSc (Hons) in ethical hacking for computer security that he completed with first-class honors. Ryan is active in the information security community, contributing to various OWASP projects and releasing his own popular tools, such as Damn Vulnerable Web App (DVWA) and WPScan. In 2013, he was recognized by his peers when he was awarded the European Information Security Magazine Rising Star Award. Ryan has also appeared on the BBC and in many magazines and online publications for his work. In the past, he was known for identifying security issues in companies such as Facebook, Mozilla, Apple, and others while conducting independent security research.

20

If there is one myth that you could debunk in cybersecurity, what would it be?

Nothing is ever "secure." There is always going to be someone smarter than you and with more resources. You could have done everything by the book—used a security development lifecycle (SDLC), had the software tested by a third party, implemented robust hardening, defense in depth, etc. etc. What you are doing here is making the software, or system, more secure, but you can never claim that something is totally "secure." And to anyone who claims their product is totally secure, what they really mean is "secure enough." And then you have to ask yourself, "Secure enough against what threat actor? Script kiddies, disgruntled employees, skilled hackers, government agencies, organized crime, and so on."

A good example of this is why the bug bounty industry exists. Take a look at the biggest companies around today—Apple, Facebook, and Google. They all use bug bounty programs with security in mind and dedicate a lot of resources to them—even after their software has been developed. That's because bug bounties work. There's always someone smarter or with more resources who, with the right incentives, will look for and identify security issues.

So, the next time someone claims that a product is secure, ask yourself, "Secure against what, or whom?"

What is one of the biggest bang-for-the-buck actions that an organization can take to improve its cybersecurity posture?
Brain power. Seriously. The more an organization's employees think about the security of their products and the security of their organization, the more secure it will be. Of course, they will need to do more than just think about security; they'll need to take action too. But by making design decisions with security in mind, they will ultimately be more secure. And to get your organization to start thinking about security, it needs to come from the top. The employees need to know the value of security, and that can come only from adequate training and creating a security culture.

"The more an organization's employees think about the security of their products and the security of their organization, the more secure it will be."

How is it that cybersecurity spending is increasing but breaches are still happening?
I don't know. Perhaps the money is not being spent in the right places?

Do you need a college degree or certification to be a cybersecurity professional?
No, you do not need a college degree or certification to be a cybersecurity professional. But I do think that degrees are useful, depending on the financial cost. My degree helped me personally, in a lot of ways. It taught me how to research, how to write scientifically, discipline, and much more. I didn't finish compulsory secondary school due to my inherent anti-establishment teenage mind. I didn't enjoy school; in fact, I hated it, so I left as soon as I was old enough for anyone to employ. University gave me, personally, a sense of achievement that I did not have before graduating, which ultimately led to greater confidence.

How did you get started in the cybersecurity field, and what advice would you give to a beginner pursuing a career in cybersecurity?
I had always had an interest in security since the first day I dialed up to the internet. The first real job I got was over Twitter. While in my first year of university, the owner of a security consulting business, not far from where I was living at the time, asked me if I was looking for work. I went down to their office and got the job. Had it not been for my tweeting about security and my involvement in the security community, I doubt I would have gotten a job so early on. At the beginning of your career, I would advise getting involved, sharing your thoughts, creating projects, and contributing to others' projects.

What is your specialty in cybersecurity, and how can others gain expertise in your specialty?
My specialty is web application security. You can gain expertise by writing secure web applications.

What is your advice for career success when it comes to getting hired, climbing the corporate ladder, or starting a company in cybersecurity?
Don't hang around if you're bored with a job. Get another job, change roles, start your own company. Life is way too short to stagnate.

What qualities do you believe all highly successful cybersecurity professionals share?
You don't need to be able to code to work in security, but in my opinion, even if your role is nontechnical, to be *highly* successful you need to know how to code. There will be caveats to this, and I'm generalizing here.

What is the best book or movie that can be used to illustrate cybersecurity challenges?
I think *GCHQ: The Uncensored Story of Britain's Most Secret Intelligence Agency* by Richard Aldrich. It illustrates the challenges in securing a state, so there is probably a lot we can learn from this book in terms of the history of security and its challenges.

What is your favorite hacker movie?
The Matrix, probably due to my age at the time it was released. It had a big influence on me and absolutely blew my mind.

What are your favorite books for motivation, personal development, or enjoyment?
I don't read as much as I'd like to, but here's a few of my favorites:

General security: *The Cuckoo's Egg* by Cliff Stoll

Technical: *The Web Application Hacker's Handbook* by Dafydd Stuttard and Marcus Pinto

Enjoyment: *Ready Player One, The Martian*

What is some practical cybersecurity advice you give to people at home in the age of social media and the Internet of Things?
Don't buy those IoT devices with internet-connected microphones and put them in your house. Keep backups. Be careful what you download and click on.

What is a life hack that you'd like to share?
Remember that everything is temporary. So take the time to do the things you love, embrace the people you love. And when times are hard, remember that they will get better.

What is the biggest mistake you've ever made, and how did you recover from it?
I tend to learn from my mistakes and then forget about them. So I can't remember any. ∎

> "We now live in a work culture of teams and teamwork being the only way to achieve success. If you can't work efficiently and positively with others, you will not climb the corporate ladder."

Twitter: @DeidreDiamond • **Websites:** www.CyberSN.com and www.Brainbabe.org

Deidre Diamond

21

Deidre Diamond is the CEO and founder of CyberSN.com, a cybersecurity research and staffing company, and the founder of Brainbabe.org, a cybersecurity not-for-profit organization. Her vision and leadership have resulted in a dramatic decrease in the frustration, time, and cost associated with job searching and hiring for cybersecurity professionals. Prior to CyberSN, Deidre was the CEO of Percussion Software, the first VP of sales at Rapid7 (NASDAQ: RPD), and the VP of staffing and recruiting for the national technical staffing company Motion Recruitment. Deidre leads with a strong commitment to transparency, equality, training, support, high productivity, and love in the workforce.

If there is one myth that you could debunk in cybersecurity, what would it be?
That cybersecurity professionals are different. We are all different in small ways and yet not different in the things that matter to success in the workplace. All humans want respect, growth, transparency, truth, training, equal opportunity, equal pay, time to decompress, and leaders who care.

What is one of the biggest bang-for-the-buck actions that an organization can take to improve its cybersecurity posture?
Have succession planning that offers training; otherwise, you will *not* retain your talent.

How is it that cybersecurity spending is increasing but breaches are still happening?

Breaches are happening because we are spending more money on technology than on people. According to our research at CyberSN, cybersecurity roles will sit vacant for an average of six months before the organization seeks outside staffing help. This means the organization's current cybersecurity team members are working overtime and not feeling successful due to a shortage of teammates. This results in poor talent retention and a weakened cybersecurity posture.

> "Breaches are happening because we are spending more money on technology than on people."

Do you need a college degree or certification to be a cybersecurity professional?

The short answer is that it depends on the company, and degrees/certs never hurt. A degree is not always needed, and yet a degree does open doors that can't be opened without one. Certifications and degrees can matter if a person is focused on obtaining a specific job title. Overall, a degree or a cert always helps and yet doesn't guarantee a job.

How did you get started in the cybersecurity field, and what advice would you give to a beginner pursuing a career in cybersecurity?

I got started through a career in sales. Thirteen years into my career of working for serial entrepreneurs, they asked me to join their startup firm Rapid7. There, I led the building of the sales, sales engineering, customer success, and talent acquisition teams. I was employee #18 and led Rapid7 from $800,000 to $50 million in recurring revenue over a four-year time period. It was through this opportunity that I fell in love with the cybersecurity community. I am a criminal justice and sociology degreed professional, so cybersecurity is super interesting to me.

What is your specialty in cybersecurity, and how can others gain expertise in your specialty?

My specialty is in sales and product vision and management. Salespeople are the closest to the customer, particularly the new customer. This means salespeople understand the real pain points of their customers and can articulate how to best engineer and build teams. Getting into sales is not hard if one has smarts, motivation, and high energy, along with the ability to truly care about how people think, feel, and perceive.

What is your advice for career success when it comes to getting hired, climbing the corporate ladder, or starting a company in cybersecurity?

My advice is to care about the soft skills, also known as emotional quotient (EQ). We now live in a work culture of teams and teamwork being the only way to achieve success. If you can't work efficiently and positively with others, you will not climb the corporate ladder. On our website at CyberSN.com, you can see a list of the EQ skills.

> "My advice is to care about the soft skills, also known as emotional quotient (EQ). We now live in a work culture of teams and teamwork being the only way to achieve success."

What qualities do you believe all highly successful cybersecurity professionals share?
The ability to communicate in such a way that others feel good about the conversation, even if they had to concede or didn't get what they wanted.

"Understanding the impact of our words and the role they play in our ability to navigate work and interpersonal relationships is a very powerful skill that will help you in life and in business."

What is the best book or movie that can be used to illustrate cybersecurity challenges?
The Art of War by Sun Tzu! I gave a keynote talk at Hacker Halted in 2017, and I named my talk W.A.R. (Words Are Risk). This was a spin on the title of this book (which was the theme of the conference that year). Our words can make or break our careers. Understanding the impact of our words and the role they play in our ability to navigate work and interpersonal relationships is a powerful skill that will help you in life and in business.

What is your favorite hacker movie?
I don't watch many fictional movies, but I did enjoy the TV show *Mr. Robot*!

What are your favorite books for motivation, personal development, or enjoyment?
The Power of Now by Eckhart Tolle and anything from the Situational Leadership Training series.

What is some practical cybersecurity advice you give to people at home in the age of social media and the Internet of Things?
Don't share things that demonstrate immaturity. Your public profile will impact your career positively or negatively; it's your choice which one it will be.

What is a life hack that you'd like to share?
For me, it was understanding that my brain is a program that chooses my emotions for me—the unconscious brain! I can choose to run the emotional program my brain has already developed at a young age, or I can reprogram it! I chose to reprogram it, and boy, did my life get much easier when I learned to consciously choose when I feel sad, mad, happy, guilty, and so on. And I get to choose how long I let this emotion live at any given time. I am 100 percent accountable to my emotions. I hacked my own brain. It was and is a constant focus.

"Leadership and life are about truthfulness and doing right by the team."

What is the biggest mistake you've ever made, and how did you recover from it?
Hiring executives who let fear guide their decision-making. Leadership and life are about truthfulness and doing right by the team. The only way to recover is to learn the traits of this type of individual, not hire those traits again, and move on! ∎

> "There's plenty of money in the world, and if that's all it took, we would have fixed cybersecurity long ago."

Twitter: @Zaeyx

Ben Donnelly

Ben has worked as a penetration tester, as a security researcher/consultant, and as the founder of Promethean Info Sec. Previously, he served as the lead developer on the DARPA-funded Active Defense Harbinger Distribution. He is also the inventor of the Ball and Chain cryptosystem and the creator of TALOS Active Defense, as well as a host of other information security tools and methodologies. Ben has assisted in the creation of content for a number of SANS courses and is a co-author of the book *Offensive Countermeasures: The Art of Active Defense*. He has worked on teams hacking such things as entire states, power plants, multinationals, and prisons. He has competed in and won a variety of InfoSec competitions, including SANS NetWars. Ben has also legally hacked the Pentagon. He has presented on his own original research at DerbyCon as well as BSides Boise.

22

If there is one myth that you could debunk in cybersecurity, what would it be?

That the preeminent contemporary problems of the field are intractable. From years of struggling with the same issues again and again, with seemingly no end in sight, a majority of the professionals in our field have thrown in the philosophical towel. I can't count how many times I've talked to highly skilled, highly knowledgeable, effective cybersecurity pros who had resigned themselves to bailing water from a sinking ship.

But we can fix these leaks! Over the course of my tenure in the field, I've written a plethora of prototypes as well as deployable solutions to problems that others had simply given up on. What got me there? If I had to sum it up in one word, I would simply say "hope."

Take the example of password storage on something like a production web server. The current accepted paradigm is to store passwords using a cryptographically secure hashing algorithm. The way hashing algorithms work—and some of the weaknesses inherent in the model—is why you see gigantic data breaches in the news, in which hundreds of millions of passwords are leaked to the Web.

> "The security for such a model has largely been shifted to the user. Websites require passwords of a certain length and complexity in order to require additional computation (more guesses) for an adversary attempting to brute force the stored form of the password (the hash). But clearly, this isn't working."

The security for such a model has largely been shifted to the user. Websites require passwords of a certain length and complexity in order to require additional computation (more guesses) for an adversary attempting to brute force the stored form of the password (the hash). But clearly, this isn't working. It seems like barely a month can go by without another large data breach.

If you walk up to most industry professionals and ask them to tell you about password security, they will generally read back to you "the book." (Obviously, there is no one single "book," but it feels like we've all read the same thing on what exactly one "should do" to secure a password.) The conversation will often end with a discussion on how "the problem" is users. Users need to have longer, stronger passwords. But is it really fair to put the onus for the security of an organization on people whose main areas of expertise are completely unrelated?

Certainly, within the currently accepted password-storage paradigm, it is true that there really isn't much more the security team can do other than work with users. So, I made an algorithm that supersedes password hashing. I don't think I'm particularly magical for having done so. I think my secret is youth and, if nothing else, (at the time) inexperience. I wrote this algorithm as a sophomore in university. I was young enough that the monotony of the day-to-day grind of securing an organization hadn't yet gotten to me. I hadn't learned to sit back and accept that the way things are is the way they need to be.

Since then, I've gone on to design a number of other such technologies in a variety of cybersecurity subdomains. I can say with complete experiential confidence that I've probably solved issues that your organization still thinks are here to stay. And I'm completely sure that there are many more paradigms waiting to be broken. These mountains can be climbed; these challenges can be met. It sounds cliché and silly to say, but truly all you fundamentally need is a little hope and an open mind.

What is one of the biggest bang-for-the-buck actions that an organization can take to improve its cybersecurity posture?

Hire good people. You will never spend money on something more effective within this domain than talented people. Cybersecurity is not a problem that can be easily solved by the application of money. There's plenty of money in the world, and if that's all it took, we would have fixed it long ago.

Technology advances every second of every day. What worked a few months ago won't work for long. What was secure a few months ago isn't necessarily secure today. Then there's the issue of sensory mapping. As humans, we're just not designed to interface with the virtual world we've created. Packets fly far faster than we can ever be expected to keep up with. Data is literally streaming down wires and through the air around you. Add on top of that the issue of abstraction and understanding—that virtual worlds are nothing like anything you've likely ever known. The execution flow for a selection of code is nothing like riding a bicycle or reading a newspaper.

You need digital Sherpas. You need people who can think rapidly and creatively, through layers of abstraction. These are the people who can actually build a solution to a complex security dilemma within your organization. These are the people who can keep track of all the latest patching requirements and standardized recommendations for all of your in-house tech solutions. These are the people with the energy and focus to predict, isolate, and mitigate likely attack vectors on your network. Always invest in people!

How is it that cybersecurity spending is increasing but breaches are still happening?

Cybersecurity as a field sits at an interesting intersection of two worlds. Due to the complexity of the underlying subject matter, there is a divide between the people who operate within the domain and those who make the decisions upon which their operations depend. That is to say, executives and decision-makers often truly do not understand the threat landscape with the level of detail necessary to make decisions that will directly repel adversaries.

A lot of our talk about threats and technologies boils down to low-resolution definitions and loose analogies. Bridging that gap between the techies and management takes effort on both sides of the table. This is compounded even more by the fact that, fundamentally, cybersecurity is not a business goal as much as it is a support activity.

When the company doesn't pocket money because your security team happened to repel an attack, it can be tempting to try to just "solve it." I've seen advertisements that target exactly this, sitting in airports, hunting for executives to walk by. They read things like "cybersecurity, solved." They're incredibly tempting. But what you have to remember is this: your adversaries *do* make money directly from this field. If you're an executive decision-maker, to you, cybersecurity might be quasicustodial. But to the threats facing your organization, this domain is a form of fundamental cash flow.

Your organization should be exactly as involved in the game as your opponents are. Just throwing money at the problem, hoping it will go away, isn't gonna solve it.

Do you need a college degree or certification to be a cybersecurity professional?

Absolutely not. What you need is know-how, nothing more. Of course, do degrees and certifications help? You betcha. At a minimum, having a selection of certifications to call from can certainly give you a hand up in the application process. When a recruiter or hiring manager reviews your résumé, they may or may not be able to parse all that you've done. Having a degree that reads "University College says he can do the cyber" instills a ton of confidence. And the same goes for certifications, although, I would argue, to a slightly lesser/more specific degree (pun intended).

But do you need a degree? Do you need an array of certifications? You absolutely, positively do not. Cybersecurity as a field is incredibly young. Academia is largely still playing catch-up in regard to how to properly train and assess individuals in the requisite skills. I know that, for me, when it came to having a degree in cybersecurity, it simply wasn't an option. I looked around for any program that seemed to meet what it was that I was looking for, and I couldn't find any. It seemed like all of the "cyber" degree options I was able to find had more to do with management or business realities than they did with cyberspace operations.

Now, here's the realization you'll want to come to: the importance of a degree or certification matters purely as a business reality. It is a way of providing tangibility to a skill set that still evades academic definition. That means it matters *who* you're trying to get hired by. You will hear some people swear up and down that certifications have been nothing short of magical for them. And in their career experience, it's likely true. You'll hear other people say that certifications and degrees are basically worthless. And in their life, in their niche, that is almost certainly true.

How did you get started in the cybersecurity field, and what advice would you give to a beginner pursuing a career in cybersecurity?

I started out in cybersecurity back in high school. I was a member of a cadet organization called AFJROTC, which is the junior version of college ROTC. As a junior, I started building a packet to apply to the Air Force Academy. One of my instructors came up to me with an offer to join a team for a new (at the time) competition called CyberPatriot. My projected career path at that point was aviation, but I figured I would give it a shot since it could help boost my Air Force Academy (USAFA) packet.

I was never one of those kids who grew up with a circuit board in my hand and my future decided. But when I learned what was possible through that competition, I was instantly hooked. I did end up turning down a shot at USAFA due to things happening with my family, and I stayed home to pursue college on my own. There weren't any good cybersecurity programs that fit what I was looking for in my entire state. So, at the time, I was feeling really adrift.

What I did manage to find was an article about the upcoming first-ever NetWars Tournament of Champions. It mentioned on the site that for the competition SANS would be inviting people who had performed well in CyberPatriot. My team had taken second at nationals. So, I wrote an email to a contact at SANS and just straight up asked if I could come compete. They said yes. So, at 18 years old, I flew myself out to Washington, DC, for SANS CDI 2012.

I think being that young and showing up at a SANS conference is pretty much unheard of, so I made a bit of a stir. I got dropped into classes to audit and prepare for the competition. I did well in the competition, though I definitely didn't win. But I immediately got offered three jobs with different SANS instructors at the conference. I took one of the offers, and the rest is history.

You can say that my performance in competitions is what got me where I am. Or you could argue that my age and the shock it brought with it was an influential part. I'm sure you're not wrong. But there's one thing that you can take away from what I did: that no matter who you are, no matter what you know, and no matter what you want, you can do it. When I saw something that I wanted to be a part of, I decided that thing was worth rejection to me, and I asked.

It doesn't matter if you've never touched a terminal before. The number-one predictor of success is easily passion. Especially today, in the age of Google, knowledge and expertise are at your fingertips every second of every day. You have no excuse for not chasing the outcomes that you want, in your career and in your life. Don't be afraid to fail. Be willing to ask.

What is your specialty in cybersecurity, and how can others gain expertise in your specialty?

I don't know if "specialty" is a word that can be accurately applied to any one of the subsets of my InfoSec skills. I wouldn't say that I really have any major "specialty."

Perhaps I have a number of specialties? Primarily, I work on the red team side of the house. As part of being a penetration tester, I've found that I need to be proficient in nearly every aspect of everything if I want to break it. I can't just skirt by on knowledge of a few tools. The engagements I find myself on require me to be not just a jack-of-all-trades but a master-of-all-trades. But, of course, that could be seen as my specialty—that I work on the red cell side of the house predominantly.

What is your advice for career success when it comes to getting hired, climbing the corporate ladder, or starting a company in cybersecurity?

Know your sh*t. There is no end to people who use buzzwords and FUD in our industry. You can use the idea of cybersecurity to exist as a professional, but it will only get you so far. There is absolutely no substitute for real proficiency. It's true that a ton of the field is tainted by a mythos collectively known as the "cult of the hacker." So much of what you will encounter in this field will be driven by bluster and ignorance. Because most people don't really know what's going on inside of their computer or on their network, it's really easy for confident, low-skill people to carve out a mild niche for themselves. Pay close enough attention, and you'll see it everywhere.

But if you actually know your stuff—if people can actually rely on you to understand and solve real problems—you will go very far. Don't fall into the prideful "cult of the hacker" trap where you start building a persona based less on your ability and more on others' perceptions of you. The day you become happy with the admiration of the uninitiated (think: managerial types who think of you as their "cyber wizard" because you know more than they do) is the day you stop growing and start getting passed up by those who are interested purely in efficacy.

What qualities do you believe all highly successful cybersecurity professionals share?

What a great question. But before I answer, let me just quickly state that I think everyone is unique. You don't necessarily have to fit a specific profile in order to be successful in any field, especially not in this one. That being said, here are some of the traits I've seen in many high-level hackers, again and again:

Curiosity: Fundamentally, hackers challenge the status quo. It would be hard to thrive in this industry without a predisposition toward radical curiosity. You want to understand why things work the way they work. You want to know if they can be made to work better, faster, more efficiently. You want to know if you can break them. You're willing to spend lots of time and precious energy learning about things you may never need to know, just because you found them interesting.

Perseverance: There are few things under the sun more frustrating than computers—from running down an obscure bug in your code to attempting to guess the memory address for an ASLR'ed binary. You are certainly going to find yourself running into what feels like a brick wall, time and time again. To be successful, you need to have the grit necessary to pick yourself up, over and over, and continue. If you love this field enough, you won't be easily discouraged, and you will succeed.

Passion: As mentioned earlier, the drive that will get you through all of the crummy parts of cybersecurity is going to be critical. But it's not just about rising above the worst parts. It's also about knowing what you want so you can seek it out effortlessly. Find what it is that drives you.

Systematizing: This one is a bit more esoteric. It's not necessarily a character trait. And to be quite clear, it's more pronounced in the "tech" types. You can easily fill a niche in the industry and completely lack this ability. Systematizing speaks to the propensity to form mental models based on an understanding of the component parts of a given thing. It's the cognitive process by which an intelligence observes a thing and breaks it down through careful study of its behaviors. This is the trait that gives tech wizards the ability to understand and build upon or break existing technologies. Rather than seeing things as set in stone, they can more easily see them for what they are and, as such, are often more apt to deconstruct them.

Novelty/sensation seeking: The people you will see at the top of any field are the ones who really love the action. You need to be in it for the journey, with the "prizes" only as wonderful side effects—extra icing on the cake. You need to appreciate getting up every morning with the sun to hit the running trail. The same is true within cybersecurity. I hack for the same reason I regularly throw myself out of perfectly good airplanes.

It's that feeling you get when you're seconds away from escalating a web shell into a reverse shell and jump to root via a kernel exploit.

What is the best book or movie that can be used to illustrate cybersecurity challenges?

Does a TV show count? Because if it does, then the answer is, hands down, Sam Esmail's *Mr. Robot*—for which the venerable Dave Kennedy (also in this book) is a technical consultant. I really can't think of any piece of media that so accurately captures and cleanly conveys the everyday realities of information age insecurity as that show. The tension is palpable, and the hacks are plausible (a huge achievement in cinema).

The show also does a great job of capturing the ways in which technology "hacks" us all every day with our manufactured consent. That you freely give your data up to Facebook or Google. That you are willing to be monitored, surveilled, and controlled. If you haven't seen it, check it out!

What is your favorite hacker movie?

So this is actually a really hard decision for me. There are a bunch of hacking movies that I really enjoy for various reasons and in various moods. I highly recommend the following list of films:

The Girl with the Dragon Tattoo: A hacker becomes involved in the hunt for a murderer in a decades-old cold case.

The Fifth Estate: Based upon plot points taken directly from the pages of the WikiLeaks saga, this movie highlights the power of people and information. It's a reminder that a single man can stop the motor of the world.

Snowden: Certainly you've heard the name, and the man is a figure of controversy. The story is well told and highlights his motivations and morality beyond just his actions. I also really appreciate this piece for putting the scale of government surveillance into context.

Blackhat: Not the best-made film by any stretch, but if you're looking for a mildly gritty action film based around mostly realistic hacking, this is it.

Hackers: There really is no greater hacking movie than this complete classic. It's campy, it's ridiculous, and it's absolutely great. If I had to choose just one hacking movie, it would likely be this one.

What are your favorite books for motivation, personal development, or enjoyment?
Anything that lets you dream. The world has grown somewhat stale. We think we know so much more than we actually do. Our trust in our institutions is largely misplaced. Read literally anything that will let you dream again. Pick up *Neuromancer*, and enjoy that they dreamed of a future with payphones. Read *Dune, Cryptonomicon, Ender's Game*, or literally anything by Tom Clancy. Find the books that make you feel good about yourself and your internal dialogue. Forget books that give you a prescription about how things ought to be or about how they are. Find the books that let you dream.

Tangentially, I cannot recommend enough, literally, any decent book about meditation. Maybe it's just me, but I've found meditation to be an absolutely invaluable skill to learn. Learning to harness the overwhelming flow of sensory information I receive has helped me to become far more effective in my everyday life.

What is some practical cybersecurity advice you give to people at home in the age of social media and the Internet of Things?
Here is a list of items you need to be cognizant of:

Location: You should never share information that reveals sensitive details about where you are, where you are going to be (exactly), or common places you visit.

This can be something as simple as posting a review about your favorite coffee shop, mentioning that you "go there every morning." That's not knowledge you want random people on the internet to be able to acquire. Be aware also of information revealed in pictures.

In some of my work in the past, I have been tasked to perform exactly this function. I was once able to identify the location of a photo down to within about ten meters by identifying the city and approximate location in the city from an old flight simulator video I once watched. I was then able to use Google Street View and the specific streetlight in the picture to figure out exactly where it was taken.

Time: You need to be aware of the importance of specific dates and times to a potential adversary. You may not want everyone on your friends list knowing when your birthday is or your anniversary or even the year of your car. Never give specifics out publicly. Little bits of seemingly harmless information can be combined to allow an attacker to impersonate you effectively.

Future actions: You should be cognizant of the possibility of someone predicting your future actions by noticing patterns in your publicly posted behavior. If you visit the same bar every Friday or if you are always posting reviews for restaurants within a two-block radius, it may allow an attacker to predict where you will be or what you will be doing. This can, of course, be exploited in many different ways. Always be willing to throw a bit of unpredictability and randomness into your posting.

Contacts: Your contacts, the people you trust, are often a direct line to you. You should be alert to the possibility of someone trying to gain your trust by working their way through your contacts. Additionally, you need to be aware that, no matter how clean your internet identity may be, if you are constantly getting tagged in photos by your friends or if your friends are posting geotagged pictures of your house, you may be opening yourself up to attack though you're doing everything right.

Trust relationships: Make sure you understand how exactly to establish trust over the Web. Adding someone to your social media profiles just because they have a number of friends in common with you? Not necessarily the best idea. What if you receive a message over Facebook from a friend asking you to add them again because their "old account" got hacked? How do you know the new account isn't someone impersonating them? The internet is a dangerous place, and there is no one else in the world who wants you to trust them more than someone trying to scam you.

Here's a secret: when in doubt, use multiple methods of communication to establish trust. It's pretty easy for someone to make a Facebook profile that looks like your great aunt. What's not easy is for them to also steal her phone number and her email. If something seems phishy, don't be afraid to insist on reaching out to the person via other means. Give them a call, tweet at them. If you get a confirmation from all of the channels through which you know them, it's almost certainly them.

What is a life hack that you'd like to share?

Binary search! We often think of algorithmic solutions as being things rightfully sequestered to the realms of academia. But you can apply computer science principles to your life in a variety of contexts. My favorite is, by far, binary search. Here's how it works: whenever you need to search through a group of things to find a specific one, most people will use the "linear search algorithm." That is, they will go through each item individually checking if it's the one.

What a binary search looks like is this: you split all of your items into two groups and then isolate both groups. You then see if the effect you're observing is still happening and which group it's coming from. Then you look at the group the effect is still emanating from and split it again. You then perform the split in half and check operation until you're down to just one element. That last element will be the sought element. The total number of checks you'll make with binary search is far fewer. With a linear search, if you have eight items to check, you'll make eight checks. With a binary search, you'll only make three. And the gains keep accelerating. If you were checking through 1,024 items, a linear search would take 1,024 checks. But a binary search would take only 10.

What is the biggest mistake you've ever made, and how did you recover from it?

Believing other people were like me. This is a mistake I have made time and time again. There is a theory that the primary driver of effective cognitive empathy (understanding and relating accurately to others) is a relationally similar mental substratum—that you and the person you are attempting to relate to are reasonably similar.

While I was growing up, I never let myself really get into the "I'm super unique" talk. It seemed egotistical, it seemed unnecessary, it even seemed antisocial. As I slowly matured, I continued to hit a wall, whereby I would sometimes completely and wildly miss a prediction on the behavior of another person. I noticed that every time I did this, it was because I was assuming they would respond like I would.

Here's what I've learned. Fundamentally, talk less. Don't be wildly open and honest with people arbitrarily. Give people space. For me, one of my stumbling blocks is in selfless motivations. People seem to have trouble understanding that I literally do things entirely selflessly, completely for the benefit of others, based on a collection of philosophical drivers. So, for me, I have had to learn to at least pretend to be selfish and seek my own ends. And to complain more. And just all the normal human things that, even if they're mildly unpleasant, people understand and can more easily work with. ■

"There's no one-size-fits-all in security, especially when it comes to securing government systems. Policy and funding are still years behind the private sector, but we're doing our best to catch up."

Twitter: @mzbat • **Website:** www.twitch.tv/rallysecurity

Kimber Dowsett

Kimber Dowsett is currently serving in the federal government, securing cloud infrastructure architecture and leading response efforts during critical security incidents. She is passionate about privacy, encryption, and building user-driven technology for the public. Named one of the 2017 Top Women in Cybersecurity by CyberScoop, Kimber has a background in information security, incident response, security policy, and penetration testing. She is an avid admirer of Chiroptera and is a connoisseur of comic books and video games.

23

If there is one myth that you could debunk in cybersecurity, what would it be?

Throwing money at problems doesn't make them go away, but it certainly helps. Security requires an investment in people, resources, hardware, software, and research. In the federal space, cybersecurity spans well beyond a hooded hacker trying to phish Google logins; we're looking at entire infrastructures in desperate need of funding before we can even begin conversations about hardening our networks and systems. There's no one-size-fits-all in security, especially when it comes to securing government systems. Policy and funding are still years behind the private sector, but we're doing our best to catch up.

What is one of the biggest bang-for-the-buck actions that an organization can take to improve its cybersecurity posture?

The defender in me immediately thinks, "logging, hardening, asset inventory, patching, detection, response," but honestly, user training almost always offers a pretty solid return on investment. Teaching users not to click things, how to recognize phishing attempts and scams, where to download software, how to secure their personal devices, and how to avoid common security mistakes are all skills that will ultimately prevent organizations from falling victim to the most common attack vectors. If I'm being honest, all the security gadgets in the world aren't going to help if my user gives up domain controller admin credentials to a well-crafted phishing email link. We, as security professionals, have a duty to our users to help them understand basic security concepts and how to spot (and report) potential attacks.

How is it that cybersecurity spending is increasing but breaches are still happening?

No matter how dedicated we are to securing our systems, there are folks out there with more time, energy, and money who dedicate their resources to finding holes in our infrastructures. In general, security folks wear several hats and are pulled in many different directions on any given day. Meanwhile, nation-state hackers have a single job with a single goal: breaching our systems. They spend their days crafting phishing emails and looking for holes in our networks. We can do our best to harden, patch, train, and test, but as long as people are part of our organizations, we have a weak link that can (and will) be exploited. That sounds more hopeless than it is, but we must learn from our mistakes and carry on.

Do you need a college degree or certification to be a cybersecurity professional?

I don't believe you need a degree or certification, but neither hurts. As a woman, I absolutely believe certifications opened some doors for me in this field. I believe that in cybersecurity, as in most professions, a good training program, whether collegiate or vocational, is critical for getting a handle on best practices. It's important to understand the rules before you break them (intentionally or unintentionally). At the end of the day, it boils down to what potential employers want to see on a résumé. Many require degrees and/or certifications. Many don't. Figure out what you want to do and choose a path that makes the most sense for you.

How did you get started in the cybersecurity field, and what advice would you give to a beginner pursuing a career in cybersecurity?

I forced my way into cybersecurity. I worked for years helping end users with technical problems, primarily malware-related, before moving on to do system administration work and managing/securing clusters. I showed up at security meetings I wasn't invited to and worked on security policies with folks who assumed I belonged in the room. I found something I felt passionate about, and I took my seat at the table. It wasn't long after receiving praise for implementing new security policies that I was able to land an actual security position and could stop worrying about being kicked out of the meetings I'd been sneaking into.

The only advice I have for beginners is to find something you're good at and go for it. Don't oversell your qualifications. Just do the work you know how to do, seek out a mentor, and set some goals for yourself. If you feel you're unable to move toward those goals with your current employer, look for another job. There are plenty of companies out there looking for junior analysts and mentees in cybersecurity.

What is your specialty in cybersecurity, and how can others gain expertise in your specialty?

These days, I'm focused on vulnerability disclosure, incident response, and response workflows. It's a lot of reading, research, and keeping abreast of active vulnerabilities that potentially pose a threat to my agency. For folks interested in this type of work, it's important to read up on vulnerability disclosure policies, gain an understanding of event versus incident, and research the ways incidents are handled within different types of organizations. I've spent time working in the security operations center (SOC), in the network operations center (NOC), and on detection and response (D&R). Digital forensics and incident response (DFIR) and capture the flags (CTFs) are a great way to get your feet wet and quickly figure out where your knowledge gaps are.

What is your advice for career success when it comes to getting hired, climbing the corporate ladder, or starting a company in cybersecurity?

Don't overstate your qualifications, but don't be afraid to toot your own horn, either. If you're really good at something, figure out how to incorporate that skill set into your résumé. Find folks who do what you want to do. Surround yourself with people willing to share knowledge. As for starting a cybersecurity company, just because you *can* do something doesn't mean you *should*. Starting a business, any business, takes a lot of knowledge, time, energy, and resources. The added layer of hiring and retaining security talent and building community trust is pretty daunting. There's a special place in Hades for charlatans who spin up security companies and offer snake oil solutions to organizations that don't know any better.

What qualities do you believe all highly successful cybersecurity professionals share?

I define success by how much a professional contributes to the community at large. It's not enough to talk about change or complain about the current state of cybersecurity; successful professionals recognize the need to mentor the next generation of talent, teach them about our generation's successes and failures, and train them to take our jobs. Success isn't defined by how well known we are or how much money we make. At the end of the day, it's defined by the generation that comes after us. Successful professionals understand it's our job to share information, not hoard it.

> "Successful professionals understand it's our job to share information, not hoard it."

What is the best book or movie that can be used to illustrate cybersecurity challenges?

The *Hunger Games* series is a pretty good metaphor for cybersecurity. All the districts are dominated and overpowered until they come together, share knowledge, and fight for a common goal. There is currently a direct assault on democracy as we know it, and it's going to take a large collaboration of researchers to preserve the sanctity of our rights as voters. I hope, one day, security researchers are able to come together to work for the common good.

What is your favorite hacker movie?

The Imitation Game. (I'll fight anyone who tries to argue it's not a hacker movie.)

What are your favorite books for motivation, personal development, or enjoyment?

I frequently turn to passages in *Quiet: The Power of Introverts in a World That Can't Stop Talking* when I'm feeling overwhelmed. I strongly encourage introverts, particularly in our field, to give it a read. For enjoyment, I love the works of William Gibson. *Neuromancer* is one of my favorites.

What is some practical cybersecurity advice you give to people at home in the age of social media and the Internet of Things?

For the everyday person, I'd say use a password manager. Avoid password reuse. These two things alone will improve your security posture. Don't download attachments from folks you don't know, and even then, proceed with caution. Don't put your entire life on social media, and periodically monitor your privacy settings to make sure you're not sharing content with unintended audiences. Set up a separate email account that's tied to your social media profiles. You shouldn't be banking with the same email login you use for Facebook. If you're feeling tech savvy, set up a separate home network to isolate your IoT devices. Your light bulbs and security cameras shouldn't be on the same network as your home and work computers. No good will come from that setup.

> "Set up a separate email account that's tied to your social media profiles. You shouldn't be banking with the same email login you use for Facebook."

What is a life hack that you'd like to share?

I travel quite a bit, and my favorite travel hack is to remove lids from my liquid makeup and toiletry bottles, place a piece of cellophane over the opening, then screw the lids on over the cellophane. I only wish I'd known about it before the Great Makeup Incident of 2014.

Another life hack for me involves social interactions. When I'm feeling anxious, I remember "HALTS" (hungry, angry, lonely, tired, stressed), and try to avoid interactions and confrontations when I find myself in a HALTS situation.

What is the biggest mistake you've ever made, and how did you recover from it?

I probably haven't made my biggest mistake yet, but the first thing that comes to mind is a minor mistake that quickly turned into a major problem. Someone on our team enabled a Slack integration with Google Docs, not realizing that all linked docs and their content would become part of our public Slack record. We caught the mistake pretty quickly and killed the integration, but the damage had already been done. Sensitive docs had been exposed, and although there was no indication they were compromised in the brief period they were publicly available, our team dealt with the backlash of that one-hour experience for nearly a year following the incident. It was brutal. That said, be careful with your application integrations, folks. A minor change is almost never as minor as you believe it to be. ■

"Once you ask, don't forget to keep coming up with new questions."

Twitter: @ronaldeddings • **Website:** secdevops.ai

Ronald Eddings

Ronald Eddings is a Silicon Valley–based cybersecurity expert, blogger, and digital nomad whose ingenuity, dedication, and ambition have all earned him the reputation as a trusted industry leader. Over the course of his career, Ronald has garnered extensive experience working at various Fortune 500 companies and mentoring a multitude of fellow professionals. In addition to cybersecurity, he is well versed in software development, DevOps, and artificial intelligence. Currently, Ronald serves as a cyber fusion engineer at a cybersecurity startup and is an active contributor to several open source projects. He also holds a BS degree in information technology and an array of cybersecurity certifications.

24

If there is one myth that you could debunk in cybersecurity, what would it be?

That macOS can't get a virus.

What is one of the biggest bang-for-the-buck actions that an organization can take to improve its cybersecurity posture?

Phishing! I've seen the best and the worst implementation for protection of phishing, and the gaps are quite large.

How is it that cybersecurity spending is increasing but breaches are still happening?

Analyst/engineer fatigue. There's not enough time in the day to exhaustively cover all aspects of an environment. I've seen a lot of competitive pay but *little* in the way of personal incentives. I think if there were more incentives—that an analyst or engineer could feel better about *personally*—they'd be more inspired to go to trainings and leave no stone unturned.

Do you need a college degree or certification to be a cybersecurity professional?
I did not have one starting out. I barely needed a high school diploma. Thanks to Marcus Carey, I've learned that this industry demands talent.

How did you get started in the cybersecurity field, and what advice would you give to a beginner pursuing a career in cybersecurity?
I started in cybersecurity when I was working at a public access TV channel—where I met MJC, Joe McCray, and Johnny Long! As a kid, I was starstruck to see three hackers in the flesh. I'm glad I seized the moment and told MJC that I was interested (the rest was history from there). My advice would be to not hesitate and ask. And once you ask, don't forget to keep coming up with new questions.

What is your specialty in cybersecurity, and how can others gain expertise in your specialty?
Fortunately and unfortunately, I have no specialty. My skills focus on threat intelligence, DevOps, and artificial intelligence. Maybe the new buzzword will be "fusion analyst."

What is your advice for career success when it comes to getting hired, climbing the corporate ladder, or starting a company in cybersecurity?
To get hired/climb/create, you must continually be present with your connections, have value to share, and, most importantly, *apply* yourself to problems you're passionate about solving.

What qualities do you believe all highly successful cybersecurity professionals share?
Being organized. If you're not organized, buffer overflow of tasks occurs.

What is the best book or movie that can be used to illustrate cybersecurity challenges?
Mr. Robot (minus some of the Hollywood razzle-dazzle), especially when looking at this TV show from a defense perspective—very tough to kick the hacker out.

What is your favorite hacker movie?
Hackers.

What are your favorite books for motivation, personal development, or enjoyment?
The ONE Thing by Gary W. Keller and Jay Papasan. *How to Talk to Anyone: 92 Little Tricks for Big Success in Relationships* by Leil Lowndes.

What is some practical cybersecurity advice you give to people at home in the age of social media and the Internet of Things?
Use two-factor authorization (2FA) and any other enhancements to force confirmation of identify whenever possible.

What is a life hack that you'd like to share?
Learn and watch videos at 3× speed.

What is the biggest mistake you've ever made, and how did you recover from it?
Not being mindful...I was constantly chasing the next technique/idea rather than reflecting on what projects fueled my passions in cybersecurity. Creating a calendar with daily events associated with accomplishable goals put my life back on track to feeling fulfilled and accomplished. ■

"People who have impressed me the most during the hiring process always highlight personal projects or their involvement in the community, even if it's not purely technical."

Twitter: @HackingLZ

Justin Elze

Justin Elze is the red team lead at TrustedSec. He has more than 10 years of experience in the information technology industry, specializing in enterprise penetration testing, network security, social engineering, and red teaming. Prior to joining TrustedSec, Justin was a senior penetration tester for AccuvantLabs, Dell SecureWorks, and Redspin—where he led numerous red team engagements and penetration tests. Justin has worked in various industries, including at internet service providers, hosting, DoD contracting, and services consulting companies.

25

If there is one myth that you could debunk in cybersecurity, what would it be?

I would say that the biggest myth about cybersecurity is that spending more money makes you more secure. Many companies are willing to spend their money on expensive products when they should focus their efforts on hiring educated and talented employees. Having a network that is properly engineered and run by knowledgeable employees has more value than purchasing products and then failing to use them properly to maximize their potential.

What is one of the biggest bang-for-the-buck actions that an organization can take to improve its cybersecurity posture?

Securing its workstations. This area is often looked at last; however, it's the main source of the majority of breaches. Companies can get creative with the desktop configuration and leverage available Microsoft features to immediately reduce end users' exposure.

> "More often than not, organizations find themselves in a situation that forces them to react versus taking proactive measures to prevent the breach from happening to begin with. This type of thinking leads to the mind-set of "We have to do something." "

How it is that cybersecurity spending is increasing but breaches are still happening?

More often than not, organizations find themselves in a situation that forces them to react versus taking proactive measures to prevent the breach from happening to begin with. This type of thinking leads to the mind-set of "We have to do something."

Unfortunately, this ends up with organizations tossing money at a problem without understanding how the problem occurred—and without hiring the most knowledgeable personnel to handle the breach. A disconnect happens between where the money is spent and how organizations actually get breached. Companies tend to fall down rabbit holes, allowing vulnerability management or other initiatives to entirely consume a department while ignoring areas where they have more exposure.

Do you need a college degree or certification to be a cybersecurity professional?

I think it really depends on the area of cybersecurity you want to pursue. In today's society, it is common for many professionals in the cybersecurity field to not have college degrees because they can show their mastery of skills through practical means, such as developing code or contributing to open source projects.

Personally, I don't have a college degree, and it has never held me back in my career. The Offensive Security Certified Professional (OSCP) certification helped me land my first information security job, or at least got me an interview. So taking certification courses may be a better way of not only getting your foot in the door, but also exposing you to different opportunities in the future through networking and staying up to date on new technologies.

> "Today, a student can go to college for cybersecurity and get a job right away, but a lot of what makes me good at what I do is my background in system and network engineering."

How did you get started in the cybersecurity field, and what advice would you give to a beginner pursuing a career in cybersecurity?

Cybersecurity has always been something I was interested in since I was really young. The path to get where I am wasn't a direct line from A to B. I started working in computer repair, moved up to system engineer, and eventually became a network engineer at a large ISP before landing my first cybersecurity job. Today, a student can go to college for cybersecurity and get a job right away, but a lot of what makes me good at what I do is my background in system and network engineering.

As far as what advice I would give to a beginner pursuing a career in cybersecurity, I would have to say be prepared to commit a large amount of your time to your career. Technology is always evolving, and the techniques we use in cybersecurity are constantly changing. You can't just jump into a job and stop learning. It's a never-ending process of developing who you are as a professional and obtaining new skills.

> "Technology is always evolving, and the techniques we use in cybersecurity are constantly changing."

What is your specialty in cybersecurity, and how can others gain expertise in your specialty?

My focus and specialty is red teaming and advisory emulation. My background as a network and system engineer gives me a better understanding of how networks and systems are built and where to look for targets. To gain experience in these areas, I would suggest following current trends in malware and exploring tactics used by real-threat actors.

What is your advice for career success when it comes to getting hired, climbing the corporate ladder, or starting a company in cybersecurity?

Getting hired for your first position in the cybersecurity industry is most likely the hardest. People who have impressed me the most during the hiring process always highlight personal projects or their involvement in the community, even if it's not purely technical. Attending conferences shows a great commitment to the industry, and I would suggest starting there if you are unsure of where to begin.

What qualities do you believe all highly successful cybersecurity professionals share?

All successful cybersecurity professionals definitely have creative problem-solving skills. It is important to be able to come up with unique approaches in order to solve complex issues. Fixes are not typically straightforward, so the capability to be flexible in your thought process is important.

> "All successful cybersecurity professionals definitely have creative problem-solving skills. It is important to be able to come up with unique approaches in order to solve complex issues."

What is the best book or movie that can be used to illustrate cybersecurity challenges?
I would say that the TV show *Mr. Robot* does a really good job of highlighting both the technical and human cybersecurity issues. The public often forgets that the user is the exploitable target.

> "I feel like this answer is cheating, but *Hackers* was a big influence in my life."

What is your favorite hacker movie?
I feel like this answer is cheating, but *Hackers* was a big influence in my life. It came out around the time I was really getting into computers. Since its release, I have probably watched it 500 times. Fun fact: I actually have a "Hack the Planet" tattoo.

What are your favorite books for motivation, personal development, or enjoyment?
Most of the books I read tend to be technology/work related. Growing up, I really enjoyed *Takedown* by Tsutomu Shimomura and *The Cuckoo's Egg*.

What is some practical cybersecurity advice you give to people at home in the age of social media and the Internet of Things?
The best advice I could give is to utilize a password manager and have unique passwords for all the websites you visit. Limiting public information that is tied to password reset questions is another area many people overlook.

> "I've found that doing something away from computers can help reset your train of thinking, and you may even come up with new ideas when you aren't expecting them."

What is a life hack that you'd like to share?
I would say to find a hobby outside of computers and cybersecurity. This can help prevent burnout. Personally, I build and race drag cars. I've found that doing something away from computers can help reset your train of thinking, and you may even come up with new ideas when you aren't expecting them.

What is the biggest mistake you've ever made, and how did you recover from it?
Well, my first computer job was at a computer repair/small IT shop. A couple weeks after I started, the owner wanted me to clone his failing laptop hard drive with an external adapter. Unfortunately, with 2.5 IDE, you can easily hook it up backward and toast the board that controls the hard drive. Luckily, the owner had made similar mistakes, so he was understanding, and I learned to double- or triple-check things in the future. ■

> "How much you spend on security relates very little to the quality of that security."

Twitter: @erratarob • **Website:** blog.erratasec.com

Robert Graham

Created: [BlackICE, IPS, sidejacking, masscan]. Doing: [blog, code, cyber-rights, internet-scanning]. Unethical coder, according to the EFF.

26

If there is one myth that you could debunk in cybersecurity, what would it be?

That it's some magic power that can be wielded without much training. As a well-known hacker for two decades, I regularly get queries asking to be taught "how to hack without all that unnecessarily complicated stuff." The queriers are looking for some button to press to instantly grant access to somebody's Facebook account, for example. That's not how hacking works. If it were that easy, then everyone would already be doing it. Instead, the ability to hack comes from studying that "unnecessarily complicated stuff." It's the very fact that people avoid the complicated bits that enable the few who actually study it to have extraordinary power.

What is one of the biggest bang-for-the-buck actions that an organization can take to improve its cybersecurity posture?

There is none. That's the "magic pill" fallacy that there exists this one thing that can be done to defend yourself. It's a variation on my answer to the previous question—that there is no easy path (to either attack or defense) that avoids all the complicated bits.

How is it that cybersecurity spending is increasing but breaches are still happening?

How much you spend on security relates very little to the quality of that security. For example, the weight loss industry is a $20 billion industry because people want to buy products to fix things rather than do what's necessary to lose weight (eat less, exercise more). The same is true of the cybersecurity industry, where customers are willing to throw money at vendors rather than do what's necessary to fix their own problems themselves. Such spending has "decreasing marginal returns." A little money can make a difference, but the more you spend, the less additional difference it makes. Most companies have reached the point where additional spending has no added benefits. This is especially true because they spend that money on the wrong things.

Security is only as strong as the weakest link. Weak links, like desktop computers hooked to the corporate network, continue to be ignored. Companies spend a ton of money trying to protect desktops rather than spending less money protecting the corporate network from compromised desktops.

> "All you need is a burning interest in technical details that most people avoid because they are too complicated and frustrating to understand."

Do you need a college degree or certification to be a cybersecurity professional?

No. All you need is a burning interest in technical details that most people avoid because they are too complicated and frustrating to understand. The wild talents of the early years of cybersecurity were solely those kinds of people because there was no degree that matched cybersecurity and no certifications.

With that said, college can be valuable in creating a more rounded person, forcing us to be exposed to concepts we'd otherwise have no interest in and forcing us to learn important details we'd otherwise skip.

How did you get started in the cybersecurity field, and what advice would you give to a beginner pursuing a career in cybersecurity?

I first started by being an expert programmer in computer networks. Both networks and programming are important skills. I then made a network security product and moved on from there. Starting first as a programmer or a sysadmin, a netadmin, or a Windows admin will teach you how systems *work*, which is an important step in learning how they *break*. I recommend several years doing one or more of these things before getting into cybersecurity. I have a low opinion of pundits/personalities in our industry who don't actually understand how any of this works.

What is your specialty in cybersecurity, and how can others gain expertise in your specialty?

My specialty is networking. Being a network administrator setting up routers and switches is a good start for that. Becoming a programmer who writes low-level network code is another way. (I mean, not creating a website using PHP/JavaScript, but something more low-level.)

What is your advice for career success when it comes to getting hired, climbing the corporate ladder, or starting a company in cybersecurity?

For getting hired, be able to point to your previous accomplishments. If you're in school, accomplish something. If you have programming skills, create a GitHub account with your code. If not, describe something that you did during an internship.

As for climbing the corporate ladder, it's hit or miss depending on the leaders above you. For some organizations, vile things will serve you, like backstabbing your co-workers, taking credit for other's work, and brown-nosing the boss. For other organizations, being an exemplary employee is the route.

The number-one difficulty in being an exemplary employee is figuring out how to deal with the fact that you're right and nobody can see it—and the fact that people won't listen to you. This frustration will burn you out and cause you to behave in ways that make everyone else unhappy as well. I could write a book on how to deal with this, but the short version is this: they (the wrong people) have the same frustration.

The simple social engineering trick is to listen to them. By this, I mean sincerely listen to them, ask honest (not leading) questions, get 100 percent of their argument out of them until they have nothing left. Then still tell them you disagree, but don't tell them why. Most of the time, they'll get on your side—not because they understand your argument, but out of the sheer gratitude that somebody, finally, listened to them. Nobody is really going to listen to your ideas, so yelling at them isn't going to help. And you don't need that anyway. Instead, displaying confidence in your own ideas, *without* trying to make others listen to you, gains you their trust.

I've gone into meetings where I've simply asked honest (not leading) questions of the opposing side, never discussing my own ideas, and walked out with easy consensus for my ideas. Of course, I likewise have some failures, but those were usually caused by factors wholly outside of my control, such as political push from some executive in the company who isn't even in the meeting.

As far as starting a company, start with friends you can trust. We all have weaknesses, and indeed, often our weaknesses are also our strengths. For example, I like learning many things, which makes it harder for me to focus on one thing. Conversely, one of the co-founders of my company focuses too much on one thing at the expense of the bigger picture. People whom you can trust, who are honest and honorable, are also important. If somebody brags about how they cheated somebody else, eventually they'll get around to cheating you, too.

What qualities do you believe all highly successful cybersecurity professionals share?

Superior technical knowledge and the ability to not be such an ass about it. To be fair, there are a lot of successful charlatans, but the real successes come from people who have technical excellence. Over the decades, I've watched how many of the early pioneers have eventually started their own successful companies or climbed the ladder. It's generally those with the best technical expertise who have done the best professionally, even as they've moved into managerial, sales, marketing, or executive roles.

What is the best book or movie that can be used to illustrate cybersecurity challenges?

None that I can think of. Mostly, I'm likely to discuss how books/movies teach the wrong lessons about cybersecurity.

What is your favorite hacker movie?

I'm going to go with *Hot Millions*, a 1968 movie starring Peter Ustinov. It's a surprisingly comprehensive hacking movie—including social engineering, computer hacking, and money laundering—from before any of us were born.

What are your favorite books for motivation, personal development, or enjoyment?

I recommend re-reading *To Kill a Mockingbird*, looking not at the angry injustice of the wrong conviction but the way the author describes the good in people who are the "enemy." Likewise, re-read Orwell's *1984*, not for what it says about government but for what it says about the common people that led to dystopia—such as the "duck quacking" concept of repeating political slogans because everyone agrees with them, not because they've put any thought or critical analysis into them.

Or, re-read *Fahrenheit 451*, paying attention to how censorship came not from the government top-down but from the people bottom-up wanting to get rid of everything that offended them.

My favorite sci fi, strangely, is Lois McMaster Bujold's Vorkosigan Saga series of books, which appears on the surface to be standard space opera fiction but is surprisingly complex underneath. What I like about the series is the concept of "honor" when all choices are dishonorable. As a cybersecurity professional, you are frequently faced with dishonorable choices, such as a client asking you to edit your pentest results or a client who you can see is clearly breaking the law.

What is some practical cybersecurity advice you give to people at home in the age of social media and the Internet of Things?

IoT vulnerabilities are hype, don't worry about it. Social media is a cancer—you like/repeat memes because you agree with them, not because you've critically evaluated their veracity/worth. Look before you repeat.

"Don't use your work email for personal things; get a personal email account. Don't use your personal/work account for financial/important things; get a separate financial email account."

What is a life hack that you'd like to share?

Don't use your work email for personal things; get a personal email account. Don't use your personal/work account for financial/important things; get a separate financial email account. That way, when you get that "PayPal password reset" message on your work or personal account, you know it's a phishing attack because it wasn't sent to your financial account.

What is the biggest mistake you've ever made, and how did you recover from it?

The real answer is that when hitchhiking through Germany in college, I didn't abandon my friends and go wherever the hot 30-something blonde was going in the red Porsche who offered one and only one of us a ride.

The more practical answer is the Witty Worm—a network worm in 2003 that took down the DoD network because of an obvious vulnerability in my code. "Recovery" was done by regression-testing code coverage—and by going on a worldwide apology tour to all our major customers. ■

> "Ultimately, there is no shortcut; you might decide to sweat it out through a master's degree or through publishing research and code on GitHub, but either way, you'll have to earn it."

Claudio Guarnieri

Claudio Guarnieri is a security researcher, artist, and human rights activist. He researches the use of technology as a means for repression and provides assistance to human rights organizations, journalists, and activists with issues surrounding computer security, privacy, and surveillance. He also plays music, creates art, and writes.

27

If there is one myth that you could debunk in cybersecurity, what would it be?

The most recurring myth I encounter is that security isn't everyone's problem. The reality is that using secure and privacy-enabling technology isn't just beneficial for yourself, but it is, in practice, an act of solidarity. If we demand technology to be better and safer, and for security to be taken seriously, we contribute to building a global ecosystem that's to everyone's benefit—including you, the company you work for, the public offices that provide you services, as well as a journalist reporting on corruption on the other side of the planet.

What is one of the biggest bang-for-the-buck actions that an organization can take to improve its cybersecurity posture?

Hire good people. They're worth it and can do a lot more for you than any box you could possibly buy.

How is it that cybersecurity spending is increasing but breaches are still happening?

The same question sounds like a definition of a bubble. We're doing a horrible job at actually building better and safer technology. We are *fixing* and *monitoring* things too much rather than investing in building more resilient foundations. Additionally, it is quite simply an industry that's being built on top of scandals and fear, and those who are exploiting this climate for a quick buck outnumber those who are genuinely in it for the long run and trying to change things.

Do you need a college degree or certification to be a cybersecurity professional?

The value of a strong education is undeniable, but it's not a prerequisite to becoming a cybersecurity professional—let alone being successful at it. Your skills, passion, and the quality of your work go a very long way. My academic career has been complicated and short-lived, and yet I managed to carve my own path. Friends of mine have pushed all the way through to a PhD and also found their way. It is very much a personal choice. Ultimately, there is no shortcut; you might decide to sweat it out through a master's degree or through publishing research and code on GitHub, but either way, you'll have to earn it.

How did you get started in the cybersecurity field, and what advice would you give to a beginner pursuing a career in cybersecurity?

I stumbled into the hacking scene in my teenage years, and eventually I stuck around long enough for it to develop into a professional industry. I also took an unusual route and ended up working in the nonprofit sector. That isn't necessarily exemplary of the financial reward that many use to define success in a profession. Truthfully, I never set out to work in cybersecurity, and my advice, particularly to younger generations, is very much consequential to that: don't rush into finding the task that will define the rest of your life.

In other words, as Moxie Marlinspike much more eloquently put it: "Be careful not to discover a career before you've discovered yourself." If cybersecurity is indeed what you really want to pursue in your life, my advice would then be to work your way through it by contributing to the larger community—be it with a tool or some novel research. For me, creating the free software project Cuckoo Sandbox was instrumental in getting my name out there and ultimately receiving the attention of all the employers I worked for.

What is your specialty in cybersecurity, and how can others gain expertise in your specialty?

I do research, primarily into malware attacks. I started becoming interested in botnets a decade ago, when Storm and Conficker were making the news, and then developed further interest in reverse engineering, malware analysis, and targeted attacks.

Malware analysts are in high demand today. Follow the public research, read other researchers' discoveries and analyses, and try to reproduce some of their results. With practice and perseverance, you'll get there. Luckily, there is so much malware out there that there is always something to research and analyze. Set up a blog, share your findings, and publish as you learn. Not only will this help you build a profile, but it'll also help you better structure your research methodology and better formulate your results.

What is your advice for career success when it comes to getting hired, climbing the corporate ladder, or starting a company in cybersecurity?

Those who work in the cybersecurity field have the immense privilege of operating in not only a highly remunerative industry but one that is constantly seeking talent. Acknowledging that privilege, I am convinced that more than finding the appropriate way to "get hired" is the importance of finding the appropriate place to contribute your time. Find a company, institution, or foundation that works on issues you deeply care about, and approach them at the opportune time with a well-prepared résumé and public record. If you lack some skills for the job, develop them. Don't be put off by a first refusal, particularly if you're applying at a large corporation. Attempt again a year later with more experience under your belt.

> "Don't be put off by a first refusal, particularly if you're applying at a large corporation."

What qualities do you believe all highly successful cybersecurity professionals share?

Humility, curiosity, passion. And a bit of stubbornness.

What is your favorite hacker movie?

Antitrust (2001) was probably the first I'd ever watched. *The Matrix* (1999) is just a classic, but *Hackers* (1995) is my all-time favorite. Seriously, I just love Johnny Lee Miller. Hack the Planet!

What are your favorite books for motivation, personal development, or enjoyment?

I mostly read books on politics and society. More recently, I started collecting and reading any possible book on surveillance—from surveillance and counter-surveillance training manuals to analysis of eavesdropping technology from the '70s, as well as academic research from the field of surveillance studies.

I do recommend, however, to read about the relationship between technology and society, as I strongly believe that we, as computer scientists, need a much stronger education on that. A classic starting point is *The Real World of Technology* by Ursula M. Franklin. Figure it out from there.

What is some practical cybersecurity advice you give to people at home in the age of social media and the Internet of Things?

Other than "Unplug that useless thing from the wall!" I generally recommend the typical things: keep everything up-to-date, enable two-factor authentication wherever you can, and use a password manager.

What is a life hack that you'd like to share?

Life hacks? Shortcuts? Nah, just take the long way, and get lost eventually.

What is the biggest mistake you've ever made, and how did you recover from it?

My adult life was built on mistakes, or rather poor decision-making. But they all turned out to be unexpected opportunities for experience and growth. Don't recover from your mistakes, just walk right through them! ∎

"Security is not a binary state. This is a mythical goal and is always a relative answer based on what threats and mitigations you have in place of your confidentiality, integrity, and availability."

Twitter: @RonGula • **Websites:** www.gula.tech and www.linkedin.com/in/rongula

Ron Gula

28

Ron started his cybersecurity career as a network penetration tester for the NSA. At BBN, he developed network honeypots to lure hackers, and he ran U.S. Internetworking's team of penetration testers and incident responders. As CTO of Network Security Wizards, Ron pioneered the art of network security monitoring and produced the Dragon Intrusion Detection System, which was recognized as a market leader by Gartner in 2001. As CEO and co-founder of Tenable Network Security, Ron led the company's rapid growth and product vision from 2002 through 2016. He helped them scale to more than 20,000 customers worldwide, raise $300 million in venture capital, and achieve revenues in excess of $100 million annually. Ron is president at Gula Tech Adventures, which focuses on the investment and advising of two dozen cybersecurity companies. Ron was honored and humbled to receive the 2017 Betamore BETA award, as well as being named a 2016 Baltimore Tech 10 Leader and a 2013 Maryland Entrepreneur of the Year by Ernst & Young.

If there is one myth that you could debunk in cybersecurity, what would it be?

Security is not a binary state. This is a mythical goal and is always a relative answer based on what threats and mitigations you have in place of your confidentiality, integrity, and availability.

What is one of the biggest bang-for-the-buck actions that an organization can take to improve its cybersecurity posture?

Keep track of what is on your network and what is used, even if it isn't yours. If you don't know what you have, it is really hard to defend it and even harder to defend something you don't know you need to defend.

"Keep track of what is on your network and what is used, even if it isn't yours. If you don't know what you have, it is really hard to defend it and even harder to defend something you don't know you need to defend."

How is it that cybersecurity spending is increasing but breaches are still happening?

It is several factors. As we consolidate more and more data to single applications, they become harder and harder to secure because an adversary is willing to wait longer or spend more resources trying to get to the target.

Many organizations still have poor cybersecurity and cyber hygiene and are easy targets for crypto-ransomware. They've always been hackable, but until the advent of anonymous ransom paying via bitcoin, it wasn't profitable.

Do you need a college degree or certification to be a cybersecurity professional?

Yes, absolutely! Cyber is the only profession where our experts claim you can do this without training. It does not occur with doctors, architects, pilots, or lawyers. Our field is so young that many of our role models don't have certifications or degrees in a cyber or network security discipline; however, for the next several generations, certifications and degrees are required.

How did you get started in the cybersecurity field, and what advice would you give to a beginner pursuing a career in cybersecurity?

I was a geek in high school and had an IBM PCjr (with the infrared wireless keyboard) as well as an Atari 400 with the membrane keyboard. I went to school for electrical engineering at Clarkson University, which was one of the first schools that required students to have a PC (a Zenith 286). I started reading *Phrack* while in the Air Force right around the time TCP sequence prediction attacks became popular. I was really interested in this and applied for an Air Force position at the NSA at the same place that Cliff Stoll reached out to in his *Cuckoo's Egg* book. While there, I fell in with a group of pentesters and got exposed to some of the smartest folks in cyber I've ever met, even though it wasn't called "cyber" until many years later.

What is your specialty in cybersecurity, and how can others gain expertise in your specialty?

I like to think I can see where people and the industry need to go and communicate this in a way that is easy to understand and motivating. I've been lucky enough to recruit some of the best people in the industry to help at companies like Tenable Network Security, and now, as an investor, I'm working on the next generation, trying to help build feedback loops where the executives of today become the mentors and investors of tomorrow.

What is your advice for career success when it comes to getting hired, climbing the corporate ladder, or starting a company in cybersecurity?

Only you can define what success is for you. There are many different paths you can take in cyber, all of which can be rewarding intellectually—making it harder for hackers and evil-doers to succeed—and all of them can be great careers. You should try to be exposed to as much cyber as possible and then commit to being good at something for a few years. We have many generalists in our field, which is necessary because of the immense amount of experience and technology that must be learned, but I really believe you should start out at something you really like—such as pentesting, incident response, IT help desk, etc.—and be good at it before you move on to bigger and better things.

> "Only you can define what success is for you."

What qualities do you believe all highly successful cybersecurity professionals share?

They all have the ability to communicate and understand perspective. They don't speak in marketing jargon, and they know that cyber is really difficult to quantify or measure. The great cyber professionals whom I respect also make it a point to train the next generation.

What is the best book or movie that can be used to illustrate cybersecurity challenges?

Spoiler alert—if you plan to read *The Three-Body Problem*, skip my answer.

There are two. First is a movie called *Colossus: The Forbin Project* (from 1970 mind you!) where an AI put in charge of our nuclear weapons has a hacking attempt made against it, and the scientists attempting the hack are ordered shot by the military police. The message here is that cyber is having increasingly real implications.

Second is a book from China called *The Three-Body Problem*. In it, a scientist figures out that the universe is actually a very scary place with advanced civilizations basically hiding and waiting to wipe out less advanced civilizations when they discover them. The same scientist figures out how to spoof a "We are here, is anyone else out there?" message from the home star of a race with a fleet on its way to attack Earth. Within a few years, that star is destroyed by an unseen, much larger advanced race. This is the model of cyber going forward. Every nation-state operates unseen in cybersecurity space. We don't know what they've recorded and what they have access to, and each is motivated by a variety of laws and national interests.

What is your favorite hacker movie?

For style and entertainment, *Swordfish*. For technical accuracy, an Italian movie called *The Listening*, in which a manual for an intelligence device created by a government contractor that can listen to anyone's phone calls falls into an unsuspecting public's hands.

What are your favorite books for motivation, personal development, or enjoyment?

Right now, I am reading Jordan Peterson's *12 Rules for Life* and have liked what I've read so far. This is the first "self-help" book I think I've read. I also enjoyed *Moonwalking with Einstein*, which is about memory and has lots of tips on having a better memory. My favorite business book to recommend to people is Ray Dalio's *Principles*.

What is some practical cybersecurity advice you give to people at home in the age of social media and the Internet of Things?

Your home network is probably safe, but for some of us it isn't. To protect yourself from this, get an iPad or Android tablet that connects only to 3G and use this for your banking, secure email, secure file saving, etc. Never use social media from this device, play games, put it on your Wi-Fi, etc.

> "Your home network is probably safe, but for some of us it isn't. To protect yourself from this, get an iPad or Android tablet that connects only to 3G and use this for your banking, secure email, secure file saving, etc."

What is a life hack that you'd like to share?

Have multiple interests, especially if you're not that great in something else you enjoy. It keeps you humble and young. For example, I'm learning and practicing the keyboard now because I enjoy it.

What is the biggest mistake you've ever made, and how did you recover from it?

My biggest mistakes are too personal to put into a book here. For the big ones, though, the best way to recover is to be honest with everyone involved and figure out the best way forward such that they won't burn you up inside or keep a grudge going with anyone.

A mistake I do like to tell folks, because it affected my college experience, was when I was trying out to be a "resident advisor." We did one of those group study exercises where we were all on an island, all had a skill and a liability, and all had to figure out who lived and died. This was my first time

> "My biggest mistakes are too personal to put into a book here. For the big ones, though, the best way to recover is to be honest with everyone involved and figure out the best way forward such that they won't burn you up inside or keep a grudge going with anyone."

doing something like this, and I did not really understand the liability part and was told that I was to play the "important architect." But I misheard it as "impotent architect." I did not get the RA job, but I listen much more attentively now and tend to assume (as in Ray Dalio's book) that if something isn't making sense, it is much more likely that I don't understand something than that someone is really being evil or deceptive. ∎

> "Do the hard work to document your enterprise and identify your information "crown jewels." "

Twitter: @Cyberjenny

Jennifer Havermann

29

Jennifer Havermann is a Deloitte client relationship executive located in Annapolis Junction, Maryland. She leads client relationships, strategy, and business development for Deloitte Central Maryland, including the intelligence community and Department of Defense clients within the community. Jennifer has more than 30 years' experience in both industry and government as a practitioner and leader in many cyber disciplines. She holds a BS degree in information assurance, a network engineering certificate, and technical certifications including the Certified Ethical Hacker (C|EH) and Certified Information Systems Security Professional (CISSP). She is an active volunteer in both the industry and community for STEM and cyber.

If there is one myth that you could debunk in cybersecurity, what would it be?
That you can just go get a degree or certification in cybersecurity and get a job right away because there are all of these unfilled jobs. Cybersecurity was a follow-on career/specialty for those who had other systems backgrounds—whether in system or network administration, programming, systems engineering, or other technical roles—that provided the necessary foundations to build cyber knowledge upon.

What is one of the biggest bang-for-the-buck actions that an organization can take to improve its cybersecurity posture?
Do the hard work to document your enterprise and identify your information "crown jewels." You can't improve what you don't know exists. So many organizations will have a breach and then try to pull information on the

impacted systems(s), only to find that it's either nonexistent or woefully out of date.

How is it that cybersecurity spending is increasing but breaches are still happening?

Money doesn't solve all problems and doesn't address the complexity of securing an enterprise; securing an enterprise requires hard work and attention to detail. The defensive professionals have a much harder job than the attackers. Defensive needs to secure everything, whereas an attacker only needs to find that one opening.

Do you need a college degree or certification to be a cybersecurity professional?

It depends on the role that you plan to fill and the knowledge you'll need to do your job. Honestly, as quickly as technology evolves, it's the lifelong learners who tend to do best in this field and have the best opportunities and longevity.

How did you get started in the cybersecurity field, and what advice would you give to a beginner pursuing a career in cybersecurity?

I was lucky to start while in the federal government, doing systems administration and becoming a "jack-of-all-trades" back when there were fewer specialties. I had an interest in cybersecurity, so I started self-teaching, taking classes, reading, and engaging with other professionals already in the field. As far as advice: never stop learning. Technical resiliency is important. Don't restrict yourself from learning different technologies. Do the reading.

What is your specialty in cybersecurity, and how can others gain expertise in your specialty?

From years of practice, I have several specialties. I'm constantly evolving in the field. Gaining expertise in any specialty requires hard work. When I did vulnerability assessment and penetration testing, I lived in that field. I learned as much as I could about different technologies, tools, and techniques. I ran a home lab with a lot of different systems in it so I could try tools and techniques in my own safe environment. I worked with a lot of others and still refer to them as my "tribe."

These people were experts in particular technologies. I'm still connected to those people to this day. Commit to the specialty you want, but be flexible about the experiences that will get you there; sometimes it looks like a lateral move, a step back, or taking on additional work.

What is your advice for career success when it comes to getting hired, climbing the corporate ladder, or starting a company in cybersecurity?

For getting hired and climbing the ladder: a willingness to do whatever is needed, grit. Those things are necessary for any career success. Be open to different work experiences, different customers (industries), or different missions (government). Look for ways to augment your experience.

For all three areas: cyber is not just about technology or solutions; it's also a business about people, so don't neglect developing your business skills. Learn contracts, how customers advertise the work, and networking. Learn how to write proposal responses, how to engage clients, effective communication skills, and project leadership/program management. Also, do both technology and business reading, as well as keeping up on current events and policy.

What qualities do you believe all highly successful cybersecurity professionals share?

- Commitment to the discipline and a desire to make things more secure and safer for all of us
- Commitment to lifelong learning
- Commitment to bettering the community and giving back, helping the next generation make their way

What is the best book or movie that can be used to illustrate cybersecurity challenges?

I'm having a hard time thinking of a "best." I will say that *The Net* (1995) was probably ahead of its time in addressing identity theft and covered a plethora of issues, albeit simplistically. It was a good overview of possibilities for its time.

What is your favorite hacker movie?

Hackers, of course. So cheesy..."Killer refresh rate" cracks me up every time I hear it.

What are your favorite books for motivation, personal development, or enjoyment?

I have a large reading list, but also look to podcasts. In the "Tribe of" spirit, I'm a huge fan of Tim Ferriss and *Tribe of Mentors,* but I also listen to the *Tim Ferriss Show* podcast and subscribe to his "Five Bullet Friday" emails. I also subscribe to a few industry/special-interest email distros that keep me abreast of what is happening in the marketplace and technology. I also use things like Coursera to take classes for my own interests.

What is some practical cybersecurity advice you give to people at home in the age of social media and the Internet of Things?

Less is more. If you don't need the IoT-enabled device, then go low-tech. If the convenience outweighs the risk, then go for it. Just remember, when using the IoT-enabled devices, there is a risk trade-off here. And less is more on social media as well. Be cognizant of how what you post could either enable a malicious actor or come back to haunt you.

What is a life hack that you'd like to share?

I'm still figuring those out! This won't sound like a life hack, but I tend to take copious notes. I figured out that my learning style involves the act of writing it down. That's the way I best learn and retain information. Using technology (laptop, tablet, etc.) doesn't have the same effect. I think "learning how to learn" has probably been my best life hack so far. You can check out Coursera's course of that name on Coursera: `https://www.coursera.org/learn/learning-how-to-learn`.

What is the biggest mistake you've ever made, and how did you recover from it?

Not getting my degree (checking that box) earlier. I think having the degree would have opened some alternative doors for me earlier in my career. I eventually got it, but I did hit the ceiling where the lack of a degree was the only barrier to other opportunities. I found a school and program that worked for me and earned a lot of credit through documenting how I obtained my experience/learning. I went full-time and worked full-time, hacking my personal schedule to knock it out as quickly as I could. It was the best investment. ■

> "To develop a successful application for today's ecosystem, security must be every member's responsibility—from managers and engineers to QA—throughout every stage of the software lifecycle."

Twitter: @TeootaHyseni • **Website:** www.linkedin.com/in/teuta-h-hyseni-12bbb42b

Teuta Hyseni

Teuta Hyseni is a security engineer at Microsoft. As a security engineer, she is responsible for leading application security projects, assessing potential flaws within applications, and reviewing the architecture of applications. Teuta started her career as a software engineer at Rackspace. After that, she moved to Denim Group, where she began working on the cybersecurity side and became fascinated with it. Teuta is committed to educating others outside of the industry on security threats and best practice, maximizing the impact of her security expertise through different talks and mentorship programs. In recognition of her efforts, she was nominated as a Security Champion of the Year in 2018 at the Women in IT Awards. As part of her passion for the tech industry and innovation, Teuta and her mentees won first place in the World Blockchain Hackathon at the Blockchain Economic Forum in 2018, a world-class competition. As an advocate for gender diversity, she also has a keen interest in motivating, inspiring, and improving women's participation in the industry.

30

If there is one myth that you could debunk in cybersecurity, what would it be?

Throughout my experience, one of the myths that I have seen is doing application security reviews as an afterthought process, meaning after the product has been developed. Although it is possible to add protection into applications post-completion, this is costly and less effective. To develop a successful application for today's ecosystem, security must be every member's responsibility—from managers and engineers to QA—throughout every stage of the software lifecycle. It is essential that each stage of the software development process has proper application security analysis performed, as well as defenses and countermeasures put in place that will result in more secure code. From envisioning through requirements, design, and implementation, to testing and releasing, security must be incorporated throughout the software development lifecycle (SDLC) to produce more secure and robust code that can better withstand attacks.

"The security posture of an organization is greatly impacted by the level of security awareness or security culture/readiness of the organization."

What is one of the biggest bang-for-the-buck actions that an organization can take to improve its cybersecurity posture?

The security posture of an organization is greatly impacted by the level of security awareness or security culture/readiness of the organization. If implemented correctly, security readiness and security awareness across the organization can be a major line of defense. If all employees are properly informed and trained regarding what to watch for, prevention, and remediation procedures, this can greatly minimize the potential security issues that could affect the company as a whole.

How is it that cybersecurity spending is increasing but breaches are still happening?

The complexity of systems has risen exponentially in the past decade. With more complex systems, the attack surface has expanded too. However, bigger investments don't necessarily imply better security defense mechanisms. For example, an expensive tool won't make a difference if the tool is not used properly and employed to serve its purpose. There should be the right combination of tools, and engineers who take advantage of these tools, to make the right decisions.

"Technology is a fast-paced industry, and a college degree or a certification won't make you a better cybersecurity professional."

Do you need a college degree or certification to be a cybersecurity professional?

Not necessarily. Technology is a fast-paced industry, and a college degree or a certification won't make you a better cybersecurity professional. There are other ways to gain knowledge and obtain different skill sets. With online learning and free courses, combined with a high level of commitment and interest, I think anyone can become a cybersecurity professional.

How did you get started in the cybersecurity field, and what advice would you give to a beginner pursuing a career in cybersecurity?

I started my career as a software engineer. Security was not on my radar until one day, at my previous job, there was a need for help with an application security assessment, and I volunteered to help. From that point on, I was fascinated with application security and how intriguing and exciting it can be. In regard to the way of thinking, one has to change the perspective, understand issues more deeply and accurately, and ponder at how an unworkable notion might become workable. To all beginners, cybersecurity is a field that requires mental toughness and resilience. However, its great reward is that you are on a mission and have a duty to protect users' private information and serve the greater good.

What is your advice for career success when it comes to getting hired, climbing the corporate ladder, or starting a company in cybersecurity?
Because the job market has become so competitive, doing well on your job, climbing the ladder, and moving forward with your career has become more challenging than ever. Depending on one's goals, advancement and recognition come as a result of a willingness and a strong desire to perform well. Once you have the willingness and the right mind-set, you will see a positive change in your career. Some of the things that have helped me on my own career path include taking initiative, being open to constructive feedback from co-workers and managers, communicating well, learning continuously, gaining trust, being results-driven, evaluating myself often, and making adjustments as needed.

What qualities do you believe all highly successful cybersecurity professionals share?
The cybersecurity industry progresses continuously and quickly, and the most important quality a successful security professional can have is natural curiosity, which leads to continual learning. Furthermore, one must have the ability to work and think fast, under pressure, and make decisions in real time.

> "Depending on one's goals, advancement and recognition come as a result of a willingness and a strong desire to perform well."

What is the best book or movie that can be used to illustrate cybersecurity challenges?
One book that illustrates cybersecurity challenges well is *Hacked Again*. This book presents the challenges that businesses and institutions deal with and the tactics used to mitigate cyber attacks—what really happens before, during, and after data breaches or security incidents.

What is your favorite hacker movie?
There are a couple of movies that I like, but I would say *The Girl with the Dragon Tattoo*.

What are your favorite books for motivation, personal development, or enjoyment?
I have a few favorite books; however, this changes often. Currently, I like *The Code of the Extraordinary Mind*, *The Future of the Mind*, *The Power of Now*, and *Phantoms in the Brain*.

What is some practical cybersecurity advice you give to people at home in the age of social media and the Internet of Things?

Cybersecurity is not just an organizational concern anymore. The number of smart devices we use and rely on at home has grown to the point where our day-to-day lives can be greatly impacted if an unauthorized malicious user gains access to them. My advice to people at home would be to use a strong password, and don't use the same password for every application. For sensitive applications, use a multifactor authenticator.

Sensitive activities, such as banking or shopping, should be done only on your device. Do not use free, unauthenticated Wi-Fi when performing such activities. The data you are sending to the browser is in plain text and can be copied easily.

Social engineering is really common. If someone calls or emails you asking for sensitive information, it's better to hang up and call the institution yourself than to trust someone on the phone.

> "The number of smart devices we use and rely on at home has grown to the point where our day-to-day lives can be greatly impacted if an unauthorized malicious user gains access to them."

What is a life hack that you'd like to share?

While I was in college, one of the biggest struggles I had was balancing sleep and study. With exams, essays, projects, and work deadlines rolling around at the end of each term, as a student, I found that napping can be a powerful tool to provide enough energy to carry me throughout the day. The schedule I used was three to four hours of uninterrupted night sleep combined with three or four power naps of 15–20 minutes between classes during the day. This is also known as a *polyphasic* sleep pattern, which refers to sleeping multiple times instead of once.

What is the biggest mistake you've ever made, and how did you recover from it?

One of my professional mistakes happened while I was a software engineer. I was assigned to a project to build a plugin for one of our products. However, the timeline was short; therefore, the project was assigned to two people in order to deliver it on time. Since we were two engineers, we were working simultaneously on codependent features. As we progressed with our projects, we failed to synchronize our code daily. We were on the second week of the project, and both of us had progressed on our feature sets, so we were asked to demo our progress. When we started to merge our code, it turned out that a lot of our code had conflicts and failed to merge. It took us a couple of days to resolve these conflicts, and on top of that, our features broke due to the merge. The lesson learned from this mistake was that, regardless of how small the project is, when working in parallel with someone else, pushing the code and merging daily is a must in order to deliver the project successfully. Hence, sometimes trying to save time backfires. In the case I just mentioned, neglecting to push and merge the code daily actually wasted time in the long run and delayed the release of the plugin. ■

> "Many companies think that "checking the box" on compliance means they're more secure."

Twitter: @tjackson78 • **Website:** ttalkstech.com

Terence Jackson

Terence Jackson graduated from Howard University with a BBA in management information systems. He is currently the chief information security officer at Thycotic Software LLC and holds certifications from Thycotic, CyberArk, RSA, Oracle, and the Identity Management Institute. He has more than 17 years' experience working in information technology and security for large and small federal contractors and as an independent consultant. Terence is also a Stars Mentor at MACH37, a Virginia-based cybersecurity accelerator. In his free time, he serves on the AV and Social Media Ministry at his church. He enjoys spending time with his wife and family, which includes his teenage son and five-year-old daughter. He's also an avid Marvel movie watcher and enjoys technology news and research.

31

If there is one myth that you could debunk in cybersecurity, what would it be?
That compliance equals security. Many companies think that "checking the box" on compliance means they're more secure.

What is one of the biggest bang-for-the-buck actions that an organization can take to improve its cybersecurity posture?
In my experience, removing local administrative privileges and application white/blacklisting goes a long way to improve security without spending a ton a money.

How is it that cybersecurity spending is increasing but breaches are still happening?

Spending is increasing; however, companies are purchasing disparate point solutions that are hard to integrate with each other and take months to deploy and configure, and teams are not properly trained to handle the emerging threats. Employees are on the front lines of this battle, but they have not been properly equipped. While there are annual security awareness trainings and phishing simulations, many times those are just to check a compliance box.

> "Employees are on the front lines of this battle, but they have not been properly equipped."

Do you need a college degree or certification to be a cybersecurity professional?

I don't believe degrees or certifications can accurately predict the success or failure of someone in cybersecurity. Just like compliance doesn't equal security, certifications and degrees don't necessarily make a cybersecurity professional. What it typically means is that you studied and did well enough to pass a test or series of tests. That's not a knock on degrees or certifications; I have both. But I think the trait that makes a person a true cybersecurity "guru" is an investigative mind-set—the drive to figure out how things work on a deeper level, often from the inside out. As a child, I would take all of my toys apart to see how they worked and then reassemble them and sometimes even modify them. I have worked with many self-trained cyber professionals who had little to no formal training, and they could run circles around some folks with degrees and certs. They were battle-tested and ready.

> "I don't believe degrees or certifications can accurately predict the success or failure of someone in cybersecurity. Just like compliance doesn't equal security, certifications and degrees don't necessarily make a cybersecurity professional."

How did you get started in the cybersecurity field, and what advice would you give to a beginner pursuing a career in cybersecurity?

I have worked in information technology my entire career, for both private-sector companies and government agencies. Security has been a component of each of those jobs, but I didn't formally pivot into cyber until 2013. I started off deploying security information and event management (SIEM) for large enterprises and helping analysts turn metadata into actionable intel, looking for the needle in the haystack. I then began consulting with Fortune 100 companies in the discipline of identity and access management, helping them secure the prized jewels—"privileged accounts." To someone pursuing a career in cyber, I would say there are many resources online to help you achieve your goal. Research the various roles in cybersecurity, find out what it will take to get to that goal, and definitely network, network, network!

What is your specialty in cybersecurity, and how can others gain expertise in your specialty?

My specialty is privileged account management (PAM) security and identity and access management (IAM). To gain expertise in these areas, one must understand that *identity* is the new perimeter, and most organizations have four times as many privileged accounts as employees. So, IAM and PAM is a lot of asking the *what, why,* and *who* in relation to access and enforcing least privilege.

> "To someone pursuing a career in cyber, I would say there are many resources online to help you achieve your goal."

What is your advice for career success when it comes to getting hired, climbing the corporate ladder, or starting a company in cybersecurity?

There are no off days. There are no eight-hour days. Security events never happen when it's convenient. In my experience, the people who accept these truths work harder and have a tenacity that doesn't stop when they leave the office. And I will say it again...*network*.

What qualities do you believe all highly successful cybersecurity professionals share?

An investigative mind-set and the innate need to help.

What is the best book or movie that can be used to illustrate cybersecurity challenges?

I don't have a movie, but the most realistic show I've seen to date is *Mr. Robot*. It highlights the threat of insiders, nation-states, and black hats. It's a phenomenal look into cyber.

What is your favorite hacker movie?

WarGames (1983).

> "Security events never happen when it's convenient."

What are your favorite books for motivation, personal development, or enjoyment?

The Bible, *The Secret, Die Empty*, and *Rtfm: Red Team Field Manual*.

What is some practical cybersecurity advice you give to people at home in the age of social media and the Internet of Things?

To enable multifactor authentication on cloud services, use antivirus, do personal banking on a separate computer used only for that purpose, use strong passwords on your Wi-Fi network, create a guest network for your IoT devices and actual guests, and use a password manager.

What is a life hack that you'd like to share?

You can make ricotta cheese at home from milk, salt, and vinegar.

What is the biggest mistake you've ever made, and how did you recover from it?

Not being comfortable in my own skin and not appreciating the gifts and talents that God had bestowed upon me. I recovered from this by being humbled and restored. ∎

"Hire the right people—especially if they're your first security person. Don't skimp; if you're going to do it, do it right."

Twitter: @cktricky • **Website:** cktricky.com

Ken Johnson

32

Ken Johnson has been hacking web apps for 10 years. He started in networking, taught himself programming, and eventually built an application security consulting company before finally leaving to work at GitHub. Ken has spoken at RSA, You Sh0t the Sheriff, Insomni'hack, CERN, DerbyCon, AppSec USA, AppSec DC, AppSec California, DevOpsDays DC, LASCON, RubyNation, and numerous Ruby, OWASP, and AWS events about AppSec, DevOps security, and AWS security. Ken's projects include the *Absolute AppSec* podcast, WeirdAAL, OWASP's RailsGoat, and the Web Exploitation Framework (wXf).

If there is one myth that you could debunk in cybersecurity, what would it be?

Self-aggrandizing. We sometimes have to accept that we're actually not that important. I feel that we do a lot to hype our unique/special culture, our silver-bullet products, the latest threats with a sexy logo and name, etc. But in the end, we're one small aspect of most businesses. Sure, some businesses specifically have to take security up a notch. For most, though, we're just one component of many in the typical business unit. I say this because, if you're a newcomer, realize this early in your career, as it pertains to your approach. If you're going to have input on a budget or give input as to the rollout of "X," take the entire picture into account. When you're overridden or dismissed by the folks working above your pay grade, try not to take it too personally. Just remember: you may have input, but at the end of the day, the business decides on priorities, and it's usually not personal. It's...*business*. It may seem like, "This is going to be soooo bad," but it's rarely as bad as you assume it will be.

What is one of the biggest bang-for-the-buck actions that an organization can take to improve its cybersecurity posture?

Hire the right people—especially if they're your first security person. Don't skimp; if you're going to do it, do it right. These are the people who are going to onboard and advocate for additional security team members. These folks will decide your overall strategy and, ultimately, whether or not it's effective.

How is it that cybersecurity spending is increasing but breaches are still happening?

Speaking as someone who has worked on both the offensive and defensive sides of the spectrum, defense has to get *every single thing right*—with zero human error involved—to successfully prevent even the smallest of breaches, whereas an attacker only needs to get lucky *once*. I believe security pros are acknowledging this.

We've seen the rise of cybersecurity insurance. We've seen more and more CSOs/CISOs emphasizing the need for having an effective incident response plan and disaster recovery strategy, as well as understanding their risk profile. That way, when a breach does occur, they are ahead of the game. To me, this is an acknowledgment that we cannot 100 percent guarantee a breach will never happen. All we can do is prepare for it and minimize the damage. I'm not saying we're sitting back and saying, "Welp, there's nothing we can do. Oh well." What I am saying is we can make ourselves hard targets, prioritize where our controls are in place, minimize our risk, and be prepared when a breach does occur.

Do you need a college degree or certification to be a cybersecurity professional?

I don't have a degree. Part of me wishes I did, just in case there ever comes a time when it might matter. To date, though, I feel I've had a pretty successful career and it hasn't mattered. If it is something you want to do for you, go for it. But I'd advocate a degree in cybersecurity is less relevant than one in, say, computer science. Take that with a grain of salt, as I do not actually have a degree. What I can say pretty definitively is that understanding the nuts and bolts of networking, programming, processors, etc. is far more practical than understanding the CIA Triad. There will be plenty of time to learn that kind of domain-specific "stuff" later.

How did you get started in the cybersecurity field, and what advice would you give to a beginner pursuing a career in cybersecurity?

I'm going to try to paint a picture without being overly long-winded. In short, I was the stereotypical "takes things apart, learn how they work, and build something better" type of kid that you hear most InfoSec folks describe themselves as.

However, there was an unflattering side to that. I was incredibly bored in school, which meant I was really lazy. In high school, I barely attended. I only did enough to graduate with a diploma...barely. School was just super boring to me unless I was in front of a computer. If it was a typing class, I'd figure out what else the computer could do. I'd finish assignments early and then find out what I could do with the computer system in front of me.

Fast-forward to my senior year, and I'm embarrassed it took that long to figure it out, but I realized I was headed for a pretty sad existence with no real prospects. I liked computers *a lot*; they brought me joy. So, I enlisted in the U.S. Navy as an IT.

The Navy taught me many things—how to sweep floors properly, the multitude of uses for Simple Green (a cleaning solution), and, most importantly, discipline. While I did enlist as an IT, I would have learned next to nothing relevant if it hadn't been for my sheer willpower to read, experiment, and stay up late following the networking crew around, running cables and asking questions. I was based in Italy for a few years, and I'd even buy Italian hacker magazines because, for whatever reason, I was drawn to what we now call "InfoSec."

When I left the Navy, I took jobs doing typical IT work until I decided to move to the East Coast for an opportunity doing security (which I didn't even know was a profession until the opportunity came about). Truly, I love programming, so I taught myself how to program. It was only a matter of time before I picked up the *Web Application Hacker's Handbook* and taught myself about web application security. From that point forward, I learned what I could, shared what I had via blogging and videos, spoke at little get-togethers, and found like-minded folks at conferences. Basically, I built the connections that landed me my first consulting gig with FishNet Security. And I've been working in AppSec ever since.

What is your specialty in cybersecurity, and how can others gain expertise in your specialty?

I work in application security, or AppSec for short. Basically, if the tech is using a web standard to communicate (web application, mobile application, thick client, IoT device, etc.), then it falls under AppSec. The most important thing to know in this area is how to write and read code. It's a fundamental requirement, since we live and breathe code.

Beyond that fundamental requirement, you need to know how to test the security of an application. It is far less risky these days to test what you're learning or reading about against a real-world website or application because of the advent of bug bounties. When I was starting, if you'd never done this professionally and were learning how to find flaws in a web app...well, you had to have a little gray in your hat. Sure, we had things like WebGoat and Samurai, but that's not the same as real targets. Nowadays, you can sign up for a bug bounty program and get cracking on real targets. The two most important books, for me, were *The Tangled Web* by Michal Zalewski and *The Web Application Hacker's Handbook* by Dafydd Stuttard and Marcus Pinto.

What is your advice for career success when it comes to getting hired, climbing the corporate ladder, or starting a company in cybersecurity?

I've been the lowest of the low on the totem pole. I've also been the co-owner and CTO of a 30-person security consulting firm, and everything else in between. The security industry is interesting in that I've found it to be a small world. Word of mouth is incredibly important. For me, I've found strong character, work ethic, and mastery of your craft will carry you incredibly far. Leave a good impression and you never know where you'll end up.

> Leave a good impression and you never know where you'll end up.

If you're starting a security company, my answer would be pretty much the same when you distill it down. What worked for me when it came to sales, recruitment, and management was all guided by the same philosophy. That philosophy is you have to maintain high standards morally and ethically for the quality of work you produce, as well as for the people you choose to work with.

What qualities do you believe all highly successful cybersecurity professionals share?
Everyone that I've seen be successful (who wasn't that .0001 percent wunderkind) did things outside of work. Whether that's speaking, writing, contributing to open source projects, podcasting, etc., all of them do something outside of their nine-to-five, which is what helps them stay relevant, so the two go hand in hand.

What is the best book or movie that can be used to illustrate cybersecurity challenges?
Genuinely, I think everyone should read *The Phoenix Project* by Gene Kim, George Spafford, and Kevin Behr. Talk about a book that really emphasizes all components of a business unit and discusses security's role in it.

What is your favorite hacker movie?
The Saint with Val Kilmer. Now, I know this isn't your stereotypical hacker movie, but the main character, John Rossi (Simon Templar), sneaks into places he shouldn't be; gains access to things he shouldn't be able to; and uses social engineering, lock picking, high-tech devices, and encrypted communications to do it. Then, he ends up trying to open-source cold fusion technology rather than have it end up in the hands of corrupt politicians, businessmen, or the mob.

What are your favorite books for motivation, personal development, or enjoyment?
Extreme Ownership by Jocko Willink and Leif Babin. Everyone should read it.

What is some practical cybersecurity advice you give to people at home in the age of social media and the Internet of Things?
Be careful what you share. Enable two-factor authentication for any social media account. Don't click before figuring out what exactly you are clicking. Ask yourself, "Do I really need an internet-connected toaster?"

What is a life hack that you'd like to share?
Two things. First, get quality sleep and focus on your work until you can't focus anymore. Then, go do something else. A good night's sleep helps me figure things out faster, and I feel better.

Working in sprints means I'm focused only on what I'm working on, and that's easier to do if I've had rest. If I've not finished whatever I'm doing before I feel my attention waning, I walk away for a bit. That way, the time I do spend in front of a computer is limited to quality time rather than getting lost in Twitter or cat memes. I think that in today's society, people prize multitasking to their detriment. Quality work requires quality focus. Get some rest and go for walks.

What is the biggest mistake you've ever made, and how did you recover from it?
Have you heard of the sunk cost fallacy? Let's just say this led me to triple down on an investment in someone and, ultimately, in a business when, in reality, I should have cut ties way earlier. There were far too many warning signs to say, "I couldn't have seen how this would play out." Instead, I just kept working harder and harder to stave off the ramifications of this person's poor personal and professional conduct. So, it took some time to forgive myself for that mistake, understand that I'm still (relatively) young, and realize there are plenty of other opportunities out there. Life is too short to dread waking up in the morning. ■

"One of the biggest myths, in my opinion, is that what hackers do requires a high level of complexity and skill. Most attacks out there are generic, and the way most organizations (and people) get hacked is through very basic things."

Twitter: @HackingDave • **Websites:** www.trustedsec.com and www.binarydefense.com

David Kennedy

33

David Kennedy is the founder of TrustedSec, Binary Defense, and DerbyCon. TrustedSec and Binary Defense are focused on the betterment of the security industry from both a defensive and offensive perspective. He also serves on the board of directors for the (ISC)[2] organization. Formerly, David was the CSO for Diebold Incorporated, where he ran the entire INFOSEC program. He is also a co-author of the book *Metasploit: The Penetration Tester's Guide* as well as the creator of the Social-Engineer Toolkit (SET), Artillery, Unicorn, PenTesters Framework (PTF), TrevorC2, and several popular open source tools. David has been interviewed by several news organizations, including CNN, Fox News, MSNBC, CNBC, Katie Couric, and BBC World News.

David has also consulted on hacker techniques for the hit TV show *Mr. Robot*. He is the co-host of the *Social-Engineer Podcast* and is featured on several additional podcasts as well. David has testified in front of Congress on two occasions concerning the security of government websites, and he is one of the founding authors of the Penetration Testing Execution Standard (PTES)—a framework designed to fix the penetration-testing industry. Prior to the private sector, David worked for the U.S. Marine Corps and deployed to Iraq twice for intelligence-related missions.

If there is one myth that you could debunk in cybersecurity, what would it be?

One of the biggest myths, in my opinion, is that what hackers do requires a high level of complexity and skill. Most attacks out there are generic, and the way most organizations (and people) get hacked is through very basic things. The biggest challenge corporations face is the speed at which they must move to conduct business. Often, information technology (IT) and security are behind the organization, so they miss things, which is where we fall into the breach categories. Companies try to sidestep building security programs by purchasing the next piece of software that's supposed to fix most of their issues, but the problems stem from the program itself.

More than anything, companies need to focus on building up their programs, which takes time, and focusing on how to detect and prevent attacks in their environment. That comes with having the right people who are skilled in understanding how attacks work, which is key to identifying the specific methods an attacker can use in order to compromise an organization.

> "More than anything, companies need to focus on building up their programs, which takes time, and focusing on how to detect and prevent attacks in their environment."

What is one of the biggest bang-for-the-buck actions that an organization can take to improve its cybersecurity posture?

Investment in skilled people is number one. The market is experiencing a shortage in talented people, which can be challenging for organizations. Having skilled people—or creating them by investing in people and training them in security—can't be emphasized enough. I've been to several organizations that have everything ranging from massive budgets all the way to the smallest. Ultimately, it's the people who make the difference in how the organization handles threats and builds its security program. I've walked into some of the largest security programs with the largest budgets and broken in within minutes—undetected. The difference in organizations where it has been a challenge to break in (and we've gotten detected in early phases of an attack) came down to the knowledge of the individuals, analysts, and the overall program and culture.

> "Investment in skilled people is number one. The market is experiencing a shortage in talented people, which can be challenging for organizations."

To me, having a budget for training, education, and awareness, and having skilled people, has the most impact on an information security program—more so than any other investment within a company. It isn't a piece of technology that makes the difference; it comes down to the knowledge and skill of the team. A team can be built from the ground up or by hiring seasoned individuals to help lead the team. Regardless, having a program that allows advancement, flexibility, training, and the ability to be challenged within information security makes or breaks the security program.

How is it that cybersecurity spending is increasing but breaches are still happening?

There does not appear to be a direct correlation between spending more money and having fewer breaches. Return on investment has always been a

"There does not appear to be a direct correlation between spending more money and having fewer breaches."

hard thing for the security industry because you are either breached or you are not. (And there may be some lag time between when you're breached and when it's detected.) It all comes down to how the investment is used and what the intent of risk reduction is. We are a risk-centric industry, and if an organization doesn't have a good grasp on what they are trying to protect, the risk factors, and the threats toward their organization, then any amount of money will not protect them.

Instead, focus spending on understanding adversary capabilities, threat modeling, and emulation—and having supplemental security programs in place that identify threats. This is where most of the investment should be going.

Unfortunately, too many companies still focus on regulatory and compliance as their primary driver—as well as purchasing technology—instead of investing in people or leveraging what they already have. What most organizations fail to realize is that when you introduce a new piece of technology, it introduces complexity. If you don't have the people to support that complexity—people with the knowledge to appropriately use this new technology—then it's a detriment to the organization, not a risk-reduction factor.

Do you need a college degree or certification to be a cybersecurity professional?

The simple answer to that is no; however, this is complex. A degree or certification doesn't attest to the skill level of someone at any stretch, but a degree or certification does show commitment and dedication to a specific focus area or an understanding of certain topics. This can be beneficial for hiring managers and human resources to be able to identify potential candidates for an organization. It's often difficult to distinguish between raw talent and a career of degrees and certifications when leveraging human resources. If a security professional were able to interview each candidate and test them on skills and capabilities, the answer would be, "No, degrees and certifications make no difference."

The truth, though, is that isn't a reality. So, certifications and degrees *do* make a difference. They help show your focus as a security professional and that you're spending time to differentiate yourself from someone else. This doesn't mean that the skills are there to meet the job requirements, but it's at least a conversation starter. If someone comes highly recommended to me from individuals I trust, I won't look at a certification or degree. However, if someone is applying blind, then they do help in understanding the skills and expertise of someone. There are also many certifications that hold more weight, depending on positions. For example, if I'm hiring someone who is technical-centric, I will look more for technical certifications that require applied knowledge to pass (such as lab simulations).

"If someone comes highly recommended to me from individuals I trust, I won't look at a certification or degree."

How did you get started in the cybersecurity field, and what advice would you give to a beginner pursuing a career in cybersecurity?

I started off not knowing really where I wanted to focus my efforts. I was always in technology, starting off programming online video games (called *multiuser dimensions*, or MUDs), and I learned a lot by self-teaching and exploring. Most important, I figured out how to program at an early age. When I joined the military, I started focusing on cybersecurity as a job. That's always one pathway into security—joining the military and getting the applied, hands-on experience that way. There are also college courses. I, for one, really enjoy the cybersecurity program at Dakota State University (DSU). The key is finding what you *enjoy* doing in security; that's the most important factor.

For most, security becomes more of a passion and hobby than it does a job or a day-to-day living. To stay up to date and learn what you need to, it's something you need to enjoy doing. Find what specialty within cybersecurity best interests you, and focus on learning that as your tradecraft. This doesn't mean you can't learn anything else, but having specializations is important. Pick up books, read them, learn and soak in as much knowledge as possible. Learning from other people's mistakes and successes can also help.

Also, communication is super important. Being able to take highly complex or technical concepts and communicate them so that everyone else can understand is part of our role. Communication and social capabilities are traits that are often lacking in the cybersecurity industry.

What is your specialty in cybersecurity, and how can others gain expertise in your specialty?

I'm not sure I have a direct specialty. Being in cybersecurity requires knowing a lot of different areas. However, if it was any, it would be *exploitation* and *post-exploitation*. I get to focus a lot on understanding attack patterns, researching new techniques, and identifying how an organization can be compromised through multiple means. Understanding attack patterns also allows me to be strong on the defensive front and help organizations build detection and prevention against a large attack surface. Programming is another. While I am a far stretch from a developer, having the ability to write tools—and automate tedious tasks or come up with new attacks—is a huge asset for people getting into the field.

What is your advice for career success when it comes to getting hired, climbing the corporate ladder, or starting a company in cybersecurity?

Take risks, trust your gut, and make calculated decisions when it comes to your career. Starting a cybersecurity company in the beginning without a lot of expertise or customers will be difficult at first.

As for getting hired, start gaining experience and differentiating yourself through your passion and drive, and things will happen. If your desire is to be highly successful in information security, going to work from 9 to 5 will not get you there. Going home and researching, taking training, reading books, networking, learning from others, and making security your passion will.

You must differentiate yourself from other individuals within the organization as well as your peers. Climbing the ladder is good, but it can also cause you to become stagnant. I notice a lot of individuals changing companies every few years to gain different experiences and challenges and to become well rounded. I personally haven't done that; I stayed for many years and then decided to start my own company.

What qualities do you believe all highly successful cybersecurity professionals share?

Passion, dedication, loyalty, ethics, communication, and drive are some of the highly sought-after skills. You can have someone who is technically brilliant but lacks drive or passion, and getting what you need to out of that person becomes challenging. I'm an advocate for the idea that you can teach a driven person anything and train them up. The ability to be a self-starter and learn information without being taught is also highly desirable. Also, being able to communicate with others and work as part of a team shows humility, and it demonstrates the ability to learn from (and teach) others.

What is the best book or movie that can be used to illustrate cybersecurity challenges?

While not directly related to cybersecurity, the book *Rework* (by Jason Fried and David Heinemeier Hansson) is more of a technology and business-centric book. I think many of the issues we run into are making things so complex that it's often to the detriment of protecting the organization. *Rework* was an inspiring book for me in that it is the exact *opposite* of what we are taught in school (or in business) on how to handle situations or hold meetings—and a lot of that directly applied to me and cybersecurity. Although cybersecurity has technical components, having a business understanding and being able to communicate how to most effectively address risk and communicate complex situations is also extremely important.

What is your favorite hacker movie?

I know this is going to be cliché, but *Hackers* is one of my favorite movies. The technical aspects are obviously incorrect, but the culture of hackers, the curiosity, and the fighting for what you believe is right is a perfect representation of how a lot of individuals are. The movie, to me, was ahead of its time and showed a lot of what was possible in the '90s with computers and what we were going to face—for example, where individuals would hack corporations to extort money and how having a high level of skill can put you in jail if you do things wrong. It was a great representation of what was to come, even if the technical aspects of the movie weren't accurate.

What are your favorite books for motivation, personal development, or enjoyment?

I really enjoy books from No Starch Press. They have many technical books that I read from time to time to keep me sharp on many topics, ranging from programming to car hacking. I enjoy reading those, even if I may not understand the topic fully, because it allows me to grasp the conceptual aspects around a topic and makes me stronger when communicating to audiences of executives. I also enjoy the book *Remote* by Jason Fried and David Heinemeier Hansson, which talks about how to build a successful company of remote employees and the things you need to do to have a good culture. For me, people are everything.

What is some practical cybersecurity advice you give to people at home in the age of social media and the Internet of Things?
When you're purchasing technology, know that it comes with a level of risk. The more technology you add to your home or that you wear, the greater the profile and footprint you have. Make sure to change default passwords, keep up to date with the latest patches, and as someone looking to get into this industry, figure out how to take them apart and hack them! Most IoT devices are rudimentary on security and super easy learning grounds for you to learn how to attack things.

What is a life hack that you'd like to share?
Life is all about balance. Maximizing your time to learn requires motivation and passion but, most important, surrounding yourself with positivity. For me, my biggest life hack is always attempting to find positives in life and what I do. Even in bad situations, using them as a way to learn how to *not* be placed in a bad situation. Family and work-life balance is the most important piece. A life hack that I use is that I will sleep in a little later and stay up later. This allows me—once the massive amount of emails have come in throughout the day—to have quiet and be focused when the kids and family are all asleep. That could be coding, reading a book, playing a video game, or trying to figure something out. You need time away from the distractions of your phone and other things to develop you. Make sure you dedicate time for you.

> "Life is all about balance. Maximizing your time to learn requires motivation and passion, but most importantly, surrounding yourself with positivity."

What is the biggest mistake you've ever made, and how did you recover from it?
When I first got into the industry, I remember I was on a penetration test for one of our company's largest customers. I attacked one of their systems, and I brought their entire network down—causing massive outages. At the time, I thought I was going to get fired and that the company would terminate all communications with us, and due to me, we would lose one of our largest customers. The customer came in highly upset, screaming and yelling—which, at the time, was something I'd never experienced. They had people running through the hallways, and it was mass chaos. It was really bad. After the dust had settled and the company recovered, and once everyone's emotions were settled, they sat me down to understand what had happened.

After explaining truthfully why these types of attacks were used, the organization found that they hadn't fully prepared for this scenario in their disaster recovery and were going to incorporate it into their program. They were super thankful and appreciated the work we did. While it caused a lot of pain for the company, calmer heads prevailed. ■

> "Nothing is going to stop a breach. I don't think there's any foolproof plan to stop them. They're going to happen."

Twitter: @diami03 • **Website:** topheavysecurity.com

Michelle Klinger

34

Michelle Klinger is a director of public cloud security living in Houston, Texas, with a bachelor's degree in organizational management and security. She has held several roles throughout her career—system/network administrator, security assessor, QSA, and security architect. In the last five years, she's made it a point to volunteer at various conferences. Michelle is a former board member of Security BSides and one of the past coordinators of the BSidesDFW conference. She can always be located by her distinctive laugh and low-cut shirts.

If there is one myth that you could debunk in cybersecurity, what would it be?
The use of the term *hacker* to encompass malicious activity or a bad actor.

What is one of the biggest bang-for-the-buck actions that an organization can take to improve its cybersecurity posture?
I don't think there is one "bang-for-your-buck" action. I think that's synonymous with a magic dietary pill. Instead, what's needed is a deliberate set of actions to create an actual information security program at an organization. This means aligning different security groups and defining what their value to the organization needs to be, as opposed to having different security groups for the sake of having them. We need to build programs, and the groups shouldn't be working in silos. We need to have dependencies between the groups, and the groups need to know what those dependencies are and establish the programs

and processes around them. It's a lot of work, but I don't think there's a single bang-for-your-buck marketing ploy. I think that's the problem we have with security; everyone's trying to find that magic bullet, and it doesn't exist.

How is it that cybersecurity spending is increasing but breaches are still happening?

Nothing is going to stop a breach. I don't think there's any foolproof plan to stop them. They're going to happen. It's how one responds to being breached—shifting one's perspective from "prevent and protect" to "respond, detect, and restore"—that is important. But I also think the spending is, again, in those perceived magic bullets, which are usually tools. They're spending a lot on tools but not developing and building programs around them. The programs should be built *first*, and then the tools should be identified as *fitting the program* versus finding the tool and then just operationalizing it without a larger program in mind.

Do you need a college degree or certification to be a cybersecurity professional?

You don't need a degree, but you definitely need a certification (one of the well-known certs) to get past the résumé triage process. Getting past recruiters and HR, who have no knowledge of the role, can be tricky without one. They tend to use keywords to filter out potential candidates, and a certification is an easy filter. The org may also have staff with certification quotas.

> "You don't need a degree, but you definitely need a certification (one of the well-known certs) to get past the résumé triage process."

I was a network admin for years, and then when I went into security, the first thing I had to do was get a security cert. That way, when my company bid on jobs, they could say they had "X" cert, or a resource with that cert. I think they're only good for meeting quotas and/or HR, but I don't think they provide much value.

How did you get started in the cybersecurity field, and what advice would you give to a beginner pursuing a career in cybersecurity?

I started in IT first. I was a network/system administrator, and this was before InfoSec was an actual profession. I was actually in IT for a security vendor, and I was the admin for their network. Eventually, the company closed down, and some of the people who worked there started their own security company doing consultative security assessments.

I think there's a benefit to starting in IT. Security is a mind-set; everything functions on some sort of IT function or IT bedrock, so coming through IT is super helpful—as opposed to just coming in and saying, "I want to learn security!"

What is your specialty in cybersecurity, and how can others gain expertise in your specialty?

My specialty was security assessments. I went to companies and assessed their security controls for maybe eight or nine years. At my current company, I started out running their assessments group, but now I've morphed into cyber risk management. Again, having security assessment experience is super helpful for doing risk, but I could not tell you how to get into risk. Risk is seen as like the third-removed cousin of InfoSec. Usually, when you tell people you're in risk, they're like, "Oh, okay." They don't see it as information security, but it is part of the governance, risk-management, and compliance (GRC) triad. As far as an organization is concerned, information security risk is the centerpiece—where understanding the company's risks and the business-making decisions based on those risks is pretty key. All of those other security programs feed into the risk program to provide metrics. My advice would be to find conferences that are risk-specific, go to those, network, and get your foot in the door.

What is your advice for career success when it comes to getting hired, climbing the corporate ladder, or starting a company in cybersecurity?

I don't have any advice for starting a company. I find a company and become loyal to it. I would never consider starting my own company.

As for getting hired, 95 percent of the jobs I got were from people I knew. There were only two companies in my career where I had to go in cold and interview. If I were going to give advice for getting hired, I would say *network*. And that all came from Twitter, which is how I know everybody who's given me a job. For our industry, networking is key. That is why it's so difficult to get into it. Everyone who gets a job is usually handed off by someone else they know. If you're going to start off in InfoSec, start networking and getting to know people, and talk about what you're interested in and what you've been working on to achieve experience—whether it's at home or in a business.

> There are some folks who've chosen InfoSec just because that's where the money seems to be. But I think a lot of us hire each other because we see the *passion* versus the need to get a *paycheck*.

If you're in IT and your role is creating user accounts and it's rote and mundane, take it upon yourself to understand what you're doing—and start doing it more securely so *you* become the security person. (Not that you bypass the security org, but you keep security in the forefront of your mind, making it clear that it's something you want to do.) Also, communicating how you've done this to others as you network shows that you're serious about security versus trying to get into the field to make some money. There are some folks who've chosen InfoSec just because that's where the money seems to be. But I think a lot of us hire each other because we see the *passion* versus the need to get a *paycheck*. If you can show your passion to others, I think that is like 90 percent of how you stand out in somebody's mind. And that's what'll make them willing to go out of their way to hand in your résumé or push you up the ladder.

What qualities do you believe all highly successful cybersecurity professionals share?

Passion and skepticism. You don't take things at face value, you question things. You're always asking "why?" Why are we doing it that way? Why does it do that? Why can't we do it this way? Also, critical thinking is such an arbitrary way of putting it, but that's exactly what it is. It's looking at something, anything that you're doing in life, and then always having a follow-up question. It's like saying, "Based on these answers, wait a minute, but what about *this*? Why *this*?" The ability to think critically and always ask "why" is a common thread among InfoSec professionals. It's like always playing devil's advocate—not to be argumentative but just to better understand.

What is your favorite hacker movie?
Sneakers.

What are your favorite books for motivation, personal development, or enjoyment?
I don't read books for motivation or personal development. Books to me are strictly for enjoyment. The Mistborn Trilogies. It was just so *different.* It was sci-fi, so think magic; but instead of having magical powers, they ingested metals—and depending on the metal that you ingested, you were able to move or do certain things. But you had to be born with the ability to use the metals. And I had never heard of that before, and I thought it was just fantastic.

What is some practical cybersecurity advice you give to people at home in the age of social media and the Internet of Things?
Situational awareness. Always be aware of what you're saying. Social media is just another dimension. Being outside, where you're at, it's all the same; it's just being situationally aware of who's around, what you're saying, and whether you want it to be overheard by someone. Social media will amplify, but again, at the end of the day, it's you saying something out loud and people overhearing it.

As for the Internet of Things, same thing. Be aware of what you're putting on the internet and your network. If you put things on your network, understand that there's a vendor that created it, and who knows if they updated. If I'm putting it on my network, it's gotta provide me some value. I'm not gonna just stick something on the network just because it's cool. For example, I have a front-door PIN that can be connected to the internet, but I've chosen not to do that because all I wanted was the ease of the PIN versus the physical key. I don't need to have it on the internet. That's the difference.

> "Be aware of what you're putting on the internet and your network."

What is a life hack that you'd like to share?
Self-care, whatever that means to you. It could be a hobby, it could be getting a massage, it's just self-care. Even if InfoSec is your hobby on the side, you're doing it for you versus doing it to get better at school or work. It's understanding that you are a person, and you take care of yourself as well. You deserve to grow and continue learning if that's your thing. If you want to learn how to do manicures for the sake of learning it, then do that. But it's finding something that makes you happy and pursuing that whenever you want—and at your leisure—while being mindful and intentional about it.

What is the biggest mistake you've ever made, and how did you recover from it?
Hindsight is 20/20. I would say I haven't made one yet. ■

"Most organizations believe they are not a target because they are "too small," "don't do anything important," and "are unknown to anybody"—or they simply think they're not a target because "they said so." This is, in my view, the biggest myth in security, which makes most of the hacks possible."

Twitter: @Marmusha

Marina Krotofil

35 Marina Krotofil is an experienced ICS/SCADA professional who has spent almost a decade on offensive industrial control systems (ICS) security—discovering and weaponizing unique attack vectors, engineering damage scenarios, and understanding attacker techniques when exploiting ICS. Marina's offensive security skills serve her well during forensic investigations, ICS malware analysis, and when engineering defenses. She previously worked as a principal analyst and subject-matter expert within the Cyber-Physical Group at FireEye (USA), as a lead cybersecurity researcher at Honeywell (USA), and as a senior security consultant at the European Network for Cyber Security (Netherlands). Between her industrial positions, Marina joined academia to pursue a doctoral degree and teach security courses at Hamburg University of Technology, Germany. She has authored more than 20 academic papers and book chapters on ICS security and is a frequent speaker at the leading security events around the world. She holds an MBA in technology management, an MSc in telecommunication, and an MSc in information and communication systems.

If there is one myth that you could debunk in cybersecurity, what would it be?
The "I am not a victim" myth. Most organizations believe they are not a target because they are "too small," "don't do anything important," and "are unknown to anybody"—or they simply think they're not a target because "they said so." This is, in my view, the biggest myth in security, which makes most of the hacks possible. Organizations that believe they are not targeted care little about

protecting their organizational assets and become the victim of various types of attacks. The least harmful consequence is that the company's computing assets become part of the botnets, used as proxy servers to hide attack origin or used for mining cryptocurrency. The most harmful consequence is when a compromised organization is used as a testing ground for sending trusted spear phishing emails, exfiltrated for sensitive customer information, or used as a stepping stone into a more protected organization via trusted communication links. Most large breaches these days are happening via third-party companies.

There is no need to go after a high-profile target via a front-door firewall if it is possible to connect to the organization "securely" via a compromised third-party VPN connection. Similarly, there is no need to exfiltrate needed information from a well-protected target company (with the risk of being detected) if one can obtain the same information from a subcontractor who only weakly protects that information.

What is one of the biggest bang-for-the-buck actions that an organization can take to improve its cybersecurity posture?

My opinion would probably be unconventional, but I formed it through my work at some large organizations—from servicing customers and from conversations with IT friends. Among the biggest bang-for-the-buck actions an organization could take is the empowerment of the so-called *champions*. Most companies typically do not have or do not dedicate large budgets for security. But, in almost every organization, there is a network admin, an IT professional, or simply a hobbyist who knows the company's infrastructure well and who has good ideas for easily implementable security controls, which could substantially improve the company's security posture (e.g., review and tune firewall rules, tighten access control, set up security logging and network monitoring, etc.).

Most of these activities require minimal financial investment, mostly consisting of the man-hours of the personnel who are willing to and capable of working on security projects. The main disappointing comments I hear from such champions is that management either does not give permission or does not allow time to be dedicated to activities related to security. Conversely, companies that are willing to improve their security are often trying to find such "champions" within their organizational units because such a person would voluntarily evangelize security.

How is it that cybersecurity spending is increasing but breaches are still happening?

I think many security professionals would give the same answer, namely, that security protections in most organizations are typically mounted as a panic-driven reaction to a breach that has already occurred, without any sort of analysis of the organization's business processes or a security assessment of the IT infrastructure. It is appealing for the affected companies to believe that a single "box" or two would be fully capable of protecting the organization from future breaches, without additional effort or human involvement. In contrast, security consultancies and service providers are having a difficult time selling their offerings because their recommended security actions require involvement of the client's personnel and a long-term commitment to implementing security programs. It's hard to change this mind-set because it is habitual to mankind in general—for example, most of us understand the value of preventively maintaining a healthy lifestyle, yet most of us still prefer a reactive approach of taking "a magic pill/smoothie/medicine" when health disorders arise.

Do you need a college degree or certification to be a cybersecurity professional?

This is probably one of the hottest questions discussed in the security community. Those who don't have a degree argue against one and vice versa. I can speak from both sides. When it comes to general/broad security topics, I am an educated professional. I actually taught security courses at the university level for 11 semesters (introduction to security as well as network, software, and application security). I also attended a couple of security courses at a neighbor university solely for my personal education. I can't emphasize enough how much I've benefited from my in-depth and broad security knowledge throughout my career. Too frequently, "security professionals" are knowledgeable in a narrow topic area only and are unable to think across the entire "defense-in-depth" spectrum. It is especially frustrating to deal with security managers who have no in-depth knowledge of security concepts and believe, for example, that the distribution of private keys via a USB stick should be "just fine."

In contrast, I am a self-taught cyber-physical hacker. My security specialization is the exploitation of industrial control systems (ICS), which are highly specialized, engineered systems. When I started, I had no idea how they worked and how they could be hacked. Also, there was little public knowledge on the topic. I became an expert in ICS engineering and security by finding ways to break these systems. A lot of talented security professionals are self-taught and earned their impeccable reputation through hacking things or in-depth security research. Because hacking requires overcoming multiple layers of security protections and finding new security flaws, security researchers typically possess in-depth knowledge in security.

How did you get started in the cybersecurity field, and what advice would you give to a beginner pursuing a career in cybersecurity?

I started my cybersecurity career by providing incident response services for malware infections in business applications (banking, retail, and others). I had my own small IT business, which provided various IT-related services and security services, and this quickly became my specialization. Often, I had to infect and remediate a test system first so that I could recover the primary application without inadvertently disrupting it. Later, I was asked to break the security scheme of a wireless sensor network protocol. This is when I discovered my passion for offensive security and decided to obtain a professional degree in the security field by pursuing a PhD. My PhD was application-oriented, meaning I closely worked with the industry on solving practical matters. This helped me to produce meaningful results and to easily get a job afterward.

As in any field, it is important to find a specialization that really excites you (e.g., social engineering versus reverse engineering, offensive versus defensive security, software versus hardware security, web applications versus network security, and so on). You could start with watching recordings of the security talks and attending local security meetups and conferences (e.g., local BSides or OWASP conferences).

Often, local events host free or affordable security trainings, which are great for starting! I personally traveled to a few conferences specifically for trainings. Many large cities around the world also have so-called maker spaces, where local communities meet for various security and hands-on activities (e.g., lock picking, hacking, crafting, building hardware, etc.). For a small price, you not only get access to a lot of expensive equipment, but you also get the unique knowledge of the local community members. Following inspiring security professionals on Twitter is another option. After you decide on a specialization, practice is extremely important. Currently, there are so many free tools, platforms, and online communities for practicing security. Working toward a security certification or two could be a good starting goal and a helpful stepping stone for eventually landing a security job.

What is your specialty in cybersecurity, and how can others gain expertise in your specialty?

As I mentioned earlier, I specialize in ICS security—specifically in physical damage. One of my key skills is offensive security—i.e., designing exploits for inflicting impact in the physical world by the means of cyberattacks. Many systems I exploit are considered to be critical infrastructures. The physical impacts I work with range from the dramatic (such as equipment breakage and explosions) to moderate (alteration of the manufactured product) to less impactful (such as short-term interruption of the operational process). I've worked with many physical applications, including chemical plants, electricity and water distribution, various smart city applications, and more.

My work consists of two parts: (1) engineering the physical damage scenario, and (2) implementing the cyber-attack, which would allow me to achieve my physical damage goal. I enjoy this field because it is highly challenging by nature. One needs to process, electrical, mechanical, and control engineering; data processing; network and embedded security; and many other disciplines to design an exploit with a specific impact. Because I began specializing in this field before it became popular (before Stuxnet), there were few, if any, educational materials or helpful resources available. I learned this field through "doing" and finding needed pieces of knowledge while engineering my attacks. I created my own experimental security platforms and often traveled long distances to talk to engineers or visit factories.

In the meantime, ICS security became fashionable, and now you can find a lot of useful resources to help you obtain and practice ICS security skills. There are a lot of talks and educational videos on YouTube, public repositories of pcaps and process data, academic papers, and even books. Several labs, which run large-scale ICS testbeds, now allow remote access for research purposes. There are also simulations of large-scale industrial processes in software or miniaturized hardware (e.g., small robotic hands). You can also find cheaper alternatives to industrial equipment. Raspberry Pi uses the same microprocessors as industrial controllers and can be easily turned into programmable logic controllers with open source software. Cheap IoT devices frequently run on the same real-time operating system (RTOS) as critical infrastructure assets. Also, more and more industrial facilities organize "open door" days and can be toured for free.

What is your advice for career success when it comes to getting hired, climbing the corporate ladder, or starting a company in cybersecurity?

What worked for me was being unique and authentic. When deciding on a security specialization, I chose the path least traveled. Nobody did physical damage. So, I picked this area and became an expert in it. To let the world know about my skills, I started presenting on large security stages around the globe. As a result, I became a natural hire for the companies who needed my expertise. I also maintain my authenticity in terms of being an innovative security professional who works very hard and who is sincerely dedicated to the field.

What qualities do you believe all highly successful cybersecurity professionals share?

Probably the number-one quality is having security (the profession) as a hobby. The security field is so complex and dynamic; defenses that worked today may become obsolete overnight. It would be impossible to be successful in security without continuous learning, which most of us are doing in our free time, simply out of passion. The number-two quality is perfectionistic attention to detail. Security protections are typically broken due to missed details or stupid mistakes caused by lack of attention. This brings us to the number-three quality, which is knowing your own knowledge gaps and asking questions. None of us has in-depth knowledge in all security areas, and we do not hesitate to reach out to colleagues. This is what makes the security community almost like a close family, because we interact a lot. Possession of the "evil bit" (the ability to think as a cunning attacker) is another quality.

What is the best book or movie that can be used to illustrate cybersecurity challenges?

Among recent ones, I relished *Skyfall*. This was the first James Bond movie that finally embraced cyber hacking as the main weapon in the villain's arsenal. To my delight, the movie features two cyber-physical attacks: (1) blowing up part of MI6 headquarters by taking control of the building's gas system, and (2) shutting down the electricity with the help of a virus, which resulted in the fail-open status of the villain's prison cell door. Also, the "oh shit" scene of the MI6 security wizard when he hastily plugged the villain's laptop directly into the MI6 network made me smile.

All security professionals have done stupid things of that caliber at least once in their career. In general, the movie vividly highlights human dependence on computerized systems and our lack of understanding of these dependencies.

What is your favorite hacker movie?

Clearly, *Hackers* is the iconic movie when it comes to representing the spirit of the security community. I really like the original *The Girl with the Dragon Tattoo*. Among others, I enjoyed two German movies, *Who Am I*, and an older movie, *23*. I am probably in the minority, but I'm not really fond of *Mr. Robot*.

What are your favorite books for motivation, personal development, or enjoyment?

I am a bookworm. I've read many books that contributed immensely to my personal development and in shaping my mind. Probably Dale Carnegie's books (luckily, he was among the few authors allowed in the post-USSR space) *How to Win Friends and Influence People* and *How to Stop Worrying and Start Living* had the biggest impact on me and served as my early life kickstarters.

Recently, I've been reading biographies of famous people, be they historical or current. My most recent was a biography of Michael Phelps. Before Phelps, I was obsessed with George Washington. In general, I enjoy books that uncover life from a previously unthought-of angle—e.g., *Freakonomics* by Levitt et al. or *Outliers* by Malcolm Gladwell. A long time ago, I read *The Manual: A True Bad Boy Explains How Men Think, Date, and Mate—and What Women Can Do to Come Out on Top* by Steve Santagati. It is such a very fun book to read, but it also perfectly shows that any system is hackable; you just need to understand how your target functions.

What is some practical cybersecurity advice you give to people at home in the age of social media and the Internet of Things?

It is extremely difficult to give advice at this point in time, as most people are still caught up in the euphoria of the benefits and the joy technology has given them. Users are not ready to hear about all the dangers of modern gadgets and social networks yet. My advice would be to realize that using the internet these days (on both PCs and mobile devices) is similar to going on vacation to a country with exotic beaches and known safety issues. What advice is typically given to people? To be aware of your surroundings and to not go to places one should not go. The use of internet-connected devices and internet services become safe when following similar rules. For example, looking for the green lock in the browser when making financial transactions (to make sure the communication is encrypted), being aware of phishing/scams and how much personal information is exposed via social media, etc. I never visit suspicious web pages and leave immediately if I accidentally land on one. When we go on vacation to a new country, we always read safety behavioral rules. Users should do the same before using the internet, internet-connected devices, and social media. There is also a great documentary to watch: *Terms and Conditions May Apply* (2013).

What is a life hack that you'd like to share?

Some individuals who do not program much or well are worried about not being able to succeed in security. You may worry less! Here is the secret: there are a lot of folks who can code well but don't know security (or any other field). Team up with them! During my studies at the University of RadioElectronics in Ukraine many years ago, I geared more toward designing and calculating complex engineering systems rather than programming their functionality. I could program well, but I did not enjoy it as much as I enjoyed the engineering part of projects. Starting when I was at university and even today, I choose to team up with guys who can program or reverse engineer well but are not necessarily experts in the task or research questions we are working on (but I am). Such collaborations are fruitful for everybody involved. In general, if I don't have a needed skill or knowledge set, I find someone who has it and form a partnership. This strategy has made me an extremely successful researcher (and, I hope, my collaborators too!).

What is the biggest mistake you've ever made, and how did you recover from it?

Over the years, I mastered the art of seeing all my mistakes as "learning experiences." However, there is one mistake I cannot forget to date. Unfortunately, I cannot talk about it because of an NDA and the privacy of the parties involved. I trusted the wrong person, and my partners and I were taken advantage of and missed a very big opportunity. My partners actually forgave me; however, I still wonder how things would be if I hadn't made that mistake.

One habitual mistake I used to make was hesitating to put myself forward and not speaking confidently about my competencies and achievements. To me, it felt like cheap showing off and bragging. I thought that people should know my name and understand my skill set from the work I'd done. It took me a while to realize that most people, even folks from within my own professional community, don't know *everything* about me. In the end, nobody has the time to read all of my papers and watch my talks. Learning to speak about my expertise and achievements was life-changing. This also helped me to gain confidence in putting myself forward more. You need to let the world know about you if you'd like to be a part of it! ∎

> "Implement the principle of least privilege—don't allow end users to be admins on their local boxes."

Twitter: @samilaiho • **Website:** win-fu.com

Sami Laiho

36

Sami Laiho is one of the world's leading professionals in Windows OS and security. He has worked with and taught OS troubleshooting, management, and security for more than 15 years. Sami's session was evaluated as the best session in TechEd North America, Europe, and Australia in 2014, and by the Nordic Infrastructure Conference in 2016 and 2017. At Ignite 2017, the world's biggest Microsoft event, Sami was noted as the Best External Speaker. He is also an author at PluralSight and the newly appointed conference chair at the TechMentor conference.

If there is one myth that you could debunk in cybersecurity, what would it be?

That security cannot be increased without lowering usability. I do believe that security is a compromise between usability, security, and price—you can get two, but you can never get all three.

What is one of the biggest bang-for-the-buck actions that an organization can take to improve its cybersecurity posture?

Implement the principle of least privilege—don't allow end users to be admins on their local boxes.

How is it that cybersecurity spending is increasing but breaches are still happening?
Most customers I meet are spending the bucks on solutions and features, although they should be spending it on training and implementing concepts.

Do you need a college degree or certification to be a cybersecurity professional?
No, I don't have one. You can learn by reading and practicing by yourself.

How did you get started in the cybersecurity field, and what advice would you give to a beginner pursuing a career in cybersecurity?
I used to teach troubleshooting and Windows internals. I started teaching security because I hated all security sessions in general. They were built to scare people but didn't offer mitigations, and they were always using insecure OS implementations—like old OS versions, full admin rights, and no full disk encryption or whitelisting.

I started by learning how computers and operating systems work. If I could recommend one book to read, it would be *Windows Internals* by David Solomon, Mark Russinovich, and Alex Ionescu.

What is your specialty in cybersecurity, and how can others gain expertise in your specialty?
I teach concepts, not features. I teach how to implement things like principle of least privilege and whitelisting. I would recommend that others watch my sessions on Channel9.msdn.com and YouTube.

What is your advice for career success when it comes to getting hired, climbing the corporate ladder, or starting a company in cybersecurity?
Sharing is caring. Learn things and then share your knowledge. Remember that it currently takes 100 people at Microsoft to know everything about the Windows OS. Networking is your most important skill nowadays. Get to know people who know what you don't.

> "Most customers I meet are spending the bucks on solutions and features, although they should be spending it on training and implementing concepts."

> "I started teaching security because I hated all security sessions in general. They were built to scare people but didn't offer mitigations, and they were always using insecure OS implementations—like old OS versions, full admin rights, and no full disk encryption or whitelisting."

> "Sharing is caring. Learn things and then share your knowledge."

"Networking is your most important skill nowadays. Get to know people who know what you don't."

What qualities do you believe all highly successful cybersecurity professionals share?
Belief in the fact that security keeps things running and more performant. If you yourself believe that security makes things hard, you've lost the game.

What is the best book or movie that can be used to illustrate cybersecurity challenges?
The film *Zero Days*, and books by Mark Russinovich.

What is your favorite hacker movie?
Zero Days.

What are your favorite books for motivation, personal development, or enjoyment?
Anything by Mark Russinovich. *Be the Master* by Don Jones.

What is some practical cybersecurity advice you give to people at home in the age of social media and the Internet of Things?
- Don't put anything on social media that you can't allow to get public.
- Use different passwords on every website, and, even better, invest in a password manager.
- Use multifactor authentication when possible.
- Don't use admin accounts for daily logons.

"Use different passwords on every website, and, even better, invest in a password manager."

What is a life hack that you'd like to share?
Use your fingerprint reader to register your index finger as your limited user and your middle finger as your admin user. This way, you can fast switch when needed.

What is the biggest mistake you've ever made, and how did you recover from it?
I missed a backup from my family photos and lost two years' worth of photos of my older daughter. ■

> "Defenders have many tools at their disposal, and attackers aren't nearly as sophisticated or well coordinated as many suggest. When defense is done correctly, I would actually argue that defenders have the upper hand."

Twitter: @RobertMLee • **Website:** www.robertmlee.org

Robert M. Lee

37

Robert M. Lee is the CEO and founder of the industrial (ICS/IIoT) cybersecurity company Dragos, Inc. He is also a nonresident National Cybersecurity Fellow at New America, focusing on policy issues relating to the cybersecurity of critical infrastructure. For his research and focus areas, Robert was named one of Passcode's Influencers, and in 2015, he was awarded EnergySec's Cybersecurity Professional of the Year. The following year, he was inducted into Forbes's 30 under 30 for Enterprise Technology. Robert obtained his start in cybersecurity in the U.S. Air Force and at the National Security Agency. While in the U.S. Air Force, he served as a Cyber Warfare Operations Officer. Robert has performed defense, intelligence, and attack missions in various government organizations, including the establishment of a first-of-its-kind ICS/SCADA cyber-threat intelligence and intrusion analysis mission. A passionate educator, Robert has authored several courses for SANS, along with their accompanying certifications. He routinely writes for publications on the topics of industrial security, threat intelligence, and cybersecurity and is a frequent speaker at conferences around the world. Robert has testified before the U.S. Senate Energy and Natural Resources Committee and is currently pursuing his PhD at King's College London, researching the industrial control threat landscape. Lastly, Robert, along with Jeff Haas, creates a weekly technology and security web comic titled *Little Bobby*.

If there is one myth that you could debunk in cybersecurity, what would it be?
That adversaries have the upper hand. Defenders have many tools at their disposal, and attackers aren't nearly as sophisticated or well coordinated as

many suggest. When defense is done correctly, I would actually argue that defenders have the upper hand.

What is one of the biggest bang-for-the-buck actions that an organization can take to improve its cybersecurity posture?

You need to hire smart analysts. Smart analysts are going to help you choose the right technologies and tell you what you need for the particular problems you're having. And they're going to help you avoid buying vendor products that you don't need. At first, it might be hard to pay the extra $30,000, $40,000, or $50,000 for a senior analyst, but they're going to give you a good return on investment, and they'll pay for themselves time and time again.

How is it that cybersecurity spending is increasing but breaches are still happening?

I'm not sure that those metrics are correlated at all. Security is increasing, and we're actually seeing, by all industry metrics, that the number of breaches are decreasing. We're hearing a lot more about breaches these days, so it seems like they are increasing, but I don't know whether that's actually accurate. It's more of a perception issue. We're also finding things that have existed for years.

Do you need a college degree or certification to be a cybersecurity professional?

Not at all. Both can be helpful for career progression purposes, but they're not required at all.

How did you get started in the cybersecurity field, and what advice would you give to a beginner pursuing a career in cybersecurity?

I got started through the U.S. Air Force, and I went into cybersecurity. Most things I actually know (and most of the skills I have) are self-taught. For people who are starting out, you can go through a decent pipeline, end up with a job, do the 8-to-5, and that's perfectly fine; there's no problem in doing that. But if you want to be one of the top performers and earn higher salaries and so forth, it's going to demand that you go outside of the normal pipeline and do a lot of self-education. The good news is, there's an immense number of free resources out there; you don't need any given pipeline to reach your goals. There's plenty out there.

What is your specialty in cybersecurity, and how can others gain expertise in your specialty?

Mine's in industrial control systems as well as threat intelligence. For both of those, I really think there's no better teacher than actually going and doing it. I think a lot of the ability to get started, especially in industrial controls, can be gained by working at places like utilities or industrial companies. Your local utility, I guarantee, is in need of people. Working at those places can give you extremely valuable experiences.

What is your advice for career success when it comes to getting hired, climbing the corporate ladder, or starting a company in cybersecurity?

Generally speaking, if you're going to progress outside of holding a salaried job, it's going to require you to go outside of your bubble, do a lot of self-education, and get involved with the community. When you start speaking publicly or writing papers or doing training for folks, it gets you noticed quickly, and it sharpens your skills. It makes you someone people are comfortable with holding those positions. For starting your own company, just add in a level of craziness, a lot of friends, and a lot of sleepless nights.

What qualities do you believe all highly successful cybersecurity professionals share?

The highly successful ones all share a passion and dedication to learning. No real expert I know calls themselves an expert.

What is the best book or movie that can be used to illustrate cybersecurity challenges?

The Cuckoo's Egg is a must-read on everybody's reading list, and then from a movie perspective, I'm not sure that we really have a good one about our field just yet. I would say people should go outside of security if they're trying to solve security issues. There are plenty of books to help with that. There's a book called *Strategy: A History* by Lawrence Freedman, but I would entirely encourage people to read the softer arts. Another one that should be mandated reading is *The Psychology of Intelligence Analysis* by Richards J. Heuer, Jr. It's not so much about personal enjoyment; it's just that nontechnical books can help you become a better technical professional.

> "When you start speaking publicly or writing papers, or doing training for folks, it gets you noticed very quickly, and it sharpens your skills."

What is your favorite hacker movie?

It'd be a faux pas not to mention *Hackers*, but honestly, I think my favorite, if I had to pick one, would be *WarGames*.

What is some practical cybersecurity advice you give to people at home in the age of social media and the Internet of Things?

I generally tell people not to fear and don't overthink it. Very simple things like using legitimate licenses for your operating system and two-factor authentication (2FA) for your account logins can really help. With the basics like that, you're going to be significantly well off as a home user.

What is a life hack that you'd like to share?

It's not really a life hack, but sort of a guiding point I tell people: the threats are far worse than you realize but not as bad as you imagine them. That kind of centers us a bit.

What is the biggest mistake you've ever made, and how did you recover from it?

I'm generally not a person who lives with regrets, but when it comes to running a company, everyday decisions that I make impact outcomes that we may not realize for a year or more. There are plenty of little mistakes and adjustments I've had to make, and not necessarily one big one. Honestly, the way to deal with it is to realize that more issues are created by *not* making a decision than by making one that might not have been perfect. It's extremely important to keep moving and to make the right call based on what you know at the time, and then just be flexible enough to adapt as you need to in the future. ■

"Institute a culture of security across your organization rather than treating it like 'somebody else's problem.'"

Twitter: @aloria

Kelly Lum

38

Kelly Lum has "officially" worked in information security since 2003 and is currently a security engineer at Spotify—where she brings more than a decade's worth of application and network security experience from the financial and government sectors to the startup space. Additionally, she teaches application security as an adjunct professor at NYU.

If there is one myth that you could debunk in cybersecurity, what would it be?

One thing that I have observed is that there is still this preconception that InfoSec is some sort of mystical art that can be done only by the rare, chosen few. It isn't just nontechnical people, either. I've walked intimidated developers and students through proof of concepts (POCs), and it's always cool to see their reaction when they get it working.

What is one of the biggest bang-for-the-buck actions that an organization can take to improve its cybersecurity posture?

Institute a culture of security across your organization rather than treating it like "somebody else's problem." Security needs to start at the beginning of every project, not in the middle or at the end. Throw less money at vendor crap and more at your talent.

How is it that cybersecurity spending is increasing but breaches are still happening?

Because folks are throwing too much money at "silver-bullet" vendor crap and not enough at attracting and empowering talented employees. But seriously, security is a complicated, moving target, and getting it right requires a lot of coordination and collaboration, and a lot of organizations aren't there yet.

Do you need a college degree or certification to be a cybersecurity professional?

Absolutely not; some of the smartest people I know in the industry got started out of high school. I believe it really all depends on your personality, career goals, and learning style. I needed the structure of a college curriculum since I tend to be disorganized and easily side-tracked. Someone who is more of a self-starter might find that kind of environment constricting.

How did you get started in the cybersecurity field, and what advice would you give to a beginner pursuing a career in cybersecurity?

In the '90s, I was a stereotypical friendless nerd who did mischievous stuff on her computer. During junior year, my university (what is now NYU Tandon) started offering the Scholarship for Service,[12] and I realized I could do those kinds of things for a living.

In addition to my day job, I'm also an adjunct professor at NYU Tandon. One of the things I always tell my students is to be curious and explore things outside of your curriculum. Attend some local meetups and try to get to know some folks in the field. Participate in a capture the flag (CTF), or read through some write-ups detailing recent vulnerabilities or breaches. Not only does this impress the heck out of potential employers, but it will broaden your horizons and expose you to areas of security you may not otherwise have known about.

> "Try to get out there and get involved with some project, group, or conference. It will help to humanize you into something more than just bullet points on a résumé."

What is your specialty in cybersecurity, and how can others gain expertise in your specialty?

I've dabbled in a bit of everything, but I have been doing application security for most of my career. I think one of the great things about AppSec is that there are so many tools and resources out there to get your feet wet. There's Google Gruyere, Damn Vulnerable Web App (DVWA), CrackMe challenges, and tons of CTF write-ups and walkthroughs, to name a handful of things.

> "I think one of the great things about AppSec is that there are so many tools and resources out there to get your feet wet."

What is your advice for career success when it comes to getting hired, climbing the corporate ladder, or starting a company in cybersecurity?

I suppose I'll just repeat the advice I gave earlier. Try to get out there and get involved with some project, group, or conference. It will help to humanize you into something more than just bullet points on a résumé.

What qualities do you believe all highly successful cybersecurity professionals share?

Curiosity, passion, and maybe—most importantly—humility. A willingness to give back to the field as you grow in it.

What is your favorite hacker movie?

It's not a movie, but the "Who is Max Mouse?" hacker arc of *Ghostwriter*. Cyberpunk Julia Stiles FTW.

What are your favorite books for motivation, personal development, or enjoyment?

I read a lot of true crime. I find detective work and forensics fascinating. Also, people leave me alone on the subway.

> "Use a password manager, two-factor authentication (2FA), and patch your crap."

What is some practical cybersecurity advice you give to people at home in the age of social media and the Internet of Things?

Use a password manager, two-factor authentication (2FA), and patch your crap.

What is a life hack that you'd like to share?

You can't get a hangover if you don't stop drinking.

What is the biggest mistake you've ever made, and how did you recover from it?

I think my biggest mistake was falling into the misconception I described earlier. I've always been surrounded by incredibly smart InfoSec folks and for the longest time had insane imposter syndrome. One day, I was sitting next to one of those incredibly smart people, and he couldn't figure out how to exploit a vulnerability he had found. I did. People tend to broadcast their successes, not the hours they spent banging their head on the desk trying to get there. When you compare yourself to other people, you're comparing yourself to that outward image and doing yourself a disservice.

Also, one time I put an OR rather than an AND in a conditional and took down a production website for about three minutes. ∎

> "We all bring something unique to the table. Diversity of thought makes us stronger to solve complex problems."

Twitter: @InfoSecSherpa • **Website:** nuzzel.com/InfoSecSherpa

Tracy Z. Maleeff

Tracy Z. Maleeff is a cyber analyst in the security operations center for a global pharmaceutical company. She earned a master of library and information science degree from the University of Pittsburgh and holds undergraduate degrees from Temple University (magna cum laude) and the Pennsylvania State University.

39

A librarian turned information security professional, she is your guide up the mountain of information as @InfoSecSherpa on Twitter. Tracy is GIAC Security Essentials (GSEC) certified and was recognized with an Information Systems Security Association Women in Security Leadership Award in 2017. She has also presented at DEF CON's Recon Village in addition to several Security BSides conferences. Tracy frequently presents to librarian and information professional audiences on information security and OSINT topics.

If there is one myth that you could debunk in cybersecurity, what would it be?

That only computer science majors or people with heavy tech experience can be employed in this industry. Information security professionals have a variety of backgrounds and educational experiences. We all bring something unique to the table. Diversity of thought makes us stronger to solve complex problems.

What is one of the biggest bang-for-the-buck actions that an organization can take to improve its cybersecurity posture?

Create a culture of security that contains empathetic and FUD-free (fear, uncertainty, and doubt) end-user training. Scared or intimidated end users will not be willing to work with the security team or self-report incidents like clicking a malicious email. Periodic phishing tests will not necessarily reinforce security, but frequent interactions with empathic InfoSec professionals within an organization will keep security on the minds of end users.

How is it that cybersecurity spending is increasing but breaches are still happening?

I have to imagine that some of it is due to the inflated, fear-based pricing of these security products. I am also inclined to believe that spending money on security helps to satisfy organizations that have to answer to a board or stockholders, and the spending is proof that they are paying attention to the problem. Whether that money is well spent is a different issue. Until cybercrime becomes a less lucrative business than cyber protection, it will always win out.

> "Until cybercrime becomes a less lucrative business than cyber protection, it will always win out."

Do you need a college degree or certification to be a cybersecurity professional?

This is a difficult question for me to answer. Prior to going into InfoSec, I was a librarian. In that world, the minimum degree required for most jobs is a master's. I became accustomed to having that high bar for entry. Degrees and certifications are definitely important for people like myself who transitioned into this industry from other disciplines. People like me need to somehow prove that we have the knowledge. I wouldn't say that degrees and certifications are necessarily requirements if the person has the correct industry knowledge and can articulate it. I believe that one of the reasons why it is so hard to find cybersecurity talent is because the traditional interviewing and résumé system doesn't exactly fit this industry, but nobody told the human resources staff and recruiters. So, perhaps to play the hiring game, having a résumé with a degree or a certification is the way to hack that system.

How did you get started in the cybersecurity field, and what advice would you give to a beginner pursuing a career in cybersecurity?

I was a librarian, mostly in law firms, for 15 years. About three years ago, I read a professional development article entitled "Future-Proofing Your Career." It made me reevaluate my goals, and I decided that I wanted to rekindle a love of tech that I never pursued in my younger years—for complicated reasons. I experimented by attending every tech meetup and workshop I could find to see if anything created a spark for me. I was introduced to the world of information security, and that spark turned into a white-hot flame within me, and I knew that I needed to make this my career change. I immersed myself in reading lots on the subject, meeting people, and attending events. I quit my library job and created my own consulting company, where I did research and social media projects with an InfoSec slant. I continued to plug away at studying and learning until an opportunity came for an interview in a security operations center. I emphasized my transferable skills and showed them my desire to learn and grow within this industry. I have now been a cyber analyst for seven months, and I wouldn't do a thing differently.

What is your specialty in cybersecurity, and how can others gain expertise in your specialty?

I would say that my specialty is a combination of threat intelligence and training/awareness. I rely on my research training in librarianship for the threat intel. My experiences in past customer-facing jobs help immensely for user training and awareness.

What is your advice for career success when it comes to getting hired, climbing the corporate ladder, or starting a company in cybersecurity?

Have good interpersonal skills in addition to creating, maintaining, and sustaining a solid professional network of people. Be able to articulate your vision or work with clarity. Set goals and be prepared to course-correct as things inevitably change.

What qualities do you believe all highly successful cybersecurity professionals share?

From what I have observed, highly successful cybersecurity professionals seem to all possess curiosity, passion, willingness to share knowledge, and a fire inside them that drives them to keep doing a job that, at times, seems like a Sisyphean task.

> "From what I have observed, highly successful cybersecurity professionals seem to all possess curiosity, passion, willingness to share knowledge, and a fire inside them that drives them to keep doing a job that, at times, seems like a Sisyphean task."

What is the best book or movie that can be used to illustrate cybersecurity challenges?

The Choose Your Own Adventure series of children's books from the 1980s. The reader was required to make choices in order to progress the story through the books. It illustrates cybersecurity challenges because the reader was presented with a situation and then had to act. Sometimes the results were positive, and sometimes they were negative. At times, the scenarios were unpredictable, and other books were more intuitive. The challenge of cybersecurity is that it presents itself with a variety of variables, unknowns, and actions to take, like these books.

What is your favorite hacker movie?

Since I'm not super-techy, I appreciate the films that explore the social engineering aspects of hacking. *Catch Me If You Can* is probably the gold standard of that genre. It's worth mentioning that *Amadeus* is also a master class in social engineering tactics and techniques, with an amazing score and period costumes.

What are your favorite books for motivation, personal development, or enjoyment?

- *The Power of Unpopular: A Guide to Building Your Brand for the Audience Who Will Love You (and Why No One Else Matters)* by Erika Napoletano
- *Bossypants* by Tina Fey
- *The Fortune Cookie Chronicles: Adventures in the World of Chinese Food* by Jennifer 8. Lee
- Overall, the works of Diana Abu-Jaber, Judy Blume, F. Scott Fitzgerald, Ernest Hemingway, and Jhumpa Lahiri bring me enjoyment

> "Regarding IoT, I advise people to be aware of what data of theirs will be used and how."

What is some practical cybersecurity advice you give to people at home in the age of social media and the Internet of Things?
Use multifactor authentication. Periodically check your privacy and security settings on social media platforms. Make wise choices when it comes to using geotagging for posts. Regarding IoT, I advise people to be aware of what data of theirs will be used and how. Know the product you are purchasing and using. Be aware of what these devices do. You don't want to spread FUD, but there is a way cybersecurity professionals can make people aware of the choices they are making by engaging an IoT device.

What is a life hack that you'd like to share?
Be courteous. Be respectful. Be punctual. Be confident. (As my mother used to say, "Act like you've been there before.") Help others. These "hacks" help create opportunities for yourself and others. We go further together.

> "Be courteous. Be respectful. Be punctual. Be confident."

What is the biggest mistake you've ever made, and how did you recover from it?
When I was in high school, I was the business editor of the newspaper. I dropped the ball on doing the accounting and was too fearful to ask for help. I kept bringing in advertising money and paying the printer, but I didn't keep track of anything. There was no impropriety other than me being a lousy bookkeeper. After six months, I came clean to the teacher who oversaw the newspaper and stated that I would fix the issue and then resign as the business editor. She refused to accept my resignation and gave me guidance and assistance on how to get the books back in order. My mistakes were that I didn't ask for help to do my job since I didn't know how and then that I let it fester for so long. I learned to speak up and ask questions without fear. It was more of a mess to clean up after six months than it would have been after a few weeks of not knowing what I was doing. It was a good lesson to learn early. ■

> "In my humble opinion, the greatest action an organization can take to improve its security stance is to move from a traditional defense-based methodology to one that assumes a breach has already taken place."

Twitter: @AndyMalone • **Website:** www.AndyMalone.org

Andy Malone

40

With a prestigious international career spanning 20 years, Andy Malone is not only a world-class technology instructor and consultant but also a Microsoft MVP and veteran conference speaker. He has spoken at notable events, including Microsoft Ignite, IT/Dev Connections, TechMentor–Live! 360, and the Cybercrime Security Forum. His passionate style of delivery, combined with his sense of fun, has become his winning trademark. Although his primary focus is security, Andy loves to talk about the Windows platform as well as the Exchange and Office technologies.

   With knowledge dating back to the MS-DOS 2 and Windows 2.0 era, there is often an interesting story to be told. But technology never sleeps, and Andy continues to work with the Microsoft product teams to create and deliver groundbreaking material on Azure/Office 365. In 2018, Andy is scheduled to deliver content in Europe, the Middle East, and the United States. He has also just published his second book, *Shadows Rising*, the sequel to his award-winning sci-fi thriller *The Seventh Day*.

If there is one myth that you could debunk in cybersecurity, what would it be?

That hackers are shady cyber criminals who live in the shadows and do the most damage. The sad truth, however, is that, in most cases, hackers are opportunists. Often, script kiddies or malicious employees who want to be bad guys have gotten hold of a tool and thought, "Hey, I wonder what this does."

Once having tasted blood, they then expand their knowledge and arsenal to attack more tempting targets.

"In my humble opinion, the greatest action an organization can take to improve its security stance is to move from a traditional defense-based methodology to one that assumes a breach has already taken place."

What is one of the biggest bang-for-the-buck actions that an organization can take to improve its cybersecurity posture?

In my humble opinion, the greatest action an organization can take to improve its security stance is to move from a traditional defense-based methodology to one that assumes a breach has already taken place. By assuming that the bad guy has already breached your network, the focus for the company shifts greatly toward detection and an information protection stance. For example, this includes adopting file classification, rights management, data loss prevention policies, and encryption. In principle, even if the bad guy obtains your data, it would be useless to him.

How is it that cybersecurity spending is increasing but breaches are still happening?

When I think of the technology that we use today, it reminds me of a box of Legos. TCP/IP, basic networking components, and most operating systems that are in use today are essentially the same as they were 20 years ago. So, in Lego-speak, this is essentially the green board that we build our businesses upon. Although we can add new services, security features, and functionality, in many cases, the basic flaws still exist—thus allowing an experienced hacker to easily circumvent an unpatched system or a poorly managed, weakly secured environment.

Do you need a college degree or certification to be a cybersecurity professional?

Absolutely not! However, that said, I would certainly recommend taking some form of certification exam, such as CompTIA's excellent Security+ certification. It provides a great grounding in cybersecurity. From there, the sky's the limit. There are a plethora of security options for you. Firstly, however, you should be aware that cybersecurity is an enormous area with many career options, and at some point, you need to pick a lane. Networking, ethical hacking, social engineering, information security, digital forensics, threat detection and response, and fraud are all possible career paths. So, have a think about what you're good at, what drives you. Then take the step toward achieving those goals. Don't worry about attending expensive classes, either. There is a wealth of online learning opportunities, from hands-on labs to video tutorials. You can also easily supplement your knowledge by obtaining self-paced books, free software, trial accounts, and demos to supplement your learning goals. Then, when you feel competent, simply take the exam. These are hosted through Pearson Vue or Prometric testing centers, and you can now even take a webcam-proctored exam at home in your pajamas.

How did you get started in the cybersecurity field, and what advice would you give to a beginner pursuing a career in cybersecurity?

To be honest, I have to take my hat off to my brother-in-law, and the author of this book, Marcus J. Carey. His tales of cybercrime and hacking really inspired me. That was 13 years ago. Today, I train, consult, and speak on various cybersecurity topics all over the world. I've become a passionate advocate of good security practices.

What is your specialty in cybersecurity, and how can others gain expertise in your specialty?

Cybersecurity casts a great shadow over business, and with so many career options, it's often difficult to make a clear choice. For me, I have four favorites: digital forensics, social engineering, identity, and access. Of these, I would say that access probably takes up a lot of my time. As a Microsoft MVP in cloud and datacenter, I teach and consult a lot on Microsoft cloud technologies, including Microsoft Azure and Office 365. At the moment, *identity convergence* is the latest buzz phrase. With so many users still using multiple usernames and passwords, identity federation and single sign-on are a hot commodity. If this is an area of interest, then of course you can take the official Microsoft courses. But, if you, like many, have a limited budget, there is a wealth of free online materials. Take a look at the excellent Microsoft Virtual Academy (`https://mva.microsoft.com/`). Other great resources include YouTube and Microsoft's excellent document repository (`https://docs.microsoft.com/en-us/`). And let's not forget Microsoft's Technical Community (`https://techcommunity.microsoft.com/`).

What is your advice for career success when it comes to getting hired, climbing the corporate ladder, or starting a company in cybersecurity?

Learn not only how to take advice but also how to take criticism. Being arrogant will never earn you friends and may possibly damage future business relationships. Like a wise man once said, never burn your bridges behind you. Learn as much as you can, and set yourself well-defined and reachable goals. Never let anyone tell you that you can't do it. Learn how to widen your business contacts by joining networking groups, as well as learning to get the most out of social media. In terms of starting your own company, don't be afraid of the challenge. Yes, it may be difficult, but in the end, it will be worth it. When you do finally get there, never forget the little guy—that one employee who stays late, that one guy who's willing to go the extra mile. A good employee is like a gold bar, precious and definitely worth holding onto.

> "Never let anyone tell you that you can't be what you want to be, or you can't do something. These people are basically in your way. You have to move past them and fulfill that dream."

What qualities do you believe all highly successful cybersecurity professionals share?

One of my pet peeves is being called an "expert." In my opinion, we're all learners here. Cybersecurity, along with technology, is like the Old West, and at

> "One of my pet peeves is being called an "expert." In my opinion, we're all learners here."

the moment, we've only just reached the frontier. It's a never-ending journey for improvement, and it's a constant game of chess against an adversary who is attempting to outwit you at every turn. Ultimately, though, as in the military world, you may win the odd battle, but the war rages on. So, for me, qualities would include the passion to succeed, determination, tenacity, and the drive to keep your skills updated, which sometimes can appear to be a constant and arduous struggle.

What is the best book or movie that can be used to illustrate cybersecurity challenges?
One of the greatest fears a person can have is the loss of his or her identity. I remember seeing the thriller *The Net*, where Sandra Bullock plays a virus and malware researcher who, as a consequence of a discovery, suddenly finds that her identity has been compromised. In just a short time, her entire life is turned upside down by a shady organization of bad guys who are attempting to infiltrate the U.S. government with a malicious software program called the Gatekeeper. That was a great movie.

> "One of the greatest fears a person can have is the loss of his or her identity."

What is your favorite hacker movie?
Oh, this is an easy one for me. The 1983 Matthew Broderick classic, *WarGames*. It's about a Seattle-based teenager who hacks into the War Operations Planned Response—a top-secret computer that is installed to help avoid the possibility of human error in a nuclear war. Of course, things don't entirely go according to plan.

What are your favorite books for motivation, personal development, or enjoyment?
You know, I have to be honest here; I've never been one for those types of books. However, in terms of inspiring moments, this is something I can share: when I was a kid, I left school with nothing, and growing up, every Thursday, I watched an old TV show called *The Paper Chase* starring John Houseman. He played an old crusty professor at Harvard Law School. He was that guy you thought would be the meanest person in the world, but in the end, he was the kindest and really cared for his students. After leaving school with no qualifications, I was inspired to further my education and eventually earn a degree. I'm sure after reading this, you'll be able to recall a moment in your life where something similar happened to you—that one person or a conversation perhaps. And if not, then use this as a model: never let anyone tell you that you can't be what you want to be or you can't do something. These people are basically in your way. You have to move past them and fulfill that dream.

> "There's no doubt that social media has changed our world, and I'm not convinced it's for the better, either."

What is some practical cybersecurity advice you give to people at home in the age of social media and the Internet of Things?
There's no doubt that social media has changed our world, and I'm not convinced it's for the better,

either. You just have to lift your head up from your smartphone and realize, "Holy crap, look at that." We're all addicted to these damn devices. Every single one of us—on trains, airports, at work, and even in bed at night—we can't put them down, and you have to ask why. But also, why are we so addicted to social networks?

I think it's because we all have an innate need to be wanted, to belong to something or someone, and perhaps this is the way the future will be. I certainly hope not. So, my first piece of advice is to detox yourself and your family from social media. In terms of the Internet of Things, treat it like any other technology. Plan for it, understand how it works, investigate its weaknesses, and ultimately learn how to protect yourself, your family, and your business from any potential vulnerabilities it may have.

> "So, my first piece of advice is to detox yourself and your family from social media."

What is a life hack that you'd like to share?

I'm a huge *Star Trek* fan. I remember an episode of *Star Trek: The Next Generation* called "Tapestry," in which Captain Picard is killed and encounters the character Q, played by John de Lancie. Appearing as God, Q listens to Picard's tales of regret and agrees to give him another chance at life. So, after transporting him backward to his early days in Starfleet Academy, Picard strives to avoid making the mistakes he made in his youth. But, of course, he ends up changing so much that he actually unravels his life, and when he's finally returned to the Enterprise, he's no longer the captain; he's a junior officer. Of course, it all works out in the end, but the lesson here was that, in life, you have to step forward, and you have to get noticed if you want to succeed. Otherwise, your life will simply drift. Don't live with regret; learn from it and move on; otherwise, it will consume you.

What is the biggest mistake you've ever made, and how did you recover from it?

Gosh, that's a tough question. I've made a few, and it depends on if you're talking about technical mistakes or life mistakes. I guess we're all guilty of those at some point. The biggest technical mistake I made was not to check that a backup had been performed at one of my major clients. So, of course, when I deleted their database by mistake, there was mayhem. They

> "The biggest technical mistake I made was not to check that a backup had been performed at one of my major clients. So, of course, when I deleted their database by mistake, there was mayhem."

were crazy mad at me. It took two days and nights of hard work to get the data back. In the end, it all worked out, and you'll be surprised to know that they are still a great customer. I can tell you after that experience, I never made that or a similar mistake again. ∎

"The reason breaches keep happening is because "we" believe that if we spend enough on security technology, we will fix the problem of being insecure."

Twitter: @MrJeffMan • **Website:** securityweekly.com/hosts

Jeffrey Man

41

Jeffrey Man is a respected information security expert, advisor, evangelist, and co-host of the security podcast *Security Weekly*. He has more than 35 years of experience in all aspects of computer, network, and information security. Jeffrey has held various information security roles within the DoD as well as private-sector enterprises, is a former PCI QSA, and was part of the first penetration testing "red team" at the NSA.

If there is one myth that you could debunk in cybersecurity, what would it be?

If I may be philosophical for a moment, I would suggest that the biggest myth in cybersecurity is the notion of *security* in and of itself—that it is a state that can be achieved or to which one can be elevated. As a more practical matter but probably equally as daunting, I would say the biggest myth in cybersecurity is the notion that cybersecurity begins and ends with *technology*. I was doing information security (InfoSec) for years before computers—and networks—came along.

While technology is here to stay and is certainly an integral part of cybersecurity, I believe there are fundamentals to understanding this thing we call "cybersecurity" that are too often misunderstood, because the understanding and application begins with a presumption about the technology. Here's a simple example: the notion of protecting your information assets too often revolves around all the information technologies that are employed within the enterprise, whereas I believe the information assets are far and away the information and data *itself* that is processed, transmitted, and stored using the information technology. In other words, we focus on the vehicle rather than the content.

What is one of the biggest bang-for-the-buck actions that an organization can take to improve its cybersecurity posture?

Taking any steps to educate the employee population about the nature of the business—and what is considered valuable by the company in terms of its information assets—and fostering an environment where every employee understands, embraces, and buys into the notion that what they do (or don't do) impacts the overall success of cybersecurity efforts. I'm not talking about compulsory viewing of an annual 30-minute security awareness video. I'm talking about systemic, core-value, company identity practices that change behaviors of employees—rewarding right behaviors and doing the right thing rather than turning a blind eye or creating a work culture where bad practices, or even breaking the rules, is rewarded or expected. How is this a "biggest bang-for-the-buck" activity? I believe it is the only thing left to do that hasn't already been done or really invested in. There's always going to be IT and IS spending, and God help the people who have to try to sort all that out in terms of the right level and focus of investment. But no amount of technology spending, ultimately, will take the place of employees understanding the goals of cybersecurity and doing their part to facilitate it in their organizations.

How is it that cybersecurity spending is increasing but breaches are still happening?

The reason breaches keep happening is because "we" believe that if we spend enough on security technology, we will fix the problem of being insecure. Innovation has created so many different ways to quickly and seamlessly share information with little to no regard (in the big picture) of how to limit or protect the "sensitive" data from falling into the wrong hands. We have bought into the notion that advances in security technologies can and are keeping up with the increased capabilities of our information-sharing technologies. But something is fundamentally broken, because too often the breaches are caused by "simple" problems—like a missing patch or a default password—that no amount of technological advancement ever seems to solve. Most of the "user" community rather blindly uses the technology with the belief that it must be secure (if they even think about security at all) or that there is so much data flying around that what they do will go unnoticed or have little to no impact.

> "Too often the breaches are caused by "simple" problems—like a missing patch or a default password—that no amount of technological advancement ever seems to solve."

Breaches keep happening because a) there is an economic motivation for criminals to keep attempting breaches, and b) they can accomplish enough success with little to no technical acumen (i.e., it's not that hard).

There is a dirty little secret in our industry as well. We spend most of our time, effort, and resources (failing) to prevent the casual or opportunistic bad guy from breaching our organizations, yet do little to prevent a determined and intentional adversary who is focused on us specifically. We generally write that off to some risk assessment that is out of the bounds of our abilities and budgets. We love the increased revenues and profitability that IT provides us while not really being able to afford what it actually takes to protect the data, information, and IT resources that we so heavily rely upon to make money. It's not cost-effective.

Do you need a college degree or certification to be a cybersecurity professional?

Do you "need" a college degree or certification to be a cybersecurity professional? Well, yes, because many organizations require this type of pedigree as a checkbox for even being considered for a cybersecurity job opening. In that sense, it is pretty much necessary. But I could just as easily say, "No, all you need is a whole lot of talent and desire and curiosity and experience, and you will succeed."

Now, I am old school and have the perspective that the best cybersecurity professionals have learned their craft through experience—that education (first) and certification (later) are not necessary at all. I still bristle every time I see certain certifications listed by individuals, and I believe that the more certifications you possess, the less likely you are to have any meaningful skills. But…I realize that not everybody had the opportunity to be in on the "ground floor" of the internet and that there are amazingly talented young people who would love to break into this industry but simply don't have the experience—and won't get it because of HR screening practices. So, while I'd like to say, "No, these aren't necessary to be a cybersecurity professional," I think that, realistically, these days you need to start somewhere, and degrees and certifications are a good way to get the foundational knowledge that will help you succeed.

How did you get started in the cybersecurity field, and what advice would you give to a beginner pursuing a career in cybersecurity?

I began my career in information security working for the Department of Defense. I ended up working in an office that conducted security evaluations of fielded (crypto) systems and ultimately the "networked systems" branch in that office—right around the time that the internet was becoming publicly available. I discovered that I possessed this thing that came to be known as the "hacker mentality"—which made me good at figuring out how to break and/or find flaws in the security. At the end of the day, it was a matter of being at the right place at the right time, but I would also attribute getting into the field to a natural curiosity that my "hacker mentality" brought about.

The advice I would give to a beginner pursuing a career in cybersecurity (or any field, really) is to make sure you're pursuing something you're genuinely interested in, that makes you happy, and not just pursuing it because it has the promise of paying well. I have met too many folks who want to get into this industry because it looks like fun and appears to be

> "The advice I would give to a beginner pursuing a career in cybersecurity (or any field, really) is to make sure you're pursuing something you're genuinely interested in, that makes you happy, and not just pursuing it because it has the promise of paying well."

rewarding for various reasons. But, they don't necessarily have the fundamental drive, the "hacker mentality," to really help them excel in their pursuits. I'm not convinced that this mentality is something that can be taught or obtained. In other words, either you have it or you don't. This doesn't necessarily mean that you shouldn't pursue a cybersecurity career or that you can't be really good at what you do. There are, after all, many aspects to this thing we call cybersecurity, and it takes many types of skill sets to move this profession forward. Nobody does it all or knows it all.

I keep coming back to finding something that you are interested in doing, enjoy doing, and maybe even have some talent for. There you will find the most success and satisfaction.

What is your specialty in cybersecurity, and how can others gain expertise in your specialty?

This is a tough question to answer. My specialty in cybersecurity is that I am a generalist; I know a little about a lot. I spent nearly 10 years of my career working as a third-party assessor, where I was hired by companies to help them build their own cybersecurity programs to meet industry compliance standards. This experience required me to become an "expert" at virtually every aspect of cybersecurity—not necessarily from the perspective of being a practitioner, but being able to see the big picture of cybersecurity and how each aspect or element fits into the overall strategy for becoming "secure" (or rather "compliant"). I encourage people to try to find jobs that give them exposure to the big picture or overall strategy of cybersecurity in their organizations. I believe that "big-picture" understanding helps you to be better at your job, no matter how big or small your role is in cybersecurity. Move around, try different things. If you can't get a job or assignment doing something different, then be an observer or volunteer (intern) to learn another aspect of the job. Ask questions. Try to see the big picture and how each element fits into it.

> "I believe that "big-picture" understanding helps you to be better at your job, no matter how big or small your role is in cybersecurity."

What is your advice for career success when it comes to getting hired, climbing the corporate ladder, or starting a company in cybersecurity?

Whatever you endeavor to do, make sure you are doing it for the right reasons. I often hear people in this field say some variation of, "It's so cool that I get paid to do what I love." That's one thing that makes this field really special and why so many want to get into the field. But, there's an old saying where I come from: "It's not just an adventure, it's a job." Perspective is everything, and that is something I often have to remind myself. Yes, you need to get paid, and yes, you should do something that you like to do, but that isn't always the case. Having a positive attitude can help, or having the ability to look beyond yourself (I think that's called *empathy*).

In terms of starting a company, I would say that you need to remind yourself of why you want to start something. Do you really want to help? Do you see a need and have a solution? Great. Go for it. Do you see a way to make millions? That's also okay for some, but I would suggest you think twice before heading down that path. The most successful *and* happy/content people I know in this industry got there because they had a vision for solving a problem and helping people (organizations) do better at cybersecurity. They made sacrifices, yes, but they also had their limits. Somebody once said, "Keep your feet on the ground, and keep reaching for the stars." (It was Casey Kasem...Google it!)

What qualities do you believe all highly successful cybersecurity professionals share?

The shared qualities of highly successful cybersecurity professionals depend on how you define success. If you define success as simply becoming incredibly wealthy, then the shared qualities too often involve being cutthroat, screwing over the customer to get the sale, and sacrificing families, friends, and personal values. Not all the time, but it is common to meet the CEO of a highly successful company who has incurred significant personal loss, generally through a divorce (or two).

On the other hand, if you define success in other ways, such as providing solutions, helping others, promoting sound cybersecurity practices, giving back to the community, or setting personal limits on what you will or won't do in terms of personal/family sacrifice, then you are going to find a different set of shared qualities. These types of individuals tend to be "real." They set limits for themselves and their employees; they encourage time off and really mean it; they reward innovation and give credit where credit is due; they have families and like to spend time with them; they are passionate not only to learn but also to teach; they are humble; they care. And they are really good at what they do from a technical perspective.

What is the best book or movie that can be used to illustrate cybersecurity challenges?

I'm not advocating that this is a particularly great movie, but Harrison Ford's *Firewall* touches on one aspect of cybersecurity that we never really talk about, at least with regard to multifactor authentication. That is the "what if somebody puts a gun to your head" scenario or, in this case, threatens your family. Not that we don't talk about it, we just don't really have a good answer for it. This is a good illustration of how cybersecurity tends to focus on stopping the inadvertent or casual hacker while doing little to stop or mitigate deliberate efforts to target *you* specifically. Nobody wants to spend the type of money it would require to "secure" everything, so we tend to ignore the fact that most organizations can't or don't protect themselves from targeted attacks.

What is your favorite hacker movie?

I'm going to date myself with this one, but I'm okay with that. I have to list two, though: *WarGames*—"Shall we play a game?"—because of its portrayal of the hacker mind-set. *Sneakers*—"My voice is my passport. Verify me."—because it was the first mainstream movie to show social engineering and physical compromise as part of penetration testing.

What are your favorite books for motivation, personal development, or enjoyment?

For motivation:

Dangerous Wonder by Michael Yaconelli

To Own a Dragon by Donald Miller

For personal development:
> *Inside Out* by Larry Crabb
> *Messy Spirituality* by Michael Yaconelli
> *The Wounded Healer* by Henri J. M. Nouwen
> *Out of the Saltshaker & into the World* by Rebecca Manley Pippert

For enjoyment:
> *The Chronicles of Narnia* by C. S. Lewis
> *With Justice for All* by John Perkins
> *A People's History of the United States* by Howard Zinn

What is some practical cybersecurity advice you give to people at home in the age of social media and the Internet of Things?

Don't fill your house with any more technology than necessary. Separate your accounts into "more" sensitive (private) and "less" sensitive, and use stronger, more cryptographically secure passwords for the sensitive accounts. Be aware of what information you possess and what you consider to be private information, and treat it accordingly. Use separate payment cards for online versus brick-and-mortar shopping. Be aware and informed of the pros and cons of implementing new technologies anywhere.

What is a life hack that you'd like to share?

Remember these two important life truths: everything matters, and nothing matters. What does this mean? Basically, it means that you should always try to see the bigger picture. It's easy for me to get spun up about major issues in my life or workplace, but I try to remember to take a "step back" and see the bigger picture—and there's always a bigger picture. A former supervisor once told me, "Don't bring up any problems that you see in the organization unless you have some idea of how to solve them." I think that's been a pretty good litmus test over the years for getting spun up about problems and issues.

What is the biggest mistake you've ever made, and how did you recover from it?

This really depends on how you define "mistake." I have certainly done things that have caused me to be pushed out or even fired from several jobs, but I don't consider any of those events to be big mistakes. I have made career choices that have not yielded the financial rewards that others have enjoyed, but I don't consider those choices to be mistakes at all. I cannot think of a single significant event, but I know that there have been times in my life when I've put myself first over my wife and family, only to find out how hurtful my actions were to those that I love and care for the most. The biggest mistake, then, was putting myself first before others in terms of decisions and actions I'd taken, which ended up being hurtful to others.

How did I recover from these times? Someone, usually my wife, pointed out my selfish behavior and how hurtful it was to others. Once I am aware, I apologize and resolve to do better the next time, and I try to remember to consider others before myself as well as what the potential impacts of my actions are. It's not a life lesson that I would say I have mastered, as I continue to disappoint and hurt those I care for the most. But it helps to keep me humble and focused on doing better the next time. ■

"Learn to code. No matter what else you do in security, it will augment your career and capabilities."

Twitter: @manicode • **Website:** manicode.com

Jim Manico

42

Jim Manico is the founder of Manicode Security, where he trains software developers on secure coding and security engineering. He is also the founder of Infrared Security and Brakeman Security and is an investor/advisor for Signal Sciences and BitDiscovery. Jim is a Java Champion and a member of the JavaOne Rock Star speaker community. He is the author of *Iron-Clad Java: Building Secure Web Applications* from McGraw-Hill and Oracle Press. Jim also volunteers for the OWASP foundation, where he helps build application security standards and other documentation. For more information, see `http://www.linkedin.com/in/jmanico`.

If there is one myth that you could debunk in cybersecurity, what would it be?
That input validation is enough to stop injection. Programmers need to master other techniques like query parameterization and proper escaping to stop the various forms of injection.

What is one of the biggest bang-for-the-buck actions that an organization can take to improve its cybersecurity posture?
Force a policy of 16-or-more-character passwords as the new minimum.

How is it that cybersecurity spending is increasing but breaches are still happening?
Hackers gonna hack.

Do you need a college degree or certification to be a cybersecurity professional?
Nope. Experience rules the roost. Can you play or not? That is the question.

How did you get started in the cybersecurity field, and what advice would you give to a beginner pursuing a career in cybersecurity?
I'm a coder first, security pro second. Learn to code. No matter what else you do in security, it will augment your career and capabilities.

What is your specialty in cybersecurity, and how can others gain expertise in your specialty?
Application security. Learn to code. The best way to learn about secure coding is to work under an architect who gets it.

What is your advice for career success when it comes to getting hired, climbing the corporate ladder, or starting a company in cybersecurity?
Chop the corporate ladder into firewood and use it to start a campfire, where you get really drunk or have some other life-altering experience where you finally decide to start your own company and become an independent consultant or entrepreneur.

What qualities do you believe all highly successful cybersecurity professionals share?
A desire to learn more! At all times!

What is the best book or movie that can be used to illustrate cybersecurity challenges?
My first security book was Gary McGraw's *Software Security*, with the yin and yang on the cover. Great read.

What is your favorite hacker movie?
The 1995 movie *Hackers* with Angelina Jolie. The fire sprinkler system going off is my first security memory.

What are your favorite books for motivation, personal development, or enjoyment?
I carry a Hawaiian language book with me when I fly. I also started reading the book *EQ, Applied*, which is a powerful book on topics we do not address enough in the security industry.

What is some practical cybersecurity advice you give to people at home in the age of social media and the Internet of Things?
Really, really long, unique passwords on all things.

What is a life hack that you'd like to share?
When you get a text early in the morning saying, "Nuclear ballistic missiles are inbound, take cover. This is not a drill," open the good stuff and spend some time with friends. We got such an alert in Hawaii recently, and it was a life-altering experience.

What is the biggest mistake you've ever made, and how did you recover from it?
You have to take me to dinner first and tell me sweet nothings before I tell you that one. ∎

"Oftentimes, it feels as though companies are quick to buy the newest "whizz-bang" tool or software that is presented as an all-in-one solution that can fix all of their problems without ensuring that the basic security checkboxes are filled."

Twitter: @0xNBE1 • **Website:** www.linkedin.com/in/kyliemartonik

Kylie Martonik

43

Kylie Martonik is a managing security consultant. Specializing in pentesting, she has seen an array of diverse environments ranging from small credit unions to large healthcare providers. Kylie has assisted security and IT teams in long-term project efforts, short-term operations, and building the road map to bring them closer to the ideal security program. Outside of work, she can be found flying her drone, playing video and board games, or actively hunting for the next action figure to add to her collection.

If there is one myth that you could debunk in cybersecurity, what would it be?

The myth I would debunk is that it's all technical work. I believe people tend to directly correlate "cybersecurity" with technical tasks or skills, such as hacking, malware reverse engineering, incident response, and so on. However, there are many other areas within cybersecurity where in-depth technical skill is not required, such as policy, compliance, and privacy.

What is one of the biggest bang-for-the-buck actions that an organization can take to improve its cybersecurity posture?

Oftentimes, it feels as though companies are quick to buy the newest "whizz-bang" tool or software that is presented as an all-in-one solution that can fix all of their problems without ensuring that the basic security checkboxes are filled. Many organizations could get the most benefit from doing the reverse. By that, I mean spending the time/money on implementing and maintaining the basic administrative policies that support information security, the standard technical tools that can improve resilience against a future attack, as well as providing proper and regular education on information security topics to their workforce.

How is it that cybersecurity spending is increasing but breaches are still happening?
Product vendors often (not all the time) push their products as the magical solution to solving information security problems. Also, the decision-makers who procure those tools may be uneducated regarding what is truly needed to implement a robust security program that would mitigate or reduce the likelihood of a breach.

Additionally, the information security industry struggles with communicating the true business risks of vulnerabilities and threats in a way that is understood by said decision-makers. When combined, this can create the perfect scenario for breaches to continue to occur.

Do you need a college degree or certification to be a cybersecurity professional?
In this current day, degrees can help a less-experienced individual break into information security. However, I do not believe that degrees are strictly required to enter the field.

How did you get started in the cybersecurity field, and what advice would you give to a beginner pursuing a career in cybersecurity?
When I was in my third year of college, I enrolled in a class ominously named "Information Warfare." Within the first month, I had popped my first shell using MS08-067 and have been hooked ever since. My advice to a beginner would be to stop wondering if you can break into information security and instead just go for it.

What is your specialty in cybersecurity, and how can others gain expertise in your specialty?
My professional journey led me down the path of a pentester, but I have had the opportunity to experience other areas of the field as well. What I would recommend to others is to go experience what you can, chase what you find interesting, and have the grit to stick through the highs and the lows.

> "What I would recommend to others is to go experience what you can, chase what you find interesting, and have the grit to stick through the highs and the lows."

What is your advice for career success when it comes to getting hired, climbing the corporate ladder, or starting a company in cybersecurity?
Build your soft skills as urgently as your technical skills. You can be the best hacker in the world, but if you can't communicate what you're doing, how you're doing it, and so on, it won't matter.

"Build your soft skills as urgently as your technical skills."

What qualities do you believe all highly successful cybersecurity professionals share?

Passion. Information security thrives when individuals are passionate about what they do.

What is the best book or movie that can be used to illustrate cybersecurity challenges?

The TV show *Mr. Robot*.

What is your favorite hacker movie?

The Matrix, with *Hackers* being a close second.

What are your favorite books for motivation, personal development, or enjoyment?

Mindset by Carol S. Dweck and the Space Odyssey series by Arthur C. Clarke.

What is some practical cybersecurity advice you give to people at home in the age of social media and the Internet of Things?

I actually struggle with this question because the standard advice of "stop reusing your password" and "enable multifactor authentication" seems to fall on deaf ears for the bulk of the population. While I would not hesitate to tell anyone this type of advice, there is still the challenge of helping them understand why it's important in terms they can understand so they actually follow it. Otherwise, I believe it can be viewed as an impediment to what they actually want to do while using computers, and there's a high chance they will revert to their "old ways."

"Information security thrives when individuals are passionate about what they do."

What is a life hack that you'd like to share?

As someone who experiences imposter syndrome, I regularly create mental habit loops to combat my brain's tendency to want to focus on the negative. If I start thinking to myself something like, "I'm not good enough" or "There's no way I could do that," I make those my triggers to say something positive to myself, such as, "But with enough time and effort, I can improve/learn." Even adding a "yet" to the end of those types of self-thoughts can be comforting and dissipate the feeling of disparity.

What is the biggest mistake you've ever made, and how did you recover from it?

Being afraid to fail. I still encounter this feeling regularly. However, I actively remind myself that failing is not a negative thing but rather an opportunity to learn and improve. ■

> "The biggest myth is that everyone—from companies to every hacker on the planet—has it all figured out."

Twitter: @divinetechygirl • **Websites:** www.christinamorillo.com and www.linkedin.com/in/christinamorillo

Christina Morillo

Christina is a New York City–based information security and technology professional with a background in enterprise-level security and identity. By day, she works as a senior program manager at Microsoft, helping organizations "do more" securely.

$$44$$

In addition to her professional work, Christina also cofounded a virtual community that is best known for boosting visual representation in the tech industry by way of an open source collection of stock photos. Christina advocates and is passionate about visual representation, connecting and creating opportunities for others, and empowering women and underrepresented folks to follow careers in security and technology. When she is not at work/traveling for work or spending time with her family, she is co-leading Women in Security and Privacy's NYC chapter, attending InfoSec meetups, or watching *Black Mirror* episodes.

If there is one myth that you could debunk in cybersecurity, what would it be?
The biggest myth is that everyone—from companies to every hacker on the planet—has it all figured out. In a field that has both breadth and lots of depth, trust me when I say this isn't the case. The one thing both companies and people have in common, besides skipping the basics when it comes to security, is refusing to admit that we don't know it all.

What is one of the biggest bang-for-the-buck actions that an organization can take to improve its cybersecurity posture?

This is subjective and greatly depends on the organization's priorities and strategy. By the way, this can also change depending on the business's needs. For Company A, this could mean enabling multifactor authentication (MFA) for all employees, while for Company B, this could mean prioritizing productivity and enabling single sign-on for all users. My point is that there isn't a one-size-fits-all approach when it comes to security.

> "CISOs are under enormous pressure to show immediate value, which results in security teams investing in and prioritizing tools they feel have a quicker ROI (like firewalls and logging) over basic hygiene."

How is it that cybersecurity spending is increasing but breaches are still happening?

CISOs are under enormous pressure to show immediate value, which results in security teams investing in and prioritizing tools they feel have a quicker ROI (like firewalls and logging) over basic hygiene.

Do you need a college degree or certification to be a cybersecurity professional?

That depends. While you don't technically need a degree to work in the field, some companies—for example, financial corporations—may require this as part of their hiring practices and corporate culture. As far as certifications, well, these are a bit controversial in that not all certs are created equal. A lot of the big-name certs you've heard of are mostly theoretical and less practical (e.g., CISSP), but they remain popular among recruiters and CISOs due to name recognition and echo chambers. If you need to level up, I'd look at SANS GIAC info security certifications. While there is massive value in theory and understanding the basics, there is no substitute for getting your hands dirty. That being said, if I had to do it all over again, I would still obtain my degree(s).

How did you get started in the cybersecurity field, and what advice would you give to a beginner pursuing a career in cybersecurity?

While attending university, I started gaining experience by interning at my school's computer lab. I then moved on to external help desk/technical support roles and gradually moved into a desktop support role. By the time I graduated with an AS in network administration and a BS in information technology, I had amassed enough experience to land a job as a network/system administrator at a technology consulting firm. While I didn't have formal security training at the time, my previous experience and insatiable curiosity led me to my first role as an information security/identity management engineer a few years later. Back when I started, there really wasn't a direct path, so I had to carve my own.

What is your specialty in cybersecurity, and how can others gain expertise in your specialty?

Thus far, most of my information security career has been building out and developing enterprise identity and access management frameworks. I have since pivoted to cloud identity and security and am focused on that these days.

How can others gain this expertise? By doing the work and building a portfolio of hands-on experience, which, by the way, does not have to look like anyone else's. That's the secret. My advice would be to map out a plan and think about what experience (not tools) are relevant. This could look different depending on the specialty, year, and what level of experience you already have. So, perhaps start off entry level and then look at self-paced SANS, CTFs, and local college courses.

> "How can others gain this expertise? By doing the work and building a portfolio of hands-on experience, which, by the way, does not have to look like anyone else's. That's the secret."

For my role, and I think for most, understanding foundational networking concepts is key. Critical thinking and the ability to break down a problem into solvable parts is also equally important.

What is your advice for career success when it comes to getting hired, climbing the corporate ladder, or starting a company in cybersecurity?

For being hired: great listening skills along with emotional intelligence. You'd be surprised by how much people love to talk, which gives you leverage. Listen, extract value, and frame your responses accordingly. Having excellent communication skills and confidence are also must-haves. Don't be overly confident or cocky, as this can be off-putting. Always do your research and tweak your résumé to emphasize why you are the best candidate for said job/project. Ask thoughtful questions, and don't be afraid to say you don't know something; it's all about how you phrase it.

> "You'd be surprised by how much people love to talk, which gives you leverage. Listen, extract value, and frame your responses accordingly."

What qualities do you believe all highly successful cybersecurity professionals share?

An insatiable curiosity and passion for making things better. Critical thinking. Seeing past shiny tech and addressing root causes. Always willing to learn, listen, and ask questions. Willing to help and guide others whether by volunteering, mentoring, or simply listening.

What is the best book or movie that can be used to illustrate cybersecurity challenges?

Black Mirror episodes.

What is your favorite hacker movie?

I don't have one, but I absolutely love *Mr. Robot* and how they incorporate real practices and exploits.

What are your favorite books for motivation, personal development, or enjoyment?

Some of my current tech faves: *Hacking the Hacker*, *The Manga Guide to Cryptography*, *Serious Cryptography*, *Penetration Testing: A Hands-On Introduction to Hacking*, *CISO Desk Reference Guide*, *2600: The Hacker Quarterly*, and many more.

For motivational and personal development: *The Subtle Art of Not Giving a F*ck*, *The 48 Laws of Power*, *The Alchemist*, *The Smart Girl's Guide to Privacy*.

What is some practical cybersecurity advice you give to people at home in the age of social media and the Internet of Things?

I start by introducing the concept of threat modeling and how this applies to the individual. I then get into basic hygiene across devices and social platforms. It can be overwhelming, so I tend to phase this out. If I had to give a practical top five, it would be these:

- Set your phone to auto-lock and set a passcode.
- Use a password manager. This is easier than having to remember to not use the same passwords, but do use hard-to-guess passwords/passphrases as needed.
- Enable multifactor authentication *everywhere*!
- Harden your home network. Reset the default admin password. Rename Wi-Fi SSID and passwords.
- Install updates across devices—do not skip indefinitely.
- Bonus: Never connect to a public Wi-Fi network, and if you must, use a reputable VPN.

> "Career-wise, don't wait on a mentor to make moves. You are your number-one mentor and advocate."

> "The biggest mistake I've made is letting my fear of failure dictate my dreams and ideas, especially after becoming a mother."

What is a life hack that you'd like to share?

Career-wise, don't wait on a mentor to make moves. You are your number-one mentor and advocate. Equally important: never check a bag and always use no-bake lasagna noodles (you're welcome).

What is the biggest mistake you've ever made, and how did you recover from it?

The biggest mistake I've made is letting my fear of failure dictate my dreams and ideas, especially after becoming a mother. Failure sucks, and where I come from, it is not celebrated because it is not an option. The only way to recover is to keep pushing myself past the point of uncomfortable by walking toward what I am afraid of and by turning my losses into lessons. ∎

"Technology is made by people. Technology is implemented by people. Technology is used (and abused) by people. So, perhaps this isn't a *technology* problem but rather a *people* problem."

Twitter: @KentNabors • **Website:** www.linkedin.com/in/kentnabors

Kent Nabors

Kent Nabors has worked in bank examinations for the FDIC and the Federal Reserve. After leading the networking infrastructure team for a national midmarket bank, he went on to build their cybersecurity practice and then served as the institution's first CISO. After more than 20 years in the banking industry, he recently took over as the cybersecurity leader for a national retail chain with more than 800 locations and a significant e-commerce presence. Kent is also the co-author of *Dissecting the Hack: The F0rb1dd3n Network*. When not practicing cybersecurity, Kent is an occasional speaker on the topic for industry, university, and civic organizations. He also does volunteer work for community cybersecurity activities. In what spare time remains, Kent owns a small business with his wife. He received his MBA from the University of Oklahoma.

45

If there is one myth that you could debunk in cybersecurity, what would it be?
When you practice cybersecurity (more on the term *practice* in a moment), you eventually realize that you cannot be successful. For someone tasked with protecting systems, this realization can (and should) grow into a question about what our organizations are asking of us. It is a far easier thing to give an assignment of "protect us" than it is to implement.

The reasons for this are legion. But I also think they can be categorized:

Technology. "You go to war with the army you have, not the army you might want or wish to have…" (Donald Rumsfeld). We work with the tools we can afford. And "afford" may not mean money; it could also mean human skill to implement or time to implement. And even if you have huge budgets and large, talented teams, the technology you work with may still not be sufficient to the task. Ultimately, technology is only a *part* of the cybersecurity problem.

Environment. David Foster Wallace gave a commencement speech in 2005. In it, he told the following joke: "Two young fish are swimming alone, and they happen to meet an older fish swimming the other way, who nods at them and says, 'Morning, boys, how's the water?' And the two young fish swim on for a bit, and then eventually one of them looks over at the other and goes, 'What the hell is water?'"

We spend so much energy trying to buy and implement systems for cybersecurity or create new procedures or produce the next awareness program, but we rarely think about the water we are swimming in. We assume far too much about what we do in a day. Even when we do things like threat modeling, we often work within walls of assumptions that prevent us from understanding what risks we are accepting. Then you realize—cybersecurity isn't possible.

Mission. We may set a mission or purpose for our cybersecurity teams, but does it align with the organization? What happens when the organization has a different risk tolerance (often unstated) than what is required to achieve the organizational mission? I have debated with leaders who want "zero risk" and then cap a cybersecurity budget at 2 percent growth in a world of threats that increase exponentially. Then you realize—cybersecurity isn't possible.

People. Technology is made by people. Technology is implemented by people. Technology is used (and abused) by people. So, perhaps this isn't a *technology* problem but rather a *people* problem. That's why there is a whole field of cybersecurity dedicated to initiatives like SANS "Securing the Human." But if we are honest with ourselves, we know no human is reliable or ultimately trustworthy. So we are tasked with implementing technologies made by *people* to protect information that *people* want to steal or destroy. Then you realize—cybersecurity isn't possible.

As for "practicing" cybersecurity, this isn't something we can achieve. The medical profession has this concept right. We "practice" medicine with the goal of improving our abilities. We have made astounding progress in medicine, but so far the mortality rate among humans has remained stubbornly stuck at 100 percent. Humility is a good trait to have for cybersecurity professionals. "On a long enough timeline, the survival rate for everyone drops to zero" (*Fight Club*).

I don't mean all of this as an "all is lost" view of the business of cybersecurity.

My intention is to show that we overstate things when we say something is "secure." Instead, we need to have an approach of active defense. There is no time when our data or systems are *secured*, but they should always be *defended*. Diligence should be our mantra more than security. That approach keeps us just enough on edge so we're always looking for how we can become better.

What is one of the biggest bang-for-the-buck actions that an organization can take to improve its cybersecurity posture?

Tell the truth. Any organization larger than three people has political issues. Somewhere past 20, you have political parties. Then you drop that organization into a marketplace of customers, regulators, activists, attackers, and so on, and suddenly truth starts to become "truthy."

It takes courage to stop a large project that a business has invested time, money, and talent in to warn them that implementing it will violate a risk principle. It takes courage to read a penetration testing report and start acknowledging you don't know as much about your organization, application, self, or adversary as you thought you did. It takes courage to listen to someone who is right, even when they don't have the highest title in the room. It takes courage to keep showing up and standing against those who would tear down what you are charged with defending. But when you do that, you have to also have the courage to call for help when you see a new threat, or a breach in the defenses, even if it will be expensive. It is so hard to learn that it will only get more expensive the longer addressing the problem is delayed.

How is it that cybersecurity spending is increasing but breaches are still happening?

We are still trying to solve the wrong problems. If you are a cybersecurity practitioner, how do you advance your career? You need to build something new. You add to the size of your security team. You implement new tech. You chase after artificial intelligence, and threat modeling, or any other buzzword that is at or near the cutting edge of the industry.

But what does your organization actually need? I bet it would benefit from the wisdom of Ignaz Semmelweis. He was the physician who made a logical leap based on observable evidence in the hospital where he worked in 1847. He noticed that women in the maternity ward got sick when examined by physicians who had just left the morgue. The physicians weren't washing their hands. He instituted a handwashing practice and illness rates fell from 10 percent to 1 percent. Of course, the wisdom of the age said he was wrong, and he was forced out of the hospital.

What kind of hero would you be if you came into a company and said, "We need to do basic hygiene, and we probably don't need to spend any new money to do it?" The company would benefit, but would it jazz your résumé? Would you be able to publish a white paper about your discovery of digital handwashing? We need to use the right tools in the right places. Sometimes that will mean new tech and new approaches. But you'd better do the basics as well. Hunting for bad actors and new threats is cool and absolutely needed. But we also need to walk around and lock the doors, patch the things, and all the other basics.

Do you need a college degree or certification to be a cybersecurity professional?

Yes and no. *No*—By the time you go through a degree process, what you learned at the beginning is already becoming outdated. And the person who taught it to you either hasn't been a practitioner in a long time or never was at all. So a degree gets you a basic body of knowledge. Perhaps 10–20 percent of that knowledge might be helpful for a while at the start of your career. The biggest thing it proves is you can endure a four-year hazing ritual.

Certifications are really good to show technical competence. They are probably better than college degrees in this regard. But they don't age well either. They also create a circular situation, where you're chasing after "credits" of some form to document that you're maintaining your certification. Ultimately, a certification is a reputation substitution scheme. I don't know much about you, but I know something about that organization, so now I know something about you. At some point, your own reputation has to be built on performance.

Yes—If you want to step from technical doer to technical leader, you need to know how to think. One of the smartest businesspeople I worked with in my career had a bachelor's degree in letters. When he told me that, my question was, "What's that?" For his degree program, he read the classics of Western literature and philosophy. We debated and worked on complex business and technical projects together, and he always asked the best questions. A degree forces you to solve problems (yes, even learning how to manage a pile of homework at finals time is a valuable career lesson).

At the start of a career, certifications and degrees can help. But if you don't create a habit of study that continues, they will be about as valuable as my long-expired Novell Network and Windows NT certifications.

How did you get started in the cybersecurity field, and what advice would you give to a beginner pursuing a career in cybersecurity?
I got in the business because of a virus infection. We had decent IT practices for the time, but we were not ready for new threats. Something got in. It didn't do any damage, but we realized the rules had changed. I was fortunate to work for an organization that learned from the experience, and we quickly flipped the priority of security. I didn't have cybersecurity in mind when I got my bachelor's degree in business management. When I added an MBA, I was still thinking about things far from the world of cybersecurity (then again, not many were thinking about cybersecurity in those days except people like Clifford Stoll).

But what I found is that cybersecurity is ultimately a people problem. That interested me. Here was this complex mix of technologies, regulations, threats, business objectives, and people. Now *that* was something I could work on. And there is one more important part of cybersecurity: if you want to be good at it, you have to see the nobility in it. We are protectors for people who don't realize they need it. In this industry, you walk around life seeing things others can't see. They need you to train your vision to see threats and rally to their defense. You have to be willing to do the work even when no one realizes what you did to protect them.

What is your specialty in cybersecurity, and how can others gain expertise in your specialty?
Hah! If you want to learn about my cybersecurity specialty, go read a history book. Seriously, my hands-on tech skills are not what they used to be. About 10 years ago, I found more of my time committed to building teams and building organizational habits around the practices of cybersecurity. There is a difficulty with this path because it is hard to see progress. You can labor for months and not see a change. Then, one day, a system admin or a tech support person, or even a front-line customer service staff member, calls and reports a security concern. The organization has learned to make security part of its habit. It's like seeing a little green plant popping out of the soil after you planted seeds so long ago you'd forgotten you'd done it.

How do you gain expertise there? Ask questions. Don't be satisfied with marching orders. Ask for context when you're given an assignment. Be curious about the mission of your business. Send a meeting invitation to a leader in your business, and ask them if they will teach you about the company. Volunteer in a community organization and meet people. We are in the networking business with *data*, but we should be in the networking business with *people!*

What is your advice for career success when it comes to getting hired, climbing the corporate ladder, or starting a company in cybersecurity?

Don't get hung up on getting credit. When you're starting out, you are playing a long-term game. You need to create and develop a brand (go read any of the great material from Tom Peters on building your brand). The best way to do that is to help other people.

Instead of working on your own accomplishments, maximize how many people you can help. Then, one day, you will look around and be amazed at how many interesting people you know, and you'll look back and see that you accomplished far more through their abilities than you could have done by yourself.

What qualities do you believe all highly successful cybersecurity professionals share?

Perpetually curious. Cybersecurity professionals must teach themselves to see the world differently. We are surrounded by systems, controls, and influences that attempt to shape human behavior. Most people walk through life not seeing these things. We need to constantly practice asking questions, learning new things, and testing, testing, testing.

One more—practice people skills. Technology can be alluring. It is interesting to learn about something and dig deeper to learn more. The deeper you go, the deeper you need to go to really understand. But cybersecurity is about accomplishing things through the skills of *people*. If you can't communicate the reason behind an action to a team, then that team won't act effectively. The tech skills you learn today will be obsolete quickly. The people skills you learn will last your entire career.

What is the best book or movie that can be used to illustrate cybersecurity challenges?

The classic book is Cliff Stoll's *The Cuckoo's Egg*. The challenge most clearly illustrated is the constant struggle Cliff faces in convincing people that there's a problem. Just because a system "works" doesn't mean it isn't compromised. The magic of his story is how he noticed one small thread out of place; he pulled on that thread and then unraveled an entire mystery.

Cybersecurity professionals need to build time into their day to pull on threads. Find the thing that is out of place—or, better yet, study what "normal" is so you'll be ready to see what *shouldn't* be there. Then ask questions. And then ask more questions. I had a boss almost 20 years ago who regularly used the "three whys" technique. It often drove me crazy and was exactly what I needed to build a mind-set of digging to find the truth underneath a surface phenomenon.

What is your favorite hacker movie?

I'm going to go older here with *Sneakers*. It's dated and the tech is rather magical, but I like the eclectic collaboration of the team. You can also take the "five mind-sets of hacking" that Josh Linkner put in his 2017 book, *Hacking Innovation*, and find every one of them in this 1992 movie. And even if you can't get past the old tech, it's still worth watching to see them talk Whistler (a blind character) through driving a van across the parking lot to save the team.

What are your favorite books for motivation, personal development, or enjoyment?

Tom Peters has built a strong community and keeps his website fresh with regular content. Every time he does a presentation, he posts his slide deck for free on his site. *The Dip* by Seth Godin is a good book about quitting. It's a great way to challenge your thinking about strategies or practices you have put into place and help decide when it's time to reevaluate. *Team of Teams* by General Stanley McChrystal is a really good book about managing in complex and dynamic environments. I really like his explanation of complicated versus complex, which has a lot of parallels in the cybersecurity world.

This question is interesting to me because I've used a variation of this in interviews—"Tell me about the last book you read." Cybersecurity professionals need to constantly read, and the material that is most timely is probably a post linked off of a tweet or GitHub. But if that is all you are reading, then you aren't learning how to think. Your reading list should be diverse and challenge how you think—just like every day on your job in this business.

What is some practical cybersecurity advice you give to people at home in the age of social media and the Internet of Things?

Keep things up to date, segment, and call a (competent) friend for help when you are in over your head. Good advice for every network. Over my career, I've been asked to help out at a lot of smaller and personal networks. The problems are so similar: default passwords, systems not patched to current level, and things on the network that should never talk with devices that hold private data.

At a minimum, keep all your devices patched. Just like you need to clean house or mow the lawn, patch your things. For the world of Internet of Things, take the time to learn how to segment them from your personal devices. Your laptop and thermostat don't need to be on the same network.

What is a life hack that you'd like to share?

Balance. Cybersecurity people work so hard at making sure the technology in our networks is kept up to date and patched, and we should be doing the same for our own bodies and minds. And we should encourage the people on our teams to do likewise.

I want people who love technology on my team. I want people who will dig into the documentation and experiment with new configurations. But I also want people who know something about the world they live in. I want them to think and have opinions and explore. When we all do that, we bring better insights to the puzzles before us each day.

What is the biggest mistake you've ever made, and how did you recover from it?

I didn't appreciate the power of time. When you face a big problem, you see the entire problem, and it seems too big to accomplish. But when you break it down and win small victories over time, you create the type of momentum that actually speeds up your success. When you are 20-something and people tell you to invest (financially or with your energy), you think you have *so* much time and you will get to that later.

When you're in your 30s, you realize you should have started in your 20s, but that's over. Then you double down on your work and effort, only to find in your 40s that you might have been investing too much in areas that weren't as important as you thought.

I know I didn't say what my specific "biggest" mistake is. That's because there were so many. And they all centered around not getting started when I should have, trying to take a shortcut to make up ground, and then putting too much effort into the wrong things. When I figured that out and started focusing on just a few things, and getting good at those, then I started to see results. Find out what is important to you and then pay the price to be good at it. If there is a barrier to your success, that's just the way the world tells you to try harder. ■

"There are definitely people from different ethnicities, women, or whoever being judged as not capable, whereas other people are given the benefit of the doubt automatically. So, those minorities may need to prove themselves a lot more, and that's when the education can come in handy."

Twitter: @wendynather • **Website:** idoneous-security.blogspot.com

Wendy Nather

Wendy Nather is a mild-mannered threat intelligence research director by day and a former analyst and CISO in the public and private sectors. Warning: This interview may contain snark.

46

If there is one myth that you could debunk in cybersecurity, what would it be?

The biggest one from my perspective is the idea that all of the users of our systems need to know as much as we do about security. Back in the early days, in the '70s and '80s, when we were first building these systems, we built them for each other. And everyone in the community had pretty much the same level of knowledge. When you designed something, you were designing it for yourself and for people who knew the same things you did. The description of an intuitive interface really made a lot of assumptions that somebody else had the same background that you did, and therefore, they would be able to intuit what you meant with something. That's completely different now. The rest of the world is using technology, and none of them understand security or IT in the same way that we do. If I could, I would kill the idea that they *do* understand the same things we do and, furthermore, that they *must* understand the same things we do. I think it's unfair to expect them to have the same level of knowledge.

What is one of the biggest bang-for-the-buck actions that an organization can take to improve its cybersecurity posture?

There's a lot of talk about the basics. If the basics were easy, everybody would be doing them. But I think they're still worth calling out, even though they are difficult. The first thing is simply knowing what you have, what it's being used for, and by whom. I recommend starting with an asset inventory—understanding what data is on those systems, who is using that data (and for what purpose), and who's using the processes running on those systems. Still, that is so much harder than it sounds. I've known so many organizations that could not keep a running inventory. You have to solve that by doing continuous discovery, because people are frequently changing the endpoints that they use, especially with virtualized systems.

How is it that cybersecurity spending is increasing but breaches are still happening?

You can certainly spend more money on something and still not be doing it right. On the other hand, you can be doing a lot of things but not spending money in the right places. We tend to equate one with the other—that if you're spending a lot, you must be doing a lot; and if you're doing a lot, it must be effective. But I don't think any of those things follow, necessarily, from that. In a lot of ways, we don't understand how to solve this problem yet. So we're throwing more money and lots of different techniques at it in the hope that we'll find the right thing—find that spaghetti that sticks to the wall—but I don't think we've gotten there yet. Therefore, spending more money doesn't necessarily equate to solving the problem.

Do you need a college degree or certification to be a cybersecurity professional?

No. As somebody who does not have a college degree myself, and the only certification I got I gave up later, I would definitely say no. Certifications and education help in cases where the hiring process involves people who don't know how to judge the capabilities of the candidates they're looking at. Things like certifications and educational degrees can help them shortcut the need to know how to judge those capabilities, and therefore, they can be useful.

They can also be useful in cases where you're hiring candidates and you have to plausibly defend against grievances and lawsuits. In that way, they can help you justify your hiring decision in an objective manner. Again, having those pieces of paper is a great shortcut and a great standard that people can agree on.

Finally, if you are an underrepresented minority and you are facing bias that forces you to demonstrate much more rigorously that you know what you're talking about (rather than someone giving you the benefit of the doubt), then, again, having those pieces of paper may be necessary. I wish it weren't, but, unfortunately, that's often the case.

There are definitely people from different ethnicities, women, or whoever being judged as not capable, whereas other people are given the benefit of the doubt automatically. So, those minorities may need to prove themselves a lot more, and that's when the education can come in handy.

How did you get started in the cybersecurity field, and what advice would you give to a beginner pursuing a career in cybersecurity?

I got into it by accident. I was managing a Unix system administrator group, and the company I was working for, a Swiss bank, decided to outsource its IT operations. I was put on a task force to figure out whether we could do that without violating Swiss banking law. So, investigating all of the security aspects of that outsourcing led to me being put in charge of regional security for the Europe, Middle East, and Africa region. That was my first security position, so that's how I got into it.

For new people today, the most I think I can offer in the way of advice is to really study technology and understand the systems that you're working with, and the applications, because you can't secure them unless you understand well how they work.

What is your specialty in cybersecurity, and how can others gain expertise in your specialty?

That's kind of tough because I think I may be one of the few remaining generalists in the field. I haven't specialized in any particular area and have instead gone very broadly with my knowledge—both because when you're a CISO, you need to understand a bit about everything that you're managing, and then, as an industry analyst, I ended up covering pretty much every area whenever anyone on my team left. I would have to take over their areas of coverage and understand what those vendors were doing and the technology they were creating. I've studied just about everything.

What is your advice for career success when it comes to getting hired, climbing the corporate ladder, or starting a company in cybersecurity?

Interestingly enough, when you start working in security, it's the so-called hard skills that will get you in the door—or understanding the technical aspects of what you're doing. But as you start climbing the corporate ladder, it's the so-called soft skills that make you a leader. You need to be able to not only engineer a system but engineer cooperation with your colleagues as well as other departments. To bring those efforts together, you need to be able to relate well to your customers (who are the business) and help design things that are helpful to them.

Also, you need to be able to influence other people to take the right security attitudes even if they don't report to you directly. Learning how to influence or socially engineer people is important. And, of course, being able to manage people and help them develop, and mediate conflict, and do all the difficult things that managers have to do with line management; all of those things are necessary if you're going to climb the corporate ladder.

What qualities do you believe all highly successful cybersecurity professionals share?

The first one I would say is curiosity, or wanting to understand how things work. And I think the second one is humility and knowing that you are never going to understand everything completely. The people who have gotten to really high positions who are very well admired and known in the industry are, for the most part, people who are very humble. I always enjoy talking with them because they are as eager to learn from me as I am to learn from them.

What is the best book or movie that can be used to illustrate cybersecurity challenges?

There are so many books, and they all seem to cover different slices of what is a really expanded whole. I don't really think there's any movie that's covered it well, and I know people who love the classics like *Sneakers* and *Hackers* and so on are going to disagree with me there, but as a professional who's worked on the defense side all this time, I've never really found a movie that I could relate to. So, I think that's long overdue.

From a facetious point of view, if I were to make a movie about the life of a CISO, a lot of it would be staring at Excel spreadsheets and turning off the notifications on your phone. It's really hard to portray, but I wish somebody could do it in a way that wasn't overly sensationalized. There are a lot of state actor attacks and sensational headlines that we see, but we don't see the really boring stuff like, "Oh, Bob has been going to the wrong website again," and "I've got to pull the logs and give them to HR, and I just hate my life right now." It'd be really interesting to get this information from a lot of CISOs and see if you could put it together into an interesting enough movie that didn't fall back into the sort of "hacker scene."

What is your favorite hacker movie?

I would have to say my favorite has always been *Real Genius*. It's not, strictly speaking, a security movie. But it sure is about hacking, and it sure is about creative people, and the ways that they interact with the world are definitely ones I can relate to. And *Real Genius* has some pretty fun songs in it.

What are your favorite books for motivation, personal development, or enjoyment?

I like a lot of science-fiction books. One that I think has helped me with motivation is called *Hardcore Zen* by Brad Warner. He is a Buddhist monk who used to be a punk rocker, and he describes how Zen Buddhism really does share a lot of the same ethos as punk rock, in that you don't just blindly trust authority, and you try to figure out for yourself what reality is. I think it's a really interesting look at a philosophical perspective.

What is some practical cybersecurity advice you give to people at home in the age of social media and the Internet of Things?

I try *not* to give them advice because it's really hard. I think the simplest thing that I tell people is this: to avoid scams, phishing, and so on, don't respond to anyone you don't know who contacts you first. I think that will cut out a lot of the problems that people tend to run into. That doesn't stop teenagers who go to really sketchy websites and end up with malware and that sort of thing, but for just about everybody else, if it's not a person you know personally, and if it's someone that's reaching out to you, don't respond in the same way that they contacted you.

What is a life hack that you'd like to share?

Sometimes I go on what I call a *data cleanse*, and I will just stop reading things, listening to things, and I put my phone away. I try to spend a lot of time without other people's words and thoughts in my head. I find that it's pretty hard at first, but it becomes relaxing the longer you do it. Today, we are so used to reading as much as we possibly can—because it's so available and it's at our fingertips—instead of picking one book and spending a week reading it and thinking about it. So, I just try to step away from all of that and try *not* to ingest as much data as possible all the time.

What is the biggest mistake you've ever made, and how did you recover from it?

I think a lot of the things we do at work or in life all seem to be the right thing at the time, and maybe in hindsight we could have done something differently, but we never really know how it would have turned out if we had. So, I try not to spend too much time second-guessing things that I did. I still feel bad about them, but I don't think about how I would have done them differently. ■

"Security is a complex problem that contains many components, and there is something for everyone. We should be open to helping and teaching all."

Twitter: @charles_nwatu • **Website:** www.linkedin.com/in/cnwatu

Charles Nwatu

Charles Nwatu is originally from Alexandria, Virginia, and currently resides with his wife and two kids in Northern California. As an information security professional, he uses his skills and experience to develop and design detection and response teams. Charles is a continuous learner and enjoys meeting and connecting with people. He also has a passion for advancing underprivileged and underrepresented communities within the STEAM community.

47

If there is one myth that you could debunk in cybersecurity, what would it be?

"Security is hard!" That would be the myth I would like to debunk. I look at security as an ongoing, evolving challenge that anyone can participate in. To start debunking this myth, I believe that, as security practitioners, we need to be explicit with our language and ensure that we are collectively speaking and using the same terminology. One of my personal goals is to reduce the barrier to entry when it comes to security and how it is explained to people. Security is a complex problem that contains many components, and there is something for everyone. We should be open to helping and teaching all.

What is one of the biggest bang-for-the-buck actions that an organization can take to improve its cybersecurity posture?

"Do less better!" Organizations should invest in performing basic security hygiene on a continuous basis. Does your organization have the ability to answer the following questions?

- What have we defined as an asset?
- How many corporate assets do we own?
- How many server assets do we own?
- What is the current software inventory of our corporate assets?
- What third-party libraries do our application or services use?
- What are the current versions of the third-party libraries that our application or services use?

I am explicit about the questions I ask so that participants in the conversation can understand what we mean and how we define it. These questions focus on vulnerability management, detection engineering, instrumentation, and monitoring. Simple investments in understanding your "assets" will help guide where and how you invest and improve your security posture.

"Organizations should invest in performing basic security hygiene on a continuous basis."

"I am probably oversimplifying this, but as I said earlier: do less better! Organizations can gain great insight by performing basic security hygiene."

How is it that cybersecurity spending is increasing but breaches are still happening?

I am probably oversimplifying this, but as I said earlier: do less better! Organizations can gain great insight by performing basic security hygiene. I see breaches as failures in our ability to understand our environments. The following quote from Matthew Syed in his book, *Black Box Thinking*, also sheds some insight into the ills that face our industry:

"Failure is rich in learning opportunities for a simple reason: in many of its guises, it represents a violation of expectation. It is showing us that the world is in some sense different from the way we imagined it to be. [...] These failures are inevitable because the world is complex and we will never fully understand its subtleties. [...] Failure is thus a signpost. It reveals a feature of our world we hadn't grasped fully and offers vital clues about how to update our models, strategies, and behaviors."[13]

In other words, throwing more money at a problem does not necessarily fix it!

Another major challenge within the security space is knowing how to effectively measure security investments. Investments are defined as tool spending, personnel hires, personnel development, process definition, and improvement. Within security, there is this concept of the "Defender's Dilemma," which basically is the idea that, as a defender, I am responsible for *all* of the things, whereas an attacker only has to find a single thing to exploit. This "single" thing could be as simple as walking into an organization and dropping a malicious USB stick, phishing, or publicly disclosing a private cloud infrastructure.

When organizations do not understand their true "asset" visibility, it is challenging to protect and monitor it. Once visibility is gained, continuous instrumentation and testing is needed to validate the organization's posture and the effectiveness of any security investments made to date.

> "When organizations do not understand their true "asset" visibility, it is challenging to protect and monitor it."

Do you need a college degree or certification to be a cybersecurity professional?

No. With that said, I do understand the importance of demonstrating your knowledge, and this can be done through many vehicles. You can do it via code, by giving back to open source projects, or through formal education. At the end of the day, demonstrating what you know as a cybersecurity professional is important; your journey is your journey.

> "At the end of the day, demonstrating what you know as a cybersecurity professional is important; your journey is your journey."

How did you get started in the cybersecurity field, and what advice would you give to a beginner pursuing a career in cybersecurity?

While attending Pennsylvania State University, I enjoyed programming, but I did not want to build applications; it just didn't excite me. During my junior year, I applied and was selected as a DISA IA scholar recipient. This program exposed me to the security side of technology, and, in particular, I loved incident response. With incident response, I had the opportunity to find the needle in the haystack, to put the puzzle together with limited pieces; I was drawn to this and have never let it go.

The advice I would give to people is that security is a way of thinking that anyone can pursue. This pursuit is your dedication to the craft. There are so many paths within security, and you should try them all. Take time to find mentors, visit meetups, or go to the various conferences. Be explicit about what you are looking for. Language matters.

What is your specialty in cybersecurity, and how can others gain expertise in your specialty?

My cybersecurity specialty is incident response. Lately, I have been rebranding incident response to detection and response engineering (DRE). It is the ability to create security tests and security sensors that act as detectors to provide analysts with data they can take action on. The response component is more than just the technical know-how; it also requires an understanding of people and how to manage an incident.

The approach I take around DRE is to always be reading and practicing. I read up on the latest attacks and various capture-the-flag write-ups, follow InfoSec folks on Twitter, and talk to red team members to understand the current attack space. Within the attack space, there will be concepts that are more applicable to your organization or area of interest. The goal is to keep learning. Security is ongoing, never static, which means there is an investment of time to keep pace with what's going on. Therefore, stay with it!

What is your advice for career success when it comes to getting hired, climbing the corporate ladder, or starting a company in cybersecurity?

The biggest advice I can give in this area is to keep learning and find what you love within security. These two things will help drive you and propel you forward.

What qualities do you believe all highly successful cybersecurity professionals share?

One of the qualities I have seen in highly successful cybersecurity professionals is the ability to explain concepts to people clearly and in such a way that people walk away having learned something new. I would also say cybersecurity professionals who take the time to think about security from their customers' perspectives (aka walking in their shoes) are the ones who ultimately develop and design thoughtful security.

What is the best book or movie that can be used to illustrate cybersecurity challenges?

Black Box Thinking by Matthew Syed. *Securing DevOps* by Julien Vehent.

What are your favorite books for motivation, personal development, or enjoyment?

On Intelligence by Jeff Hawkins. (Marcus J. Carey recommended this to me, and as a detection and response engineer, I think this book is important.) *The Secret* by Rhonda Byrne. *Start with Why* by Simon Sinek. *Black Box Thinking* by Matthew Syed (an awesome book recommended to me by Bob Lord).

What is some practical cybersecurity advice you give to people at home in the age of social media and the Internet of Things?

Keep your systems up to date—desktop, laptop, mobile, game systems. If it connects to a network, keep it up to date. When it comes to passwords, use password managers, passphrases, and two-factor authentication on all your accounts. When it comes to social media, what happens in the dark will come to light. So if you don't want it on the Web, don't do it.

What is a life hack that you'd like to share?

I'm not sure if this is a life hack or more just being a parent, but any free time I have I quickly decide how I want to spend it on myself. I divide this into three things: personal development (technical), personal development (fun), or family development. This thinking just helps me prioritize my time. I love my family and being a security practitioner, but time is a limited commodity.

What is the biggest mistake you've ever made, and how did you recover from it?

While working on a security project, I made a comment along the lines of, "If you want to run this security tool effectively, the organization will need to staff three to four team members." I did not realize, at the time, who was around me when I made that statement, and that statement was used to push for additional budget for these new hires. The only thing was that our budget had already been approved for the year, and the funds were taken from somewhere else. My director at the time called me in to discuss the ramifications of how my statement was used. From that point on, when it comes to scoping security projects properly, I make recommendations up front on what is needed to install, tune, and mature a security capability. ■

"In theory, practicing security means taking low-cost baby steps in every area possible, treating time spent practicing security as a small, incremental investment that grows."

Website: www.flyingpenguin.com

Davi Ottenheimer

Davi Ottenheimer is the founder and president of flyingpenguin, with more than 20 years' experience managing global security operations and assessments—including a decade of leading incident response and digital forensics teams. He is also a member of the faculty at Institute for Applied Network Security (IANS), serves on the board of a couple of security startups, and guest lectures at St. Pölten University of Applied Sciences. In 2012, while consulting with VMware engineering, Davi co-wrote the cloud security book *Securing the Virtual Environment: How to Defend the Enterprise Against Attack.* Lately, he is the head of product security for a popular database company and has been working on his next book, *The Realities of Securing Big Data*, about the societal risks inherent in unsecured machine learning and AI.

48

If there is one myth that you could debunk in cybersecurity, what would it be?

I sometimes hear people attempting to prove our folk tales and fables false. It is tempting to use personal expertise to debunk fantastical-sounding cybersecurity stories of inhuman skill, unearthly severity, or the astronomical likelihood of attacks. Yet, behind all of our reality-based arguments to dispel some awful-sounding threats—advanced persistent threats (APTs), nation-states, corporate mercenaries, or hackers in hoodies—lies the ancient issue that mythology actually is a great way to educate and inform.

Instead of debunking myths or making them disappear, what if we acknowledged their purpose and adjusted them to carry messages further in the direction we want to go? We could, instead of debunking, strive to enrich allegories like the myth of the solo genius attacker, or "rock-star" hackers. We also can improve upon the myths of talent scarcity and the myth of rising complexity in cybersecurity. What I'm saying is that our industry should portray myths using more human tragedies with complex narratives—inherently fallible and plagued by self-imposed vulnerabilities—to further the art of cybersecurity mythology. Years ago, I came up with "Ctrl-Alt-Delete When You Leave Your Seat" and won some awareness competitions with it. If I added a giant red penguin mythology to this phrase to make it stickier and someone started saying "giant red penguins are not real," I would be very sad about the state of our industry.

What is one of the biggest bang-for-the-buck actions that an organization can take to improve its cybersecurity posture?

I'd love to pull out some particular technology-focused action here, such as patching. Quick, everybody patch everything. Done. However, decades of experience tells me the biggest bang truly comes from setting up a reliable, repeatable discipline of practicing security. (A little wax on, wax off leads even a scrawny kid to achieve the seagull pose, for those of you who remember *The Karate Kid*.)

In theory, practicing security means taking low-cost baby steps in every area possible, treating time spent practicing security as a small, incremental investment that grows. It's like insurance, just without the adversarial lawyers writing exclusion clauses to ensure their employers' margins. In reality, some organizations take a long time to accept that security will do more good than harm, so they never truly accept the concept of practicing it regularly. These organizations hope for lottery-style returns on spending instead of treating security as small steps worth doing daily. This is backwards, of course, since perfection in pose comes from *practice*.

Two things generally push organizations out of the allure of a lottery-style approach—either friendly regulators bring fines for lack of practice or unfriendly adversaries bring breaches. This is why I say initiating disciplined, incremental approaches is one of the lowest-cost, best-result actions an organization can take—whether we're talking about patching, encryption, identity management, education, logging, or anything else. Organizations that do not regularly practice security tend to throw money away for tactical diversions and stopgaps after harm has already been done. They also tend to be blind to the strategic problems that manifest, while regular practitioners frequently report results to management. Course correction becomes harder the further you go without a safety check.

> "Course correction becomes harder the further you go without a safety check."

All that being said, each organization will still have to prioritize actions, and that really depends on specifics that come from practicing threat modeling (a part of every security action). Sometimes more bang comes from patching, while other times the bang would be biggest from logging. No matter what the organization chooses, their posture will improve the most with the least cost if they act early on—creating a discipline of practice and assigning resources to it, no matter how small.

How is it that cybersecurity spending is increasing but breaches are still happening?

If increased spending meant that bad things would stop happening completely, economists would probably lose their minds. America spends more on healthcare than other countries, and yet it has worse health and a shorter life expectancy.

This has also been linked to attempts by American politicians to gamble on private ventures that profit from harm, in much the same way that antivirus companies have delivered so little value to customers while making investors rich. Coincidence? Market analysis tells us people spend for a myriad of reasons. Leaving the market without regulation has been repeatedly proven ineffective in getting people to spend on things that reduce harm. Instead, we've learned that below a certain level of control (regulatory guidance), the probability of harm goes *up* dramatically—like driving a car faster than 12 mph without a seatbelt. The best "nudge," then, is spending above a reasonable threshold (regulatory guidance) to keep things minimally and predictably safe, even during high performance. This is far more effective than giving companies complete free reign and hoping that will eliminate all breaches.

I tend to speak about cybersecurity in terms of automobile safety because there's so much data to work with, and it's not very controversial (anymore). There's ample proof that increased seatbelt spending significantly reduced injuries. If I remember right, the drop was initially 50 percent. After that, no matter how much manufacturers were willing to spend on seatbelt technology, there was only negligible improvement. So, regulators shifted to requiring airbags and found yet another big drop in harm. The history of seatbelts thus becomes a good case study for cybersecurity spending—better results come from teams collaborating on more science-based regulations and raising our baselines in predictable areas. This has been the effect of California's Database Security Breach Notification Act (SB-1386) as well as the Payment Card Industry Data Security Standard (PCI DSS).

Interestingly, a 2018 survey by Adobe found that 83 percent of the 500 private and public cybersecurity professionals polled agreed that government regulations have a positive impact on cybersecurity.[14] With a social-good focus on the compromises necessary for regulation, also known as *good governance*, there is a reasonable chance that increased spending will reduce the pace of breaches, as we have already seen with some of these early regulations.

Do you need a college degree or certification to be a cybersecurity professional?

Oh, economics again. Whenever someone asks me if you need a certification to work in security, I ask them whether they would trust a website that doesn't use HTTPS, because that's a certificate system they ostensibly believe is essential to verifying whether a site is professional. To be fair, our cybersecurity industry's attempt to build a highly reputable certificate authority (CA) was sidetracked by "businesses" that realized you can get wealthy by charging large amounts of money to hand out weak and untrustworthy certs. A bit of a loophole, yet the point still stands. I mean, universities apparently had the same idea as shady CA companies. Obviously, you don't need or want an untrusted degree or certificate to prove you're a professional.

With that said, when an authority is undermined or compromised, you are likely better off building your own proofs. All that means is, yes, choose wisely which authority is proving your authority, even if that means yourself. I still know system administrators who offer excellent reasons for only trusting "self-signed" certs, and I have been enjoying the latest wave of administrators who believe the cost of SSL certs should be zero. College degrees for free? What? Can we call them "cert socialists?"

The whole model of requiring certification raises an economic reality that standards should be designed to provide a lower-cost means of proof in order to enable a freer exchange of information. In that sense, a college degree says you accomplished something finite and measurable, and it presents proof in a known format that could get you hired. Likewise, certification from an authority can dramatically reduce the cost of proving that you are who you claim to be. Should you happen to find less costly or easier methods of proving yourself, then you could end up ahead of the game. Most people still have to play this game because it's their best option, if not their only option, and because the authority model isn't completely broken.

How did you get started in the cybersecurity field, and what advice would you give to a beginner pursuing a career in cybersecurity?

This seems like a follow-up to the previous question. First, I have to give a shout-out to my family. Hi mom! For as long as I can remember, computers have been around. My great aunt proudly showed me photos of the "computing group" she managed in the 1950s, and one of my great uncles managed bulk power (nuclear) computing systems, while another talked of his U.S. Army days running copper telco lines behind enemy lines. Thus, I have always thought of computers in terms of international relations and war, sort of like it was going to be my generation's piston engine. My grandfather was an electrical engineer and apparently worked with some of the first U.S. Navy computing systems before he started a company that worked with silicon manufacturers. Both of my parents, by way of teaching at a university, offered me inexpensive access to computers, and we communicated by email. By the time I was leaving high school in the 1980s, I was already toying with laptops and building my own low-cost "kit" computers, and...hacking.

To put things in perspective, I was likely seen as the *least* technical among those around me. My sibling was a SunOS administrator, and back then, as a kid, I thought it was fair game to try to get around whatever access obstacles were in the way of playing *Netrek*. Hackers were treated as playful, mischievous, or malicious instead of as career-minded creative types. My first decision in terms of career was to *not* pursue my family's interest in computers and instead strike out on my own to make a mark in another field. To my grandfather's dismay, I walked away from computer science, let alone electrical engineering, and took up philosophy and political science and ended up in history. In the end, I suppose the most influential thing to kickstart my career in cybersecurity was a very wise graduate school adviser, who noticed I was always hacking around the empty lab systems. He suggested I leverage computers for a livable wage instead of just academic degrees. I believe he put it as, "Life's comforts come more easily in computer jobs, and when you get tired of that, you can always come back and suffer through a PhD."

> "Find time to break things and try to put them back together, repeatedly."

The moral of the story, and the advice I always try to give beginners, is this: find a way to the financial comforts that will allow you to be creative and curious with computers. Find time to break things and try to put them back together, repeatedly. Cybersecurity is all about shifting contexts, trying the unusual and undocumented things others might take for granted. It's also about communicating results in a way that helps people see what they were blind to before. The best people I've worked with in cybersecurity don't give up easily because their curiosity is vast, and they try the most things because their creativity runs deep.

On that note, when I finished graduate school and headed to California, I stopped to visit my great uncle. Since he was nearing retirement from his computer operations career, I figured it would be a bonding moment to tell him I now was off to start my own career as his was winding down. He looked at me and laughed, his big mustache quivering as he snickered, "You think you'll get hired to work with computers with your history degree?! That's a new one." A week later, I walked into a subsidiary of Space Applications—a Digital (DEC) VAR I found in a phone book—told them about my love of hacking macOS and TCP/IP, and they hired me on the spot because the context of computers was shifting and they needed security-minded distributed systems people like me. A few months later, I was hand-delivering cutting-edge Unix systems for rocket research to high-security campuses and responding to Windows NT breaches. The rest is...history.

What is your specialty in cybersecurity, and how can others gain expertise in your specialty?

This looks like a trick question to me. Instead of *specialization*, which felt limiting, I've always been eager to learn anything anyone was willing to throw at me.

Expertise also seemed relative, instead of absolute, so a specialization opportunity depended on the expertise of those around me. On a project—or an engagement where a team has to divide and collaborate—I'll take a special assignment, like being a cloud expert. Yet beyond that, I like to keep up on everything. I have to admit that writing a book on cloud security in 2012 (*Securing the Virtual Environment*) generated a lot of engagements where I was asked, "What's special about cloud?" Rather than push cloud as my specialization, I'd usually say, "It's mostly the same concepts, just a different context."

When it comes to specialization, I've always felt it was better to learn every position and rotate through them. The downside to being a cyber pastoralist (or shepherd) is the feeling of having the reset button pushed all the time. You need to have a strong support system to survive a really big reset. It can be incredibly humbling for an expert generalist to stay competitive with specialists all the time.

The upside is you never feel tempted to believe the myth of talent shortage or the myth that cybersecurity is becoming too complex to keep up, because working up through levels of complexity is what makes you tick. So, if I had to pick, I would stay curious and avoid over-specialization. That has been my specialty, and for the last five years, it has meant having fun breaking big data systems, advocating for encryption solutions, and hunting bad and unsafe machine learning (ML) and AI. I look forward to others establishing specialties in these areas and showing me how much of a generalist I still am. That way, I can pivot to that security thing no one is good at yet.

What is your advice for career success when it comes to getting hired, climbing the corporate ladder, or starting a company in cybersecurity?

I shifted from academia to the business world, and the best advice I can give for career success, which I learned through trial and error, is to have empathy for customer pain. Every job I've ever held has started with someone saying they had a need and asking if I could help. Same for starting a company in cybersecurity. When you find a lot of people have a problem, and if you can think of a solution that reduces it at a reasonable cost, then you have a product or service worth selling. Also important to starting a company is putting the right team together and knowing how and when to pivot from failure. I don't think I'm saying anything novel or unique here, so I'll end with a couple thoughts about corporate ladders.

First, corporate ladders tend to be unfair by design. Those at the top are controlling who they'd like to see coming up behind them, reflecting their values. Thus, historically, it's been a sordid mess of racism and misogyny. Choosing to leave and start one's own company has made more sense for excluded groups, instead of taking fruitless steps in a game fixed against them. The Chinese Exclusion Act of 1882 is linked directly to Chinese working in America leaving corporate ladders and starting restaurants and laundry services instead (because they became their own bosses). Cybersecurity had very short ladders initially, so achieving a role as an industry leader almost always meant starting one's own company for executive/top experience. Even by 2000, 30 years after cybersecurity had started, there were almost no ladder-climber role models to learn from; very few had reached a true top and stayed there.

Second, corporate ladders really are social engineering exercises, which makes them an interesting aspect of security. Those who are best at it could turn out to be insider threats, and security teams might be in a position of building safety checks to flag and investigate competitive ladder climbers who use methods counterproductive to corporate values. That might sound a bit Machiavellian, so I'll just circle back to my point about specialization. Some like to stay on a rung and become specialists, never wanting to climb out of it. That actually has value we should recognize, which might be easier if we call it a form of specialization. Others want to jump rung to rung and move along in their career, expanding as generalists across rungs. My advice is if you want to be the latter, earn those steps by being the best you can at that level/rung of specialization. Unlike a physical ladder, each step in the corporate ladder is different, and moving up a level usually requires some artifact or proof of worth.

What qualities do you believe all highly successful cybersecurity professionals share?
Brevity.

What is the best book or movie that can be used to illustrate cybersecurity challenges?
The word *hacker* itself comes from horses pulling carts in London centuries ago. So, I'm tempted to list illustrations of transportation challenges of bygone eras, such as license plates on cars to stop them from committing crimes and driving away. Instead, I'll say *Metaphors We Live By* by George Lakoff, a cognitive linguist, which was a popular book when I was in college. Lakoff makes the argument that we really shouldn't be saying "attack" and "breach" when we talk about cyber, unless we actively recognize where these terms come from and how they convey certain powerful meanings.

Another recommendation is *Zen and the Art of Motorcycle Maintenance*, a fictional autobiography from the 1970s about value systems and technology. Ironically, the author was writing computer manuals as his day job while he wrote this book at night about how to define the quality of journeys that are dependent on machines.

What is your favorite hacker movie?
One favorite is *Until the End of the World*. It's a pretty clever/artful attempt to predict the social future of technology, including security, which is strangely

accurate. I've watched *Blade Runner* far too many times, and I'd still place *Until the End of the World* ahead of it on most lists. *The 414s: The Original Teenage Hackers* documentary, about being a curious kid in 1983, is a favorite since it tipped the scales and turned all the 1970s anti-hacking bills into the big Computer Fraud and Abuse Act (CFAA). On that note, *23* (also known in Germany as *Nichts ist so wie es scheint*) is a favorite because of what it ironically gets wrong about the 1989 death of infamous hacker Karl Koch. I also have to mention my mother's movie, *The Quorum*, even though it's not strictly about computers. However, it does allude to the hacker mentality—with funny anecdotes to the police raids in 1964 where 73 people were arrested for things like playing guitar out of tune. *The Vula Connection* is also a favorite because the story is so intense and inspiring. It's about an anti-apartheid group in 1985 that used encryption to penetrate the "fortified borders" of South Africa. Can I have more than one favorite?

What are your favorite books for motivation, personal development, or enjoyment?
I read whenever I get the chance, especially poetry, which is why I founded Poetry.org in 1995. Decoding the meaning of poems in many languages is something I try to practice often for personal development. One of the weirdest feelings is spending hours translating a poem into a different language and then realizing you hate it once you get the intended meaning decoded. I look at it like an ancient version of unpacking malware. As for books, I have a lot of favorites. *Fire in the Night: Wingate of Burma, Ethiopia, and Zion* is one of them. *Nathaniel's Nutmeg* is another. It's highly motivating to learn how people overcame adversity through technology in the past and to explore the tragic mistakes they made along the way—ones that we should avoid even to this day.

What is some practical cybersecurity advice you give to people at home in the age of social media and the Internet of Things?
Think ahead of the curve. People are trying to figure out how to patch IoT like a Zenith TV repair expert trying to learn desoldering. Today, society has shifted away from repairing technology products to simply replacing them with new ones. That mentality is going to significantly affect the safety and security decisions in IoT, as people succumb to economic decisions that innovate around product rotation and disposal practices instead of repairs. It kind of makes sense when you think back to the economic reasoning that created patching in the first place. (In 1968, IBM realized software patches were less costly than hardware fixes.) So, your cybersecurity strategy in IoT will probably look increasingly like quick and inexpensive rotations to avoid even the slightest complicated/skilled fix.

Social media is looking similar to me the more it evolves down two paths. Either engineers are building tools that allow new concepts in privacy (e.g., rapid iteration and transitive contexts) or companies like Facebook are literally trying to push society back into the Dark Ages (operating as police-state tyrants, forcing constant identification/tracking on their users, and pushing propaganda in the most self-serving ways).

Future social models we need to gravitate toward allow people to control their multiple online identities in ways where they never lose control of their own data. The European Union is doing great work to that end with its General Data Protection Regulation (GDPR), which promotes privacy as a human right—floating the concept of "right to erasure"—and basically telling the Facebook executive team to get a clue about ethics. For now, the best practical advice is to delete Facebook from all your devices and convince others to do the same. Stay in touch with others using less "sticky" tools that let you easily rotate in and out. For example, contacts can be easily imported and exported with the Signal chat application. I know it sounds counterintuitive to some, so hopefully the IoT example helps illustrate why a quick replacement of a platform is as desirable as easily replacing devices.

What is a life hack that you'd like to share?

It always amazes me to think that the seminal study of wolves in the 1960s, which spoke of Alpha and Beta types, was updated and corrected by its author to clarify that *Alpha* means *parent* and *Beta* means *child*: "The female predominates primarily in such activities as pup care and defense and the male primarily during foraging and food-provisioning."[15]

More generally, Alpha represents a *caregiver*. When people throw around that they're an Alpha, they never seem to be familiar with the correction to the study and so are not referring to a desire to be a parent who feeds and defends Betas—let alone values and cares for others. My life hack has been to see those who are most likely to care for the people around them as the Alphas and those who care only for themselves as Betas. Not that the world has to be neatly divided into caregivers (leaders) and care receivers (followers), but this method has increased my productivity by refocusing my attention on empathy and compassion as natural leadership traits, even within the most competitive, dangerous, and wild environments.

What is the biggest mistake you've ever made, and how did you recover from it?

Back in the 1990s, I was doing global penetration tests on large organizations of every type. At some point, a very large manufacturer hired me to find flaws that would impact their bottom line. Fiddling with ping packets, I was trying to be sure I had enumerated every possible ingress point they could have. I wasn't going to give up easily, despite repeatedly facing setbacks with all the time zones powering down systems on local schedules—foiling my attempts to scan the world and get a comprehensive map within a deadline. Then, one early morning, I heard word that warehouses were down across Asia.

More to the point, I was hauled into an operations group meeting and asked to explain how my tests were going. Apparently, my pings had overflowed the JetDirect kernel used by HP printers, which meant "pick slips" in the warehouses went silent. I was thrilled! Nothing could be shipped. Also, I was devastated. Holy moly, I'd just crashed delivery of stuff I could only imagine had a cascading effect...scary. Fortunately, because they powered everything down and back up again daily, printing started again the next day. My persistence had found these isolated devices as well as a vulnerability that impacted the company's bottom line. They were super unhappy with the vulnerability until I framed the test in terms of professional early-warning, and we set about improving what we would today call IoT devices.

In those days, we couldn't lean on regulations to force good hygiene, so it took a bit of social engineering. Despite causing an outage, and perhaps because of the way we quickly explained and recovered from it, they hired me soon after to break their AS/400, which, unfortunately, I did almost immediately. ■

> "As an industry, we know how to build secure infrastructure, applications, and processes. What is hard is changing our behaviors and habits that are decidedly insecure."

Twitter: @BrandonPrry • **Website:** www.volatileminds.net

Brandon Perry

Brandon Perry is an engineer and consultant focusing on helping organizations secure their applications and network infrastructure. In his free time, he enjoys writing Metasploit modules and playing guitar.

49

If there is one myth that you could debunk in cybersecurity, what would it be?

The myth that security is hard. Maintaining secure networks, building secure applications, and running secure organizations aren't hard things. Securely encrypting and decrypting data is easy. People do these things every day. As an industry, we know how to build secure infrastructure, applications, and processes. What is hard is changing our behaviors and habits that are decidedly insecure. Security isn't hard. It's people that are hard, and they aren't going anywhere anytime soon.

What is one of the biggest bang-for-the-buck actions that an organization can take to improve its cybersecurity posture?

Start making implementation and process decisions assuming there *is* a breach instead of assuming there isn't one. Installing patches shouldn't be determined by whether an asset is "internal" or not, as if the internal network is any more secure than the external perimeter of the network.

"Security isn't hard. It's people that are hard, and they aren't going anywhere anytime soon."

How is it that cybersecurity spending is increasing but breaches are still happening?

It's easy to spend money on the wrong things in information security. And even if you buy the right things, it's easy to misconfigure them. Testing to make sure those complex security products are configured correctly is expensive and hard to do objectively. Not many organizations do it, so they never know the product was misconfigured to begin with.

However, correlation isn't causation. It could easily be that the organizations that aren't getting breached are vastly outspending the organizations that are. I think you'll see a difference in how upper management perceives security spending at these two different types of organizations as well. The organizations that aren't getting breached invest in their security, while the organizations that are getting breached minimize the cost.

Do you need a college degree or certification to be a cybersecurity professional?

I think the obvious answer is no to both degree and certificate. The non-obvious answer is that all of the work that goes into getting accredited is still absolutely required, if not more so. And expect to constantly feel like you're missing something that your more "lettered" colleagues aren't. It's not imposter syndrome; it's just realizing you don't have the same base of knowledge as those who went to school or are more classically trained.

How did you get started in the cybersecurity field, and what advice would you give to a beginner pursuing a career in cybersecurity?

After high school, around 2007, I started as a regular web application developer for C#/ASP.NET. I've subsequently stuck out like a sore thumb in InfoSec for being a proponent of C# and Mono/Xamarin for building tools, and C# has only recently (as of 2018) become an interesting language for red teams/offensive security researchers (you can't beat luck). After a few jobs writing C# apps, I ended up trying to go to college, but failed spectacularly. Unfortunately, I had become enthralled with computer security and how exploits worked. In my free time, I began writing Metasploit modules. This work got my foot in the door at Rapid7, and my C# experience played well with the Java-heavy stuff at R7. I guess that technically was the start of my career in InfoSec.

I don't like to give advice, but someone told me something once when I was about 20 that really stuck with me: "Work hard for the next 10 years so you can party for 40 after that instead of partying for the next 10 years and working hard for 40 catching up." You'll never have as much free time or energy to pursue hobbies or gain experience as you do when you're younger and just starting out.

What is your specialty in cybersecurity, and how can others gain expertise in your specialty?

Application security, with a particular focus on web applications. Many people who do what I do started out hacking in the beginning, and many aren't very strong coders—let alone understand how to architect complex applications. I was fortunate enough to begin writing code on a daily basis for eight hours a day, five days a week, while learning how applications were built and architected straight out of high school. This gave me a huge leg up in learning how exploits worked because I knew how to read code and was fluent in it. It also has given me insight into how layers within applications work with (or against) each other, which leads to a certain intuition about where vulnerabilities may lie or where a weakness can be abused.

Serious application development experience can give you a much better grasp on where to look for—and how to exploit—novel and unique vulnerabilities.

What is your advice for career success when it comes to getting hired, climbing the corporate ladder, or starting a company in cybersecurity?

I try not to give advice. I've been fortunate to get my foot in the door at companies early on in my career through personal relationships. That allowed me to gain real skills in the workplace before many of my friends. I didn't go to college; I just started working after high school. I've not sought titles or positions; I've only pursued jobs I felt I would feel fulfilled in. My jobs have always been technical; I've never managed people, so climbing the corporate ladder and starting a company are out of my wheelhouse. In the end, it's as much (if not more) *who* you know as it is *what* you know.

> "I've been fortunate to get my foot in the door at companies early on in my career through personal relationships."

What qualities do you believe all highly successful cybersecurity professionals share?

I think that depends on what your definition of *successful* is. Risk management skills, I think, are a universal need across InfoSec. Some people may think you need to constantly publish work to be considered successful. We aren't in academia, and there's already a lot of poor and misleading security content out there anyway. Practical attacks from 15 years ago still work consistently today. Maybe successful means your organization is more secure today than it was yesterday. By that standard, you've never heard of the most highly successful security professionals out there. I don't want to assume qualities, but I'm sure they are hardworking and underappreciated.

> "Risk management skills, I think, are a universal need across InfoSec."

What is the best book or movie that can be used to illustrate cybersecurity challenges?

I'm going to include a TV show here: *Star Trek: The Original Series*. In Kirk's own words: "Risk is a starship's business. It's what we do." The Enterprise as a whole is an organization that has to operate securely, maintain security, and, in some instances, enact security on short notice. Kirk relies on luck a bit more than I like, but, considering the odds, I think his threat model allows it. It's good to be good, but it's better to be lucky.

What is your favorite hacker movie?

Caddyshack. Tons of hacking. It's the first instance of the Gopher protocol (years ahead of its time). The film also makes an excellent example of false positives and their potential effects (using a pool and a chocolate bar).

What are your favorite books for motivation, personal development, or enjoyment?

Free to Choose by Milton Friedman

Basic Economics by Thomas Sowell

The Meditations (particularly Book 2) by Marcus Aurelius

I read a lot of American and world history pre-1950. Did you know people had security problems before computers?

What is some practical cybersecurity advice you give to people at home in the age of social media and the Internet of Things?

Again, I try not to give advice, but I do want people to realize this more: you are not the only person who has access to your phone and the data on it, even if you are the only person currently accessing your phone. This doesn't mean you shouldn't use your phone and that you should live in a cave. Many of us rely on our phones to a large degree, and there are certainly security enhancements our phones make to our lives (multifactor authentication is one example). However, all of the cheap, insecure phones that we don't want in rich Western countries will end up in the countries with a lot less money, with governments that would love to have remote access to their population's phones. These phones are often the only computer a family (or multiple families) has and can be the only access to news or communication outside of their immediate community. As the richer countries are able to buy more secure phones or mobile devices, the cheaper, more insecure phones will end up with those who need the security the most.

> "Again, I try not to give advice, but I do want people to realize this more: you are not the only person who has access to your phone and the data on it, even if you are the only person currently accessing your phone."

What is a life hack that you'd like to share?

Don't start sentences until you know how they are going to end.

What is the biggest mistake you've ever made, and how did you recover from it?

I feel like "mistake" implies I regret something and wish things had turned out differently. I'm not sure I've had events in my life that I wish had turned out differently or I wish hadn't happened at all (at least professionally, and mostly personally). I think it's important to realize every situation has something you can take from it and learn. Even if learning is painful, I'm not sure it's ever regrettable or a mistake. As engineers, the term *bug* is just a euphemism for "mistake." Of course, every bug is a learning opportunity for someone, and I doubt I'd find many disagreeing with that. ■

> "If more organizations focused on doing the basics well, rather than focusing on fancy new technologies, we'd be better off."

Twitter: @gdead • **Website:** cycleoverride.org

Bruce Potter

Bruce Potter is the CISO at Expel and founder of The Shmoo Group, and helps run ShmooCon. He has been doing cybersecurity for more than 20 years and can best be summed up as a "jack of all trades, master of none." Bruce has dabbled in network security, wireless and mobile security, AppSec, product assessments, pentesting, and risk management—with many of his ramblings ending up as DEF CON talks over the years.

50

If there is one myth that you could debunk in cybersecurity, what would it be?

There are myths? I think there are a lot of bare truths out there that people choose to ignore. Like the fact that while antivirus isn't perfect, it's still necessary. Like the fact that we've known how to build secure systems for 40+ years, but the economics and business motivations aren't there to do it. Like the fact that closing the workforce gap not only needs to focus on training and professionalization, but it also needs to address advances in technology as well. Maybe the myth is "We have myths." The reality is we're terrible at recognizing the truth.

What is one of the biggest bang-for-the-buck actions that an organization can take to improve its cybersecurity posture?

Do the basics. Patch, limit use of USBs, and use two-factor authentication (2FA). These are huge. If more organizations focused on doing the basics well, rather than focusing on fancy new technologies, we'd be better off.

How is it that cybersecurity spending is increasing but breaches are still happening?

You can only buy the products that exist. We can't buy secure products because our developers can't build secure systems. So, all the later lifecycle security spending is just putting good money after bad. It's necessary to try to hunt down adversaries, patch vulnerabilities, and do all the things we know to be "cybersecurity." But the reality is, without more secure building blocks, we'll keep having breaches, no matter how much we're spending.

Do you need a college degree or certification to be a cybersecurity professional?

Nope. That doesn't mean it's not a good idea to have one, though. I struggle with the multiple ways we try to measure what people know in this space—college degrees, certs, demonstration of personal projects—they're all fraught with danger. Undergrad degrees didn't exist 12 years ago, so anyone over the age of 34 is unlikely to have an undergrad degree in cybersecurity. Certs are both a test of what you know as well as a *hugely* profitable thing for the certifying bodies. And doing things on your own time means that the industry expects you to have a totally fucked-up work-life balance. I don't have a good answer for knowing whether a person is capable of doing their job.

The best answer I have is, "Find someone who knows more than you, and have them interview the person." It's very much a per-person call as to what you know and how you'll fit into an org. That's hugely unsatisfying and fraught with opportunities for bias and discrimination.

How did you get started in the cybersecurity field, and what advice would you give to a beginner pursuing a career in cybersecurity?

I got started because one semester I helped the on-campus supercomputing center track down a person who had used our VAX system to break into their Cray. The very next semester, I was almost expelled because I used the command "<username>" to let a friend use my shell to kill a runaway process they had created. (The supercomputer folks thought "su" could only "switch user" to root and figured I had hacked their system.) That's when I realized security was a very nuanced area, and I wanted to learn more.

As far as how to get started, as Nike says, "Just Do It." I never asked permission or waited for someone to tell me what to do. I just did shit I found interesting. Turns out it was all cybersecurity related, and it all worked out. But I did very little asking when I was young. I just did what made sense to me and learned from it.

What is your specialty in cybersecurity, and how can others gain expertise in your specialty?

Erm...uh...risk management these days? I've done a lot of stuff, and it's hard to think I have a specialization. Really, in non-IT security roles, I think that's important. A broad base of knowledge gives you a lot of flexibility to help your company and your customers. (IT security is different and requires domain knowledge of the tools and products in the space—very much a different animal, IMO.)

What is your advice for career success when it comes to getting hired, climbing the corporate ladder, or starting a company in cybersecurity?

Do what you love. Don't feel like there's a particular path you need to follow or a progression of skills/knowledge/jobs. At one point in my career, I went from being a pretty deep-level software security consultant—helping people build secure systems at a fundamental level—to doing security operations for service providers because I wanted to do ops for a while. Those two dots definitely aren't connected in most "corporate ladders," but I loved both jobs and learned a ton from both, and I could actually apply a lot of what I knew in both. When the time came to quit ops and do something else, I did so unapologetically. It was time to move on. I then did IC/DoD stuff, started my own company, sold it, did the CTO thing, and now I'm the CISO in a startup. That's not a path, but I've loved it.

What qualities do you believe all highly successful cybersecurity professionals share?

Heh...the willingness to say "fuck it." To do the right thing for yourself and others, even if it's not the easy thing. We battle people and orgs that are not trying to do the right thing. In fact, they're trying to do the opposite. So, becoming wed to a plan or a course of action makes us unable to respond to threats, both tactically and strategically. Getting an idea, knowing it's right, and saying "fuck it" leads to much better places.

What is your favorite hacker movie?

Die Hard 4. I saw that and thought, "Yeah, that could happen."

What are your favorite books for motivation, personal development, or enjoyment?

Trout fishing books. Learning to tie flies and catch trout is my current "keeps me sane" hobby.

What is some practical cybersecurity advice you give to people at home in the age of social media and the Internet of Things?

First, realize you're not a target. If you are a target, you know. You're a director of an agency or a CEO or something; 99.999 percent of the time, you're not a target. Knowing that, don't worry about the security of your IoT device. Worry about the company providing it to you, their cloud service that feeds it, and what they're going to do with that data. If you don't pay them by the month, you probably can't trust them. Don't use it if you don't pay for the service (looking at you, Amazon and Google). Use Apple products. Seriously. They're hard to hack, a small part of the market, and just not attractive to mass-market attackers.

What is a life hack that you'd like to share?

That the term *life hack* isn't really a thing. It's just learning. Some things you learn are cooler than others, but binning knowledge into different buckets isn't useful as a tool. You're better off just learning what you want and not worrying if it bubbles up to the level of being a "life hack."

What is the biggest mistake you've ever made, and how did you recover from it?

I can't think of a lot of "big mistakes" I've made. I've made a bunch of small ones that, when added together, equaled something much larger. I think the biggest mistake you can make is not recognizing the little mistakes. Not being honest with yourself about what you're doing and whether you're doing the right thing. In the end, letting a million little cuts add up is just as bad as one large one...and much more likely. ∎

> "Invest in educating employees. Awareness goes a long way in a world where lying and social engineering are the keys to most doors."

Twitter: @EdwardPrevost • **Website:** edwardprevost.info

Edward Prevost

51

Edward Prevost started with computing at a young age when his uncle (a professor) gave him C and BASIC textbooks. Having only school computers, he mostly theorized and scribbled on paper. Fast-forward and today Edward uses his powers to help organizations stay secure in cyberspace. He also enjoys wrestling, powerlifting, soccer, RPGs (not the grenades), comics, sci-fi, epistemology, and making people laugh.

If there is one myth that you could debunk in cybersecurity, what would it be?

I would want the world to know that Marcus J. Carey does indeed hack better while bearded and that sometimes, just sometimes, it's not actually China or Russia that did it.

What is one of the biggest bang-for-the-buck actions that an organization can take to improve its cybersecurity posture?

Invest in educating employees. Awareness goes a long way in a world where lying and social engineering are the keys to most doors. This also applies to technical awareness. Encouraging, paying for, or otherwise providing employees opportunities to become more technically astute is money and time well spent.

How is it that cybersecurity spending is increasing but breaches are still happening?

As the depth and breadth of complexity in computing increases, no amount of spending is going to make that stop growing. Most compromises can be reduced to basic awareness failures. As long as there is a deficit in awareness, there will continue to be a steady increase of breaches. We need a massive cultural shift in the sharing of technical information and partnering across all industries if we really want to see breaches slow down.

> "Most compromises can be reduced to basic awareness failures. As long as there is a deficit in awareness, there will continue to be a steady increase of breaches."

Do you need a college degree or certification to be a cybersecurity professional?

Lulz...nope.

How did you get started in the cybersecurity field, and what advice would you give to a beginner pursuing a career in cybersecurity?

I was blessed to be exposed to computing at a young age whilst helping my father at the Rensselaer Polytechnic Institute (RPI). Although I had been involved in InfoSec from a young age (thanks to RPI), I began my career pursuing nursing. Then, in God's good providence, I was given an opportunity to move into application security at the very hospital I was working at.

My advice would be to look into everything! Security is applicable in every industry and practice, and there may be one specifically that you'll find most enjoyable and rewarding over all the others. And if you're looking into InfoSec for money, stop and think. On average, one will spend more time with co-workers and working over the course of their life than with their own immediate family. Don't plop yourself into InfoSec only to be regretful or embittered later. It can be lonely, long, and monotonous.

What is your specialty in cybersecurity, and how can others gain expertise in your specialty?

If I were to have a specialty, it would be the ability to tackle multiple specialties. I've spent an embarrassing number of hours looking for POP POP RET, identifying bad characters in protocol calls, reading, studying, social networking, building things that don't work and some that worked too well, and playing in my home lab. It worked for me, but it may not for you. I found these practices to be the most efficacious way for me to gain new and useful skills, both technical and interpersonal. Try things out. Feel out various pedagogical patterns, see what fits you, and then keep drinking it up.

> "Try things out. Feel out various pedagogical patterns, see what fits you, and then keep drinking it up."

What is your advice for career success when it comes to getting hired, climbing the corporate ladder, or starting a company in cybersecurity?

Remember your roots, and always think rationally. There are many people along the way who will want to say they "know" you or will want to be around when you're executing on something "cool." But you know who *really* "knows" you, and they'd be there regardless. Remember them; and as much as possible, keep hanging around them, because none of us gets out of this whole thing alive, and a friend is always a great thing to have.

What qualities do you believe all highly successful cybersecurity professionals share?

Genuine compassion and a never-ending desire to learn. They also all seem to tolerate reading for nefariously long periods of time.

What is the best book or movie that can be used to illustrate cybersecurity challenges?

Alice in Wonderland. Creative thinking and an approach to problems that allows for unique and differing ways to solve the same problem.

What is your favorite hacker movie?

The Computer Wore Tennis Shoes (1969).

What are your favorite books for motivation, personal development, or enjoyment?

- *The Scriptures* (66 books of the Textus Receptus) by God
- *The Christian's Daily Walk* by Henry Scudder
- *Where the Sidewalk Ends* by Shel Silverstein
- *What Color Is Your Parachute?* by Richard Nelson Bolles

What is some practical cybersecurity advice you give to people at home in the age of social media and the Internet of Things?

Don't click stuff!

What is a life hack that you'd like to share?

Find out what part of the day you prefer to labor. Are you a night owl, an early bird, or a daytime dog? And do what you can to facilitate working during that time.

What is the biggest mistake you've ever made, and how did you recover from it?

The Ninth Commandment requires us to always tell the truth... I was the security lead for a *very* large advertising effort taking place during a national sporting event. I had failed to secure a form for a certain type of attack. When I realized this, I quickly notified every team I could. Unfortunately, several of the attacks happened. Thankfully, secondary protections prevented serious damage. I humbly recognized my failure during the large post-event debrief and was voted to receive a prestigious award for my cross-team efforts and honesty. ■

"Fail hard, and fail often. You're going to mess up, and that's okay. Just remember to learn from those failures so you don't repeat them."

Twitter: @SteveD3 • **Website:** about.me/SteveD3

Steve Ragan

Father. Hacker. Journalist, covering national security and information security.

52

If there is one myth that you could debunk in cybersecurity, what would it be?

I would like to see a few myths done away with. The first is that zero-day vulnerabilities are the ultimate risk and should be one of the top focal points when developing a security program. That's just not true. In fact, most attacks will originate via phishing, exploiting weak or improper controls, or leveraging existing (old) vulnerabilities.

Another myth I'd like to see done away with is the concept that security should come second or that breaches are just "the cost of doing business" within an organization. Being willing to accept a data breach because you refuse to dump legacy code or apps, or have some desire to keep a few Windows NT boxes on the network, is just backward thinking.

What is one of the biggest bang-for-the-buck actions that an organization can take to improve its cybersecurity posture?

Hands down it's limiting access and controlling user permissions. Least privilege does more to strangle malware than any endpoint product could ever do. The problem is most organizations can't or won't do this because their users complain or suffer workflow issues. And even if the workflow issues are imagined, the constant stream of tickets related to admin rights drags the help desk down to the point that it's just easier to let people have elevated access.

There's also the problem of remote workers (who usually request admin rights) and executives who will not work with anything less than administrator access.

How is it that cybersecurity spending is increasing but breaches are still happening?
The budgets are spent on shiny boxes and checkbox-based security solutions. It's great to have a FireEye or CrowdStrike appliance, but if said products are not tuned or used to their full potential, they're essentially bricks. The fact is, most security purchases require massive investments in resources (people, money, infrastructure), and once they're purchased and installed—provided they meet expectations and/or requirements—they're left alone. It isn't hard to get past defenses if you have valid credentials, which are usually phished, guessed, or located in password dumps. (LinkedIn's data breach has led to countless secondary incidents because people recycle passwords.)

Do you need a college degree or certification to be a cybersecurity professional?
I don't believe so, no. While a degree or certification will help and lately does get you past the HR firewall, it's your drive, passion, and experience that push you forward in security. Most of us working in InfoSec today started out as IT; security was something that landed in our laps, and it was sink or swim. Not to push the "get off my lawn" narrative, but when I was coming up, we didn't have security-based classes in college, and computer science was mostly the basics.

How did you get started in the cybersecurity field, and what advice would you give to a beginner pursuing a career in cybersecurity?
I came into work one day and had a choice: do security or get a new job. So, I started with endpoint defenses, then moved to a firewall, and so on. I ended up in a dual role, as I ran the help desk and the security team (on paper, the security team was just me really), but it was educational.

> "For those just starting out, I would say find something about security you're passionate about and chase it."

For those just starting out, I would say find something about security you're passionate about and chase it. If you're into phishing and social engineering, develop something no one has—a new awareness program or method of attack—and keep building. One other bit of advice is to fail. Fail hard, and fail often. You're going to mess up, and that's okay. Just remember to learn from those failures so you don't repeat them.

What is your specialty in cybersecurity, and how can others gain expertise in your specialty?
Social engineering and socially based attacks. After that, I would say my other specialty is network engineering. I would suggest reading as much as you can about human reactions and responses, what makes people tick, and how they act under pressure. There are a lot of social engineering books on the market, but I'd skip them and start with psychology and sociology first. I've found that those topics help me more than anything. You have to be comfortable talking to people and talking to them about anything. As for the engineering stuff, most of my training was hands-on. I learned by breaking and fixing.

What is your advice for career success when it comes to getting hired, climbing the corporate ladder, or starting a company in cybersecurity?

Do it. Just run out there and do it. Fall flat on your face, stand up, and keep pushing. Security is hard; IT is too. But none of us working got here without learning a few lessons along the way—including some that were learned the hard way. Honestly, my successes are great, but I treasure my failures. I learned more that way. When you're looking for a job, don't sweat the interview. Relax and be ready to show why you deserve a spot on the team. Showcase your talents and skills, and explain how you solved a really challenging problem. Most of all, remember it isn't bragging if you've done it or can do it and have proof.

What qualities do you believe all highly successful cybersecurity professionals share?

The ability to learn. The ability to adapt. The ability to realize they know nothing and are still students, even if they've got 20 years on the job.

What is the best book or movie that can be used to illustrate cybersecurity challenges?

There have been a few movies that have come close, but I can't really think of any. Honestly, if they were realistic, they wouldn't be entertaining. No one wants to see someone sit at a computer for days randomly typing and hitting the Backspace key over and over.

What is your favorite hacker movie?

Hackers. It was awesome 20 years ago, and it's awesome now.

What are your favorite books for motivation, personal development, or enjoyment?

I like reading Mack Bolan novels and Mitch Rapp novels. They're good for long flights. Both are spy thrillers.

What is some practical cybersecurity advice you give to people at home in the age of social media and the Internet of Things?

Limit what you share and how you share it. There is nothing wrong with having a few close friends on one platform and thousands of others on another platform. So: Facebook (close friends/family) and Twitter (everyone else). On Facebook, lock it down, keep it out of public view, and only share with the group. On Twitter, keep things basic and simple; try to avoid having deep conversations about sensitive stuff. As for Internet of Things...change your default passwords.

What is a life hack that you'd like to share?

Only check social media and email at the top of the hour. Make this a habit and you'll get more done at work.

What is the biggest mistake you've ever made, and how did you recover from it?

I formatted the CEO's laptop and lost about 1.5TB of MP3s and movies when I was working the help desk. Lucky for me, she had a backup at home, so I was able to restore them. ■

Twitter: @s7ephen • **Website:** iot.security

Stephen A. Ridley

53 Stephen A. Ridley is a security researcher with more than 10 years of experience in software development, software security, and reverse engineering. In the last few years, he has spoken on these topics and presented his research on every continent except Antarctica. Stephen and his work have been featured on NPR and NBC, as well as in *Wired*, *The Washington Post*, *Fast Company*, *VentureBeat*, *Slashdot*, *The Register*, and other publications. Stephen has authored a number of information security articles and co-written several texts. The most recent of these is *Android Hacker's Handbook*, published by John Wiley & Sons. He has guest lectured at NYU, Rensselaer Polytechnic Institute (RPI), Dartmouth, and other universities on the subject of software exploitation and reverse engineering. Stephen is on the programming/review committees of USENIX WOOT, Securing Smart Cities, and BuildItSecure.ly. He also serves on the board of IndySci.org, a California 501(c)(3) nonprofit devoted to making "open source" pharmaceuticals a reality.

If there is one myth that you could debunk in cybersecurity, what would it be?

From a big-picture perspective, I think the biggest myth is more of this pervasive notion that security will eventually be "solved." It permeates cybersecurity product marketing, and it's ever present in the tension between internal security staff and the rest of the organization. It is *always* there, and try as we might, we can never eradicate this. We can, however, get "good enough." By throwing all threats and attack types on the board and seeing where the large clusters are, we can definitely take minimal steps toward eradicating those big clusters of risk. Cybersecurity is really just a niche version of "risk and quality assurance."

What is one of the biggest bang-for-the-buck actions that an organization can take to improve its cybersecurity posture?

Risk is really relative to the organization. I learned this when working as a consultant (first at Matasano and then at Xipiter). A *good* consultant and cybersecurity subject-matter expert, who acts as a trusted advisor to an organization, doesn't go in with a script of remediations and techniques. Instead, he or she empathetically looks at the organization (and what people in that organization care about most) and then pulls from his or her knowledge to help build a plan to strike at the "center of mass" of those risks. One thing is true, though: the best "bang-for-the-buck" security measures (no matter what kind of organization) have one commonality—simplicity.

For example:

- At McAfee, I developed secure coding practices for all of the company's worldwide developers. And the best thing we did there was make it easy for devs to use secure coding practices by publishing safe libraries for them to use (Java, C, C++). We also did simple checks at the time of code commit. This killed *tons* of bugs.

- At Xipiter, we advised hardware/IoT companies to just use simple tamper switches that will inform you if someone has opened a device and to disable business logic in the firmware.

- At Senrio, we created a simple passive asset identification and anomaly detection network monitoring solution that helps people see all the things on their network (even things that they didn't know were there). Asset identification isn't a "sexy" InfoSec problem, but it is what people currently lack.

All of these things have simplicity in common, no matter what the organization. For the standard enterprise, I would say the biggest bang for your buck is *visibility*. You can't protect what you don't know is there. Don't assume you know how everything is interconnected and how your users are *actually* using resources—gather intel first. Identify assets. See how they communicate. And from there, start snipping bad practices. Visibility is key; you can't protect what you can't see.

How is it that cybersecurity spending is increasing but breaches are still happening?

This is a great question, and I possibly have a different opinion on this. Spending is definitely being driven by awareness of "the art of the possible" growing within the organization. However, I think the breaches are "still happening," or even happening more often, for reasons we might not think of.

As an example, between 1988 and 1996, breast cancer rates skyrocketed. In fact, other kinds of cancer rates have increased dramatically, even within the last few years. On the surface, this paints a very gloomy picture. And, in fact, there are many predatory product companies and charitable orgs that use this in their marketing. But when you actually dive into the research, you learn that the cancer rates themselves never increased. It was the *detection rates* that increased. In the case of breast cancer, between 1988 and 1996, mammography had a renaissance. Computing was getting cheaper, and some of the niche tech also got dramatically cheaper, so the equipment was less expensive to operate and became more abundant. For other cancers, machine learning and image analysis techniques exploded in the early 2000s, and this dramatically increased detection rates.

So, I offer that example to explain what I believe is happening in cybersecurity. I contend that the breaches were already happening. And the reason these incidences have seemingly increased is because our visibility into the problem has also increased.

Do you need a college degree or certification to be a cybersecurity professional?

I don't believe you need a degree to be good at cybersecurity. I will, however, say that some of the best cybersecurity professionals I have met came from *other* well-educated technical backgrounds first (CS, mathematics, robotics, even civics). The things that are most important are drive, the ability to logic/reason your way through a challenge, and being willing to try crazy things.

How did you get started in the cybersecurity field, and what advice would you give to a beginner pursuing a career in cybersecurity?

The best advice I can give to cybersecurity newcomers is "Trust your technolust." Trust that excitement you feel when you sit down in front of a screen full of colorful text. Trust the excitement you feel when you think about networks and computing, and even future-leaning stuff like virtual reality (VR), augmented reality (AR), and artificial intelligence (AI). All of those things are your engine. They fuel your passion, and it's your passion that's going to make you work harder and late into the night, giving you those "eureka moments" that help you level up.

Also, get good at reading people. You'll waste a lot of time trying to learn from people who you'll later discover don't really know as much as they let on. Stay true to what it is you want to learn, and if you find someone you can learn from, latch on and drain them of everything. And then, the hardest thing…stay true to yourself. Don't pretend to be anyone else as you learn from them. Your vision and your perspective are going to help you find *your* novel solutions.

What is your specialty in cybersecurity, and how can others gain expertise in your specialty?

For the last few years, I have been running a product company. So, these days, I spend a lot of time in front of customers or helping people understand what we are doing and how it relates to cybersecurity. My love and passion, however, is reverse engineering/exploitation. I love building tools that do neat things. Exploits, or "software lock picks," are probably my absolute favorite. But, in general, I love just understanding how a technology works. There comes a point in every great project when you get goosebumps and have that epiphany moment. I love that feeling; I'm addicted to it. The best way to learn is to self-teach and find others in your niche who you can learn from. And *play, play, play.* You have to play to learn. Set up things at home, or in a place where you can freely experiment. No matter what part of InfoSec you want to specialize in, I have found this to be the commonality.

What is your advice for career success when it comes to getting hired, climbing the corporate ladder, or starting a company in cybersecurity?

Starting companies is overrated, I think. It's really just something you do because you realize that it's the only path to "creating the thing" or "doing the thing" you want to do at any appreciable scale. I don't want to piss in anyone's cornflakes, but I personally don't think it's any fun to start a business "just because." There has to be a driver or a reason, and the company is simply the vehicle for that.

That said, I think the most important thing in building a career in InfoSec (aside from building a reputation as someone who "knows their stuff") is to have empathy for people. Read them, understand where they're pointed; and if it aligns with what you want to do, fly formation with them for a bit. I think staying genuine and honest and professional is the most important thing. Then, when it's time for you to break formation and fly solo or join a new formation, do it in a way that makes everyone feel comfortable and happy to welcome you back again.

What qualities do you believe all highly successful cybersecurity professionals share?

Success is overrated. I would challenge people to look for *excellence* over success. Success is the *end*, but excellence is the *journey*. I try to align myself with people who have rectitude, speak honestly, and have demonstrated that they know how to intelligently navigate tough spots. I would say the rarest and most valuable gem is a person's ability to "get it done." There are *a lot* of people who just do busywork or throw a lot of smoke and glitter in the air. But if you see people executing or "doing what it takes" to get to the objective, that is really the rarest quality I have seen in people, regardless of career path. Smart people can do anything. So, if you have to filter, look for smart people who can get dropped into new environments and achieve the objective without a lot of handholding and realignment. These people are rare. And you'll likely want to work with them for the rest of your life in some capacity or another.

What is the best book or movie that can be used to illustrate cybersecurity challenges?

Wow, there are lots of great books out there. When I was in grade school, I fell in love with William Gibson's work. Now, as an adult, I've since gone back to re-read them, and they were almost unreadable. Hah! I guess my point is this: don't necessarily look for self-help books or books in which some successful person tells you what they think. I've gotten the most fuel and rejuvenation from books and movies that fed my technolust. They made me dream of new technologies and ways to use technology. I think it's that forward thinking that fuels you to improve and evolve tech instead of just "accept that this is how it is."

What is your favorite hacker movie?

My favorite hacker movie...oh, man. I spent many years toiling in obscurity because, at the time, manga and anime were really the only place I could fully indulge in "techy sci-fi futurism." I loved the now-famous Ghost in the Shell manga series (and animated 1995 movie). *Roujin Z* was another favorite. *Patlabor, Bubblegum Crisis, Battle Angel Alita*, and *Memories* by Katsuhiro Otomo are also amazing.

There were some great, cheesy hacker movies like *New Rose Hotel, Johnny Mnemonic*, and *The Lawnmower Man*. Then, when I was in high school, *Hackers* came out. And as much as I made fun of that movie, I secretly loved it. It made me read *The Cuckoo's Egg* and *Three Days of the Condor* and all these other books. As I neared the end of high school, *The Matrix* was released, and that movie just confirmed what I had spent most of my young life consuming in obscurity. I finally got to show my family what it was that I was thinking about, and watching and reading, in all these strange movies and books. *The Matrix* put cyberpunk in the mainstream, and after it, I had to do less explaining. And lastly, *Sneakers*. By far the best. And my man Branford Marsalis did the soundtrack!

What are your favorite books for motivation, personal development, or enjoyment?

Three books that blew my mind were *Hyperspace* by Michio Kaku (which I read in the latter years of high school), *The Elegant Universe* by Brian Greene, and *Linked: The New Science of Networks* by Albert-Laszlo Barabasi. These three books were like gateway drugs to thinking about life and the universe in new ways, especially that last book. More recently, as I'm getting older, the books that have really resonated with me and my career are *Zero to One* by Peter Thiel, *Essentialism: The Disciplined Pursuit of Less* by Greg McKeown, and *Venture Deals* by Brad Feld—and one or two others by Brad Feld that relate to business. *The Black Swan* by Nassim Nicholas Taleb and *Blink* by Malcolm Gladwell are also great recent books for me. *Tragedy and Hope* by Carroll Quigley is also an amazing read.

What is some practical cybersecurity advice you give to people at home in the age of social media and the Internet of Things?

I travel a lot internationally, and one thing that astounds me is how much American consumers really believe the marketing spin—especially as it relates to IoT and social media/online services. For example, consumers in Asia, and the European Union think Americans are crazy for buying cellphones that only work with a given service provider. They just don't stand for that. Ironically, America is where most (if not all) of this technology innovation originated, because Americans are largely the most entrepreneurial in the world, and our government fosters this in a lot of good ways.

That said, once these products get to market, American consumers are woefully unprepared to think critically about them. They tend to suspend disbelief very easily, so it has led to a whole glut of privacy-violating online services and products (especially in IoT). The best advice is to just think critically. Why put an always-on microphone and camera in your house just because it can help you get recipes when your hands are kneading bread?

What is a life hack that you'd like to share?

Life hacks are so abundant these days, it's hard to think of anything good. Maybe get an Imgur account. It lets you skim funny images in your downtime, and every few days a gallery of cool life hacks will pop up.

What is the biggest mistake you've ever made, and how did you recover from it?

The biggest mistakes I've ever made stemmed from not trusting my gut. I think, especially as an entrepreneur, you want to do what is best for the business, which means fully recognizing that your decisions may not be the best course of action. So, naturally you seek other opinions and more information to double-check your decision-making—or defer to someone else to make the decision. In virtually all of these cases, I have regretted the outcome or had to expend extra energy to undo the mistake.

I'm still learning how to navigate, but I've definitely gotten better at decreasing the deliberation time when my gut is pointing in a different direction. And to that end, I think it's extremely important to "re-center" yourself, whether that's spending time with family, going to church, or crushing it at the gym. Whatever it is, I have very recently learned (within the last six months) that you have to *forcefully* take time to re-center yourself. That means saying, "No, I can't take that important call right now because I have to get to the gym." Otherwise, if you don't take that time, even your "gut decisions" will be completely wrong. ■

> "I had the skills necessary to apply for the positions, but it was the people I knew who introduced me to the people who were hiring."

Twitter: @da_667

Tony Robinson

Tony Robinson is a security professional with expertise in threat intelligence, malware triage, and network security monitoring. Tony is the author of *Building Virtual Machine Labs: A Hands-On Guide*, as well as a course instructor for an online training course of the same name. Tony has a decade of combined experience in information technology and information security positions. When he's not working, he can be found traveling with his wife, Rebecca, and two basset hounds, Henry and Sam.

54

If there is one myth that you could debunk in cybersecurity, what would it be?

There is no such thing as "unhackable." There is only mitigation of risk, reduction of risk, and acceptance of risk. The only unhackable, 100 percent secure system is the one that is powered off.

What is one of the biggest bang-for-the-buck actions that an organization can take to improve its cybersecurity posture?

Situational awareness. And what I mean by that is proper software and asset inventory management. Companies pay untold amounts of money to large security vendors with solutions that promise to passively collect and index both your asset and software inventory over time, but oftentimes, these solutions are extremely flawed. Keep track of what is running, where on your network it's running, and what hardware (or cloud) it is running on.

Companies pay untold amounts of money to large security vendors with solutions that promise to passively collect and index both your asset and software inventory over time, but oftentimes, these solutions are extremely flawed.

It makes patch management and vulnerability management loads easier if you have this information on hand and regularly updated.

How is it that cybersecurity spending is increasing but breaches are still happening?

Focus is being applied in all the wrong places. Companies don't want to have to hire people to manage the balance between usability and security; they want a magic, machine-learning AI turnkey solution that they can drop in place and forget about, not realizing that this is not how cybersecurity works. Machine-learning AI turnkey solutions don't tell you that you have RDP exposed all over your perimeter. These solutions don't tell you that the IoT firmware you're shipping in the latest internet-enabled device you're bringing to market with an ancient version of the Linux kernel is a terrible idea. These solutions don't tell you that one of your users who happened to use their company email address for registering to a service that got breached also reused their company password on this service, and the service did not hash their passwords, so the hackers who acquired those passwords are coming for your company next.

Companies would rather pay for cybersecurity insurance and just accept that breaches are inevitable rather than do anything more than the absolute minimum required to pass compliance and/or acquire said cyber insurance policy. That being said, while the bar is still low, vendor solutions are exorbitantly priced—if not for the hardware and software, then for the licensing and/or support that is mandatory for running whatever appliance or solution the business has bought into.

Do you need a college degree or certification to be a cybersecurity professional?

If you had asked me this at the beginning of my career, I would've told you that getting a degree is kind of pointless. There are so many hoops you have to jump through—core curriculum and electives—just to get that piece of paper, not to mention the mountains of debt. It's a huge ask in this day and age of record-high tuition rates, combined with record-low tuition assistance and relaxed rulings on predatory loan practices. I had professors who, at the time, I thought were crazy and gave me stupid assignments. But my college experience made me more well rounded. I learned to see alternate points of view. I learned to write well-thought-out research. I learned to present an argument. I learned communication by necessity. Those communication skills are invaluable. I learned public speaking at college, and the more I talked at security conferences and the more I wrote well-thought-out blog posts, the better I got, and the more respect I was given.

Soft skills, written communication, and oral communication are extremely important with regard to cybersecurity careers. You can be the smartest security professional ever, but if you are unbearable to work with and are incapable of reading your audience to determine how you should interact with them—and/or unable to relate problems to them in a way that they understand—then you're not going to get far. I learned how to do a lot of that in college. Most will tell you that you don't need a degree to excel in cybersecurity, but I also want to point out that a degree and/or certifications will not *hurt* your chances of success either. If someone gives you a hard time because of the education you have or the certifications you've acquired, there's a good chance that you dodged a bullet.

How did you get started in the cybersecurity field, and what advice would you give to a beginner pursuing a career in cybersecurity?

Cybersecurity as a field of research and employment is as deep as it is wide. The best advice I can give is to experiment. There are so many more resources available than there were when I graduated nearly a decade ago. CTFs, wargame exercises, free and cheap training, conferences all over the world, and so on. Take advantage of all of those cheap and free resources. Be sure to attend conferences and build your social and/or professional network. Having that network of peers is extremely important. As your network grows and people learn of your skill and expertise in a particular cybersecurity niche, they will come to you with questions relating to your expertise. And you, in turn, can approach them with questions and/or problems that fall outside of your expertise, and you will be able to rely on their expertise to guide you. Not only that, my network of peers is what allowed me to acquire practically all of my information security positions. I had the skills necessary to apply for the positions, but it was the people I knew who introduced me to the people who were hiring.

What is your specialty in cybersecurity, and how can others gain expertise in your specialty?

My primary expertise is in network security monitoring (NSM). To be even more specific, I have a lot of experience when it comes to network intrusion detection and prevention systems (NIDS/NIPS). To make a long story short, these systems inspect network traffic looking for anomalies. If anomalies are found, an alert is triggered, the traffic is often logged, and an analyst is somehow notified. The analyst is then responsible for further investigating the alert(s) and determining whether they represent a problem and require further investigation and/or response (true positive). If the event was a false alarm, then the analyst determines whether the alert requires tuning or needs to be disabled. The best advice I can give for learning more about NSM, IDS, and IPS tech would be to experiment. Try out the security onion distro, try your hand at incident response and packet analysis exercises—like the ones available on malware-traffic-analysis. net—and familiarize yourself with Snort, Suricata, and BRO IDS and IPS platforms.

What is your advice for career success when it comes to getting hired, climbing the corporate ladder, or starting a company in cybersecurity?

As I mentioned earlier, having a network of friends, peers, and professionals you can rely on, and who rely on you, is important. The more people who rely on you and know of your expertise, the more of a community pillar you become, and the easier it is for you to attain a career and/or be considered successful.

What qualities do you believe all highly successful cybersecurity professionals share?

As a cybersecurity professional, I find that good verbal and written communication skills are extremely important. Additionally, one should have good soft skills, such as being able to read your audience, showing empathy, and generally being willing to demonstrate not only that you are human but that you understand the other difficult aspects of running a company or organization. You need to be able to communicate risk in a way that people can understand. They need to understand why the problems you are bringing up are things that should be resolved as soon as possible.

> "There exists a common mantra in law enforcement and/or counterterrorism called "Follow the money." If you follow the money, more often than not you find the bigger bad guys who are financing an operation, and your efforts usually pay off a bit more."

There exists a common mantra in law enforcement and/or counterterrorism called "Follow the money." If you follow the money, more often than not you find the bigger bad guys who are financing an operation, and your efforts usually pay off a bit more. I believe this concept also holds true for cybersecurity. You need to be able to communicate issues you find in terms of risk to mission-critical resources. For a government organization, this may be classified information or personally identifiable information (PII). For a private-sector organization, this is likely intellectual property or systems that generate revenue. If you can relate your problems in terms of the risk they pose to sensitive data or revenue generation, there is a better chance of your message being heard and acted upon.

What is the best book or movie that can be used to illustrate cybersecurity challenges?
As old as it is, and as cliché as it might seem, Cliff Stoll's *The Cuckoo's Egg* is a classic book that illustrates a lot of the same cybersecurity issues we see today, nearly three decades later.

What is your favorite hacker movie?
I'm not really one for hacker movies, so let me pick the absolute worst hacker movie I've ever seen: *Blackhat*.

What are your favorite books for motivation, personal development, or enjoyment?
When it comes to enjoyment, I have a tendency toward fantasy. *A Song of Ice and Fire* and *The Kingkiller Chronicle* are some of my favorites. When it comes to professional development, I prefer books published by No Starch Press. They are wonderful reference books to have on hand.

What is some practical cybersecurity advice you give to people at home in the age of social media and the Internet of Things?
Resist the Internet of Things as much as you can. Not everything in your home requires an internet connection.

What is the biggest mistake you've ever made, and how did you recover from it?
One time, I violated company policy at a former employer. This misinterpretation of the company rules cost me my job. The same day I was officially let go, I had dozens of job offers lined up, and it was thanks to my network of peers connecting me with opportunities quickly. This is why I say it's extremely important to have a good network of peers who rely on you and know you by deed and reputation. The effort you put into helping others always finds a way to come back to you. ∎

> "If you don't work for a company that supports a good work-life balance, find another company to work for."

Twitter: @davidrook • **Website:** securityleadership.ninja

David Rook

David Rook is the European security lead at Riot Games. He has worked in technology for 18 years and in the information security space full-time since 2006. Before moving into the computer games industry, David held various application security roles in the financial services industry. He has presented at leading information security conferences, including DEF CON and RSA.

55

If there is one myth that you could debunk in cybersecurity, what would it be?
The perception that cybersecurity is an incredibly difficult technical problem. Most of the issues we want to prevent often require very low-tech solutions, or the control needed is simple. The hard part comes in changing the behavior of people and the company culture.

What is one of the biggest bang-for-the-buck actions that an organization can take to improve its cybersecurity posture?
Based on what I've seen work in my time in cybersecurity, I'd say my top four would be:

- Reduce the access employees have to the minimum needed, and implement multifactor authentication everywhere you can.
- Implement solid patch management.
- Provide a password manager license (and training!) for your employees.
- Speak to people and teams. Make yourself and your team approachable and open to collaboration.

How is it that cybersecurity spending is increasing but breaches are still happening?

I feel this one is quite simple. It's accurate to say spending is increasing, but I feel most companies spend in the wrong places. For example, I could count on one hand the number of tools and services I think are really impactful and game-changing in the application security world. I don't think many in cybersecurity would argue with me if I said most products and services we buy really aren't that useful. They don't stop the threats we really worry about, and they do almost nothing to change the behaviors of people, which is the root cause of most issues.

Do you need a college degree or certification to be a cybersecurity professional?

My short answer to this question, as someone who didn't go to college or university, is no; but I could be biased. The longer answer is still no, but having a bachelor's, master's, or even a PhD can of course be beneficial. I think if you want to land your first cybersecurity job in a large tech company like Google, then a degree is very likely a requirement.

If you don't have the option of getting a degree or, like me, had no interest in going to college or university, you need to think about how to make yourself stand out. When I'm hiring, I don't view standing out as proving you know X, Y, and Z, but I do want to see a demonstration of your passion for security. If you're a developer wanting to move into application security, as an example, I'm going to look for blog posts on this topic, maybe application security–related projects in your GitHub, and potentially things like contributing to open source security tool projects. To be clear, I expect to see this kind of thing from every candidate, but I feel if you don't have a degree, it's vital you do this.

How did you get started in the cybersecurity field, and what advice would you give to a beginner pursuing a career in cybersecurity?

I had already been working in various IT roles, from basic support to IT manager, between the ages of 16 and 21. I initially worked in a warehouse loading large tubs of glue onto vans when I was 16. Then later, in the IT manager role, I started to ask questions about the security of our infrastructure, account security, password policies, and so on. That led me down the rabbit hole that is cybersecurity! I read everything I could get my hands on and leveled up the security of the company I worked for. I also did a few security certifications (look away now, those of you who feel certifications are useless), but having a CISSP helped me get my first cybersecurity job interview. That turned into my first full-time cybersecurity role in 2006, which focused on infrastructure and network security.

My move into application security was partially because of my inquisitive nature and partly by accident. The company I joined started to realize application security was something they needed to focus on, and they suggested I give it a try. I tried it, loved it, and worked in that area of cybersecurity for the next 11 years!

So, my advice is this: always be on the lookout for opportunities to learn, don't hold yourself back, and don't be afraid to ask questions and give it your all. If possible, find a great mentor in the area you're interested in and make the most of the advice they give you and the doors they may open.

What is your specialty in cybersecurity, and how can others gain expertise in your specialty?

My specialty is application security. I've been working in cybersecurity since 2006 and in application security full time since 2007. I think nowadays it's probably easier than ever to learn and practice some of the skills needed to work in application security. I would encourage anyone interested in this area to participate in bug bounties. These programs will allow you to develop the breaking skills needed in application security whilst also earning some money. If you are able to concisely explain, in a language developers understand, how to prevent these issues from occurring in the first place, you'll really be setting yourself up for success.

You can develop those fixer/building skills in a few ways. If you submit bug bounty reports, do your research on how to fix the issue you've found. As someone who has run a public bounty program, I can tell you people appreciate guidance on how to fix the issue you've found. Being able to code is also a huge help for anyone working in this field. The team I built at Riot spends a large chunk of its time writing software that helps developers produce secure products. If you can code, you should learn how to write secure code and fix security vulnerabilities. I'm sure pretty much any open source project would welcome you with open arms if you offered to find and fix vulnerabilities for them.

For instance, the Open Web Application Security Project (OWASP) obviously has some great resources. I love the cheat sheets in particular, and they participate in the Google Summer of Code project. If you take part in this, you'll work with some of the leading people in application security, write code for some of the biggest open source projects in our field, and get paid for doing it.

What is your advice for career success when it comes to getting hired, climbing the corporate ladder, or starting a company in cybersecurity?

I'm specifically going to focus on attending and speaking at conferences, the mind-set of technical knowledge being king, and the fact that engaging with people and collaboration are often looked down on in this industry. I will tell you that, in my own experience, doing less of the first two and developing my own people and collaboration skills accelerated my career growth and earning potential way more than increasing my technical expertise ever did. I would never tell people to stop attending or speaking at conferences or continually improving their technical knowledge. Those are all useful, even if I do often question the value people truly get out of most conferences.

I would encourage people to think about what really improves security and changes security behaviors in a company. We're ultimately trying to change the mind-set and behaviors of people, so any technical controls we try to implement fail to really address this. Look to work with people from different backgrounds and different industries.

Finally, speak to people. If you ask smart questions and actually meet people face to face to talk about security, their concerns, and what you can do to help them, you'll be surprised at how useful that is. You really need to learn how to engage with non-tech influencers, what those people care about, and how you can get them to buy into security. After a certain point in your career, the people you work with and want to influence really don't care about a stunt-hacking talk you gave/attended at BlackHat. It's important for people to learn that early on and focus on developing the soft skills alongside the tech.

What qualities do you believe all highly successful cybersecurity professionals share?

The best cybersecurity professionals I know all share a small set of qualities. They're all very passionate about ensuring that people are safe and secure; effectively, they want to protect people from harm. They also tend to be very curious and driven, as in they always want to continue learning and, more importantly, share their knowledge.

What is the best book or movie that can be used to illustrate cybersecurity challenges?

The Phoenix Project. I think the head of information security in that book demonstrates exactly what cybersecurity professionals *shouldn't* be like, but often are. If you read that book and set out to be the opposite of that character, you'll set yourself up to be successful in this industry. I think the book does a great job of outlining the kind of challenges we all face daily—just don't turn into that kind of cybersecurity professional. Next to our Dublin Information Security team, we have a quote from Rich Smith (@iodboi) that says, "If security introduces blocking to the org, it will be ignored, not embraced." This always helps us deal with the challenges that our jobs bring without turning into "that security guy" and being bypassed.

What is your favorite hacker movie?

It has to be *Hackers.* Who doesn't want to share floppy disks with friends and hack things while rollerskating and listen to The Prodigy?

What are your favorite books for motivation, personal development, or enjoyment?

I have a few different ones in mind. I always recommend *The Checklist Manifesto* to new people on my team. I've found checklists to be very beneficial in my personal and professional life for more than 10 years now. I include this on the reading list for any new hires I make to my team nowadays. We work with complex systems, and security teams are often smaller than they need to be. It's easy for us to overlook simple things because we're so focused on finding the doomsday vulnerabilities in our products. By integrating checklists into your life, you're not trying to dumb things down; you're actually making yourself better at your job. We often have an ego problem in cybersecurity, which probably stops many people from adopting a simple checklist. Let me put it this way: if checklists are fine for the pilots who fly you around the world, the architects who design the office you work in, and for doctors and surgeons who may care for you one day, they sure as hell can be used for your next security review.

I found *Chaos Monkeys* to be a fantastic read, covering the early days of Facebook and the funding model for startups in Silicon Valley. It's a great read for anyone in tech and/or anyone looking to launch their own startup.

From a personal development point of view, I'm going to pick a book that changed my early thinking at Riot Games. *Switch: How to Change Things When Change Is Hard* is a book I read soon after joining Riot to build its application security program. The bright spots story really got my attention because it was simple but effective. How often do you see cybersecurity teams scratching their heads about a specific team or person's bad security behavior? If we focus more on what makes the good people and teams good, we can potentially learn how to level everyone up. When we ran application security focus groups with a behavioral psychologist at Riot, we found what made our good teams good. The teams that needed to improve lacked the knowledge and resources that the good teams had. Those were the things that made the good teams good. That made crafting a road map pretty easy for us!

Leading Snowflakes is my final recommendation. It helped me make the transition from being a security engineer to being a security leader with people-management responsibilities. It helped me figure out what my days should look like and how to redefine value/good work in my mind. It's a must-read for anyone making the transition from a purely technical role to one where you manage and develop others.

What is some practical cybersecurity advice you give to people at home in the age of social media and the Internet of Things?

I think it's largely the same things people have been recommending for many years now. It's the simple things we often overlook. If people ensured that all of their computers, phones, devices, and so on were patched, that would help significantly. If people used password managers and two-factor authentication (where available) on their accounts, they'd be significantly more difficult to attack.

What is a life hack that you'd like to share?

My advice is to figure out what you need to do to look after yourself. All of the best leaders I know in this field have a significant hobby outside of cybersecurity. It can be working out at the gym, playing games, going surfing, or arts and crafts. It doesn't matter what it is, provided it disconnects you from this weird world we live and work in.

Take time off from work; you've got very little to gain from killing yourself for a company and so much to gain from relaxing and enjoying free time. That also extends to not keeping an eye on emails, Slack, etc. all hours of the day. Turn it all off. In fact, if you can, don't even have that stuff on your personal devices. If you don't work for a company that supports a good work-life balance, find another company to work for.

What is the biggest mistake you've ever made, and how did you recover from it?

The biggest mistake I ever made in my professional career is ultimately a story about me being arrogant and making assumptions. As I mentioned earlier, I used to work in infrastructure and network security, which involved owning our production firewalls. I was cleaning up firewall rules that weren't being used, and I felt like I had a solid plan: I checked our logs to see which rules were being used. If I didn't find an entry in the logs, I assumed the rules weren't being used, so they went on my list to be disabled.

I did all of the relevant change-management paperwork and waited for the next maintenance window. I logged into the firewall, removed all the unused rules, and pushed my changes. A few minutes later, all of our service-monitoring systems started turning red. No customer payment transactions were being processed. I was asked if my changes could've caused this, and arrogant young David said, "No, I only disabled rules that weren't being used, right?"

Well, it turns out I'd made a *big* mistake. The top rule in the list allowed our web servers to connect to our database servers, and that's one of the rules I removed. We didn't have logging enabled on that rule because of the amount of noise it would've generated. I trusted the logs too much and never really looked at the rules I was removing. Once I'd realized it was my mistake, I rolled back the changes and held up my hands—I had caused a service outage for some very large companies.

The lesson here is don't be arrogant like I was, and don't make assumptions. We're all very capable of making mistakes, and if we're pushing ourselves to be better, we *should* make mistakes. However, some mistakes, like this one, are definitely avoidable, so now I double- and triple-check important things before making a move. ∎

"Truly knowing how to operate something lets you define how it should be secured in terms your colleagues will easily understand. Read, test, test in real life, and iterate."

Twitter: @gepeto42 • **Website:** caffeinesecurity.com

Guillaume Ross

56

Guillaume Ross is an experienced information security professional, providing services to an array of organizations as the lead consultant and founder of Caffeine Security, Inc. Having worked in multiple verticals, from Fortune 50 to startups, Guillaume's specialty is providing the right security program and architecture for each specific environment and company.

If there is one myth that you could debunk in cybersecurity, what would it be?

That attacks are advanced. They're never more advanced than they need to be, and that means they are frequently very basic, as companies have a hard time doing the so-called "basics" well. Managing hundreds, thousands, or often many more systems well is hard work, and it's not something any product can do on its own. Unfortunately, when people get breached, they rarely claim they were successfully attacked by a very simple technique targeting default passwords, SQL injection, and unpatched, exposed systems. The more sensationalist headlines are often the most popular.

What is one of the biggest bang-for-the-buck actions that an organization can take to improve its cybersecurity posture?

Deploying a multibrowser strategy. For example, prevent the use of browsers with plugins enabled on anything but internal and whitelisted websites, and force the use of a modern browser, such as Edge or Chrome, with a hardened configuration to access the Web. That's free, and more effective than a lot of expensive products.

How is it that cybersecurity spending is increasing but breaches are still happening?

Many security problems are caused by a lack of IT hygiene and software security issues. Unfortunately, a lot of cybersecurity spending goes to "advanced/next-gen solutions," monitoring, and discovering more issues rather than improving the health of IT systems. Improving the quality of configurations, and the speed at which systems can be reconfigured, has a huge security impact. But that would often be seen as IT or development spending, while security teams, unfortunately, often only deploy more third-party software to try to bolt security onto fundamentally unsafe systems.

Do you need a college degree or certification to be a cybersecurity professional?

Not having one won't stop you if you're motivated, but it may make employment in some very process-heavy environments much harder to obtain. Still, many companies would be glad to hire someone who's shown they can get stuff done, that they understand security, and, most of all, that they understand how to effectively apply it within a company's environment. The less experience you have, the more useful that degree or certification will be—but so would participation in open source projects, community events, or security research.

How did you get started in the cybersecurity field, and what advice would you give to a beginner pursuing a career in cybersecurity?

I had always been interested in technology, networking, and security. When I started working in IT, I was still interested in security, but back then I didn't even know it was a full-time job. I simply assumed that every IT person at the large bank where I worked *had* to be amazing at security. When I realized that wasn't necessarily the case, I focused on understanding how to secure every technology I worked with to the best of my abilities. I got involved in more security projects and finally made the jump to full-time security.

What is your specialty in cybersecurity, and how can others gain expertise in your specialty?

Planning entire security programs, and on the technical side, securing corporate environments in large companies, especially around end-user workstations and Active Directory. Securing all this is important, and yet, the most difficult part is not necessarily the technical aspect of locking it down but rather doing it in a way that does not break the business.

The best way to learn how to do this is to pick a smaller environment, or a subset of a bigger one, and try to improve it a bit. Iterate, read all the vendor documentation you can find, and try to improve a few areas every week. Knowing how things work is a skill that can sound almost too obvious to be worth mentioning, but truly knowing how to operate something lets you define how it should be secured in terms your IT colleagues will easily understand. Read, test, test in real life, and iterate.

What is your advice for career success when it comes to getting hired, climbing the corporate ladder, or starting a company in cybersecurity?

If you have little experience, participate in community events and publish research and/or tools for the community to discover. As a hiring manager, I highly value this type of involvement, and as someone starting out, there is no barrier to entry.

What qualities do you believe all highly successful cybersecurity professionals share?

Being curious and motivated. Also knowing how to communicate not only the issues but the proposed improvements as well. A combination of technical skills and soft skills is a great way to get the important stuff done: improving security.

What is the best book or movie that can be used to illustrate cybersecurity challenges?

Home Alone will show you that, with enough motivation, anyone can defend himself from common attacks. All it takes is thinking outside the box. Kevin didn't even need to buy anything "next-gen!"

What is your favorite hacker movie?

WarGames is a great hacker movie, but *Office Space* is closer to the day-to-day of many security teams.

What are your favorite books for motivation, personal development, or enjoyment?

As someone who has been consulting for many years, *Professional Services Marketing* by Mike Schultz and John E. Doerr and *Managing the Professional Service Firm* by David H. Maister are two very useful books I read in the last year. Consulting practices, such as law firms, have been providing services pretty much since Emperor Claudius abolished the ban on fees. There is a lot to be learned from the experience of people selling services, even if it's in other professions.

What is some practical cybersecurity advice you give to people at home in the age of social media and the Internet of Things?

Keep your systems up to date, use a password manager, enable two-factor authentication (2FA) where you can, and most of all, keep offline and offsite backups of your most important files.

What is a life hack that you'd like to share?

Find an app to manage to-dos that works on your main computer and your phone and that supports geofencing. That way, you can easily be reminded about a specific email when you get to work in the morning, but it will also remind you to pick up some whiskey next time you drive by the liquor store. Anything that allows you to offload the mental load of having to remember things on your own helps you focus. If you're trying to secure an organization or system, you already have enough things working against you; no need to risk forgetting things or wasting brain cycles trying to remember.

What is the biggest mistake you've ever made, and how did you recover from it?

On the *first morning* of the *first day* of a new job early in my career, while trying to update software for an employee having issues with timesheets, I rebooted the employee's computer. But it did not reboot; I simply saw a new desktop background all of a sudden. I realized I had rebooted a remote terminal server with hundreds of users. What I thought was her desktop just wasn't.

I recovered by rapidly informing our director of IT, the help desk, and getting ready to downgrade what I had accidentally upgraded when the server came back up (there was a reason it was running a specific version). I felt quite stupid, but I would've felt even stupider trying to hide my own reckless action. ∎

"Once you've reached a point in life where your financial needs are met, the source of your happiness shifts from more money to whether your role provides you with the opportunity to grow with an organization that has a culture that makes you excited to get up in the morning and immerse yourself in it every day."

Website: www.linkedin.com/in/bradleyschaufenbuel

Brad Schaufenbuel

Bradley Schaufenbuel is VP and CISO at Paylocity. He has held security leadership positions at numerous companies in the financial services and technology industries over his 22-year career. Bradley has MBA, JD, and LLM degrees; is a licensed attorney; and holds 23 professional certifications. He is a prolific author and speaker and serves on the advisory boards of multiple venture funds and startups.

57

If there is one myth that you could debunk in cybersecurity, what would it be?
The myth I would debunk is that cybersecurity success is largely the result of buying and implementing new technology. Vendors especially would like us to believe that if we just bought their wares, we would be secure. Many security leaders share this belief. Their cybersecurity programs consist of an endless search for silver bullets, punctuated by cycles of technology implementation projects. In reality, an effective cybersecurity program depends on people, process, and technology, in that order of importance. Even the best security technology is useless without repeatable processes in place to manage it. Even the best security processes are useless without good people to execute them. People are what make the difference between a world-class cybersecurity program and an ineffective one.

What is one of the biggest bang-for-the-buck actions that an organization can take to improve its cybersecurity posture?

I have gotten the best return on investment from security awareness training. Creating a culture of security is absolutely essential to cybersecurity defense. Almost all successful penetrations rely on human weakness. Think phishing, social engineering, and human error. You can spend a fortune on technology controls, which can all be defeated by an attacker simply finding one careless insider. Training is relatively inexpensive, but an army of diligent human firewalls is priceless.

> "I have gotten the best return on investment from security awareness training."

How is it that cybersecurity spending is increasing but breaches are still happening?

There are two reasons that cybersecurity spending is increasing but data breaches are still happening. First, security leaders are not spending money on the right things. There is often little correlation between unmitigated risk and the investments organizations are making. For example, most organizations allocate the bulk of their cybersecurity budget to mitigation of externally perpetrated attacks, despite the fact that the majority of breaches are the result of malicious or careless insiders. Second, attackers work together better than defenders do. Malicious actors of all types cooperate in an extensive interconnected digital underground. However, most defending organizations go it alone, maybe consuming threat intelligence from others but rarely contributing anything to a shared defense. Legislation limiting liability for intelligence sharing and the growth of information sharing and analysis centers/organizations (ISACs/ISAOs) are helping, but there is still a lot to do.

Do you need a college degree or certification to be a cybersecurity professional?

No. You do not need a college degree or certification to be a cybersecurity professional. In a field with negative unemployment, raw talent is often enough. That being said, I would highly recommend both. An employer needs some way to weed out candidates and validate that individuals know what they say they know. Although by no means perfect, there are few better ways to obtain independent, third-party validation that a candidate possesses some base level of skills than through the completion of an objective certification process or a formal degree program.

Beyond that, the successful pursuit of education and certification also is an indicator that a candidate possesses the maturity and persistence to set a long-term goal and achieve it. If a person claims to be a cybersecurity expert, then they should have no problem passing a certification examination. The unwillingness to put that knowledge to the test may be an indicator that they are not as knowledgeable as they claim to be.

How did you get started in the cybersecurity field, and what advice would you give to a beginner pursuing a career in cybersecurity?

The term *cybersecurity* did not exist when I entered the field more than 22 years ago. It was just referred to as "security" or "IT security." There were no formal educational programs for security. If you knew a lot about all aspects of technology and had a defensive mind-set, you just found your way onto a security team.

I started my career as a system administrator at Arthur Andersen LLP, one of the "Big Five" accounting and auditing firms at the time. When the internet was commercialized in the late 1990s, I joined a new team focused on designing "internet architecture," where I became familiar with network security concepts. The combination of system administration and networking expertise allowed me to make the move onto the security team. Once there, I never looked back.

I think it is a lot easier to get into the cybersecurity field these days, as there are now formal programs (academic and trade oriented) that are focused on giving individuals the skills they need to break into the field. If going back to school isn't in the cards, there is no substitute for simply immersing yourself in the field. You can join professional associations dedicated to security, attend security meetups and conferences, teach yourself the skills you need on your own time, and invest in your own professional certification. If you show initiative and demonstrate a passion for the field, a security leader like me, desperate for talent in a tight labor market, is going to notice it and give you a chance.

What is your specialty in cybersecurity, and how can others gain expertise in your specialty?

At this point, my "specialty" is security leadership (i.e., conducting the security orchestra). I have served as the head of the security function for quite a few years now. Earlier in my career, however, I specialized in many areas within security, including ethical hacking, IT audit, risk management, forensics, security management, IT governance, privacy, strategy, architecture, and IT compliance.

If your goal ultimately is to become the top security leader within your organization (or another), you need to be familiar with all of the major specialties within security. At the very least, you need to know enough to determine whether a vendor or co-worker is giving you a line of crap (I call this level of mastery "BS detection"). Add to that fine-tuned communications skills, diplomacy, and political tact, and you are well on your way to becoming a CISO. If your goal, however, is simply to be the best within a single area of specialty (and there is nothing wrong with that), then I would suggest educating yourself on that specialty, hanging out with people already in that specialty and learning from them, joining professional associations dedicated to that specialization, getting certified in that area of specialization, and so on.

What is your advice for career success when it comes to getting hired, climbing the corporate ladder, or starting a company in cybersecurity?

My advice for career success is to aim high and think big. If you are looking to move up in your current organization, perform the functions of the role you aspire to and not just the one you are in. When leaders are looking to fill a leadership position below them, they try to imagine how potential candidates will perform in that role. Leave nothing to the imagination and actually demonstrate your ability to do the job before you are asked to.

When searching for a new role, don't allow overly specific requirements in job descriptions to deter you. Hiring managers often make the mistake of treating a job description as a "wish list." They throw everything they can possibly think of in there in case the perfect candidate comes along. Instead of weeding yourself out, apply anyway and focus on demonstrating that you are capable of doing everything your prospective employer is asking for.

Finally, exude confidence. Creating the perception that you know what you are doing is often as powerful as actually knowing what you are doing. Don't be afraid to take on your dream job before you think you are prepared for it. If you have a passion for the field and an insatiable appetite for learning as you go, you'll be fine.

What qualities do you believe all highly successful cybersecurity professionals share?

There are four qualities that I believe all highly successful cybersecurity professionals possess. First, they never stop learning. This field evolves incredibly fast, so you have to be constantly learning to avoid obsolescence. Second, they have excellent communication skills. Cybersecurity professionals are regularly called upon to explain complex technical concepts to non-technical people. It takes a knack for communication to do this well. Third, they collaborate well with others. Cybersecurity professionals must work with individuals throughout an organization—IT, legal, compliance, auditors, HR, operations, sales, marketing, etc. Lone wolves don't go far in this field. Finally, they demonstrate a passion for the field. Cybersecurity can be a stressful calling. If you don't absolutely love what you do, you won't last long in this field.

What is the best book or movie that can be used to illustrate cybersecurity challenges?

The book that can best be used to illustrate cybersecurity challenges has got to be *The Cuckoo's Egg* by Clifford Stoll. I realize this is one of the oldest (if not *the* oldest) book about hacking. Although the technology discussed is dated, many of the main concepts (e.g., the methods used by a hacker to cover his or her tracks, the difficulty of following an attacker who is moving laterally within a network, the extraordinary skill and determination required of defenders, etc.) are as true today as they were in 1989.

What is your favorite hacker movie?

WarGames is my favorite hacker movie. Seeing Matthew Broderick show Ally Sheedy how to war dial and hack into a Pentagon computer in 1983 changed my life forever. Fascinated by what I saw, I saved up my money and bought a 300 baud modem for my Commodore 64 personal computer. Soon I was completely engrossed by the world of underground dial-up bulletin board systems and sharing software hacks with fellow "BBSers." Ultimately, this fascination with digital communications networks turned into a career in security that has served me very well. Oh—and it didn't hurt that I had a huge crush on Ally Sheedy.

What are your favorite books for motivation, personal development, or enjoyment?

I enjoy real-life drama and I am an entrepreneur at heart, so I love to read nonfiction books about the spectacular rise and fall of innovative businesses. Not only is reality often just as interesting as fiction in the world of business, making for a fun read, but there are often lessons to be learned from the mistakes of the past that can be applied to solve current problems. Three such books are *Commodore: A Company on the Edge* by Brian Bagnall, which follows the rise and fall of Commodore Business Machines in the fledgling personal computer market of the 1980s; *Barbarians at the Gate: The Fall of RJR Nabisco* by Bryan Burrough and John Helyar, which describes the leveraged buyout of RJR Nabisco in 1988; and *The Smartest Guys in the Room: The Amazing Rise and*

Scandalous Fall of Enron by Bethany McLean and Peter Elkind, which covers the rise and fall of Enron in the energy sector in the early 2000s.

What is some practical cybersecurity advice you give to people at home in the age of social media and the Internet of Things?

The best cybersecurity advice I have to give to people in the age of social media is to resist the temptation to overshare information. As a society, we seem to have lost any appreciation for our own privacy. This is especially true of younger generations. We post a ton of information about ourselves on social media. That information can in turn be utilized by malicious actors to discern passwords, socially engineer us or others, and steal our identities. Learn to use the privacy settings of the social media sites you use and/or just be a little more discreet about what you share online. The entire world doesn't need to know everything about you.

I have similar thoughts about IoT. It has become clear that there are inherent weaknesses in most IoT devices. From connected cars to thermostats, these devices often are not designed with security in mind, and there is usually no mechanism to update them when vulnerabilities are found. So, take the time to assess the risk before connecting everything you have to the internet.

What is a life hack that you'd like to share?

My life hack is to always remember that although you may have little control over what happens to you in life, you are always in control of how you react to it. In other words, don't worry about trying to change something you have little control over (e.g., what others say and do to you, the weather, the business cycle, etc.). Focus only on that over which you do have control (e.g., whether you are going to let that uncontrollable circumstance negatively affect you). Too many people go through life stressing over what is happening to them when things do not go to plan rather than focusing on what they can learn from the situation and how they can use adversity to improve themselves and become a better person in the long run.

What is the biggest mistake you've ever made, and how did you recover from it?

The biggest mistake I ever made was leaving a job that I absolutely loved for the wrong reasons. I was at an organization with a great culture where I was working with extremely talented people, learning a ton, and growing professionally every day. I left that role to take a position with a firm with a more conservative culture and little opportunity for professional growth, based largely on the prestigious reputation of the firm and a significantly more attractive compensation package. I learned the hard way that when it comes to career satisfaction, culture trumps compensation every time.

Once you've reached a point in life where your financial needs are met, the source of your happiness shifts from more money to whether your role provides you with the opportunity to grow with an organization that has a culture that makes you excited to get up in the morning and immerse yourself in it every day. In other words, the extra money does not make up for feeling professionally unfulfilled. Fortunately, there is a happy ending to this lesson. The company I loved felt the same way about me, and I was given the opportunity to return, which I gladly seized. I refer to the episode as my "career mulligan." ■

"People rely too much on technology to protect them instead of looking at how their actions (or inaction) make them vulnerable to attack."

Website: www.linkedin.com/in/chinyere-schwartz-9155bb10

Chinyere Schwartz

58

Chinyere Schwartz is an information system security officer (ISSO) currently employed by SRC Technologies, Inc. She has been working in information security for a little over seven years and became interested in the field while working for the human resources help desk at the U.S. State Department in Washington, DC. In addition to working, Chinyere is a wife and mother of two children. She met her husband at Howard University while they were both working on their BS degrees in electrical engineering. She has been married to her husband for over 11 years, and they have a soon-to-be-10-year-old daughter and a 3-year-old son. Chinyere enjoys spending time with her family and friends, learning about new things, and relaxing.

If there is one myth that you could debunk in cybersecurity, what would it be?

I think one of the myths that, unfortunately, is still hanging around out there is that "It can't happen to me." People rely too much on technology to protect them instead of looking at how their actions (or inaction) make them vulnerable to attack. If you consistently accept the updates on your cell phone (thinking your phone is secure) but turn around and download apps from untrusted sources, you've potentially opened yourself up to some unknown threat.

What is one of the biggest bang-for-the-buck actions that an organization can take to improve its cybersecurity posture?

At the end of the day, the same actions that were used to protect an organization before the term *cybersecurity* became popular are the actions that need to be taken to protect an organization now. Ensuring that security is "built-in" instead of "bolted-on" goes a long way toward a healthy security posture. When security controls are implemented in the design, build, and test phases of the architecture, features such as unnecessary ports/protocols/services are turned off and best practices are followed regarding account management, auditing, identification, and authentication—just to name a few.

> "Ensuring that security is "built-in" instead of "bolted-on" goes a long way toward a healthy security posture."

How is it that cybersecurity spending is increasing but breaches are still happening?

I think that may be a symptom of where the money is getting spent. It's when more of the budget is used for a particular solution, but you don't purchase the maintenance plan that includes software/hardware/firmware updates (especially if it's proprietary). Or you hire more IT personnel, but you don't have a patching plan in place, which could require implementing an automated solution and subsequently re-engineering your architecture in order to become and/or stay compliant.

Do you need a college degree or certification to be a cybersecurity professional?

Depending on where you work, having a degree and/or certification is still required (especially if it's a STEM-related degree). Some places may take years of experience, but again, it definitely depends on the customer and sector.

> Depending on where you work, having a degree and/or certification is still required (especially if it's a STEM-related degree). Some places may take years of experience, but again, it definitely depends on the customer and sector.

How did you get started in the cybersecurity field, and what advice would you give to a beginner pursuing a career in cybersecurity?

I was interested in becoming an ISSO when I did help-desk work with the State Department. My supervisor was an ISSO, and one day he and our lead SA had to confiscate a person's machine. I was curious and asked him about it, and he gave me the basics of that aspect of his job and told me I wouldn't like it because it was mainly paperwork. I was still interested and, initially, when the opportunity presented itself, I had all the credentials except the certification (Security+), which was a requirement for the position. I quickly got my certification and was hired. I've been doing ISSO work ever since—about seven years now. For someone beginning or pursuing a career in cybersecurity, I would encourage them to do their research on which aspect of this field they want to be a part of. Do you want to be on the defensive side or offensive side? There's a lot out there to be a part of—you have to look at what best suits you.

What is your specialty in cybersecurity, and how can others gain expertise in your specialty?

I am an information system security officer, and my role is responsible for ensuring that the organization adheres to security policies and procedures that protect it from both internal and external threats. As far as gaining expertise, while you don't have to be technical, it doesn't hurt. When you get hands-on experience configuring security policies on systems, it helps a person (in my opinion) understand the challenges that are sometimes involved in making a decent security posture a reality.

What is your advice for career success when it comes to getting hired, climbing the corporate ladder, or starting a company in cybersecurity?

Be honest about what services you can and cannot provide for the customer. Be a team player and self-motivated. If you love what you do, there is an inherent level of motivation to not just be good but to become great. Also, be consistent—that illustrates dedication.

> "Be honest about what services you can and cannot provide for the customer."

What qualities do you believe all highly successful cybersecurity professionals share?

Staying informed and dedicating time to perfecting your craft.

What is your favorite hacker movie?

WarGames. I loved this movie, and it really had me thinking about what was possible in the world of computers. (Mind you, the first time I laid hands on a computer was in the early '90s when we saved everything on 3.5" floppy disks while learning DOS—I'll leave it there.)

What are your favorite books for motivation, personal development, or enjoyment?

I don't get a chance to read nearly as much as I would like, but the last good book I read was *The Last Lecture* by Randy Pausch and Jeffrey Zaslow. Randy Pausch was a professor of computer science, human-computer interaction, and design at Carnegie Mellon University, and the book details a series of topics in his lecture titled "Really Achieving Your Childhood Dreams." A month before the lecture, he was told that his pancreatic cancer was terminal, so it became the last lecture he gave.

What is some practical cybersecurity advice you give to people at home in the age of social media and the Internet of Things?

Not to state the obvious, but stop posting your life on social media! You don't know who's monitoring you. Also, update your devices and really look at the services running on them. Do you know what those apps are, who installed them, and what other apps have dependencies on them? Ask yourself if you really want it running on your device. ■

> "Not to state the obvious, but stop posting your life on social media!"

> "Now there are a lot of myths that need debunking in InfoSec, but if I were to choose just one, it would be that using vendor products (antivirus, firewalls, gateways, etc.) to protect yourself, or your organization, is enough."

Twitter: @sehnaoui

Khalil Sehnaoui

59

Khalil Sehnaoui is a Belgian-Lebanese information security consultant and hacker who specializes in the Middle East. He's also the founder of Krypton Security, an InfoSec firm that helps test companies' security strengths, weaknesses, and loopholes. Khalil is a member of the Chaos Computer Club (CCC), Europe's largest association of hackers, and was featured in *The Guardian's* video series *The Power of Privacy*, as well as on National Geographic in the series *Breakthrough*, Season 2 Episode 2, "Cyber Terror."

If there were one myth that you could debunk in cybersecurity, what would it be?

For all intents and purposes, let's first agree to stop using the word *cyber*. It holds no real meaning anymore and has been overused by the media, trying to make the internet sound scary and basically trying to wrap a complex system into a single word rather than really trying to understand it. In this particular case, we will be talking about information security, or InfoSec for short.

Now there are a lot of myths that need debunking in InfoSec, but if I were to choose just one, it would be that using vendor products (antivirus, firewalls, gateways, etc.) to protect yourself, or your organization, is enough. The correct approach to information security must include not only products, but product training, regular penetration testing, regular security assessments, user-awareness training, research, regular updates, and constant monitoring of your networks and applications, etc.

What is one of the biggest bang-for-the-buck actions that an organization can take to improve its cybersecurity posture?

As far as I'm concerned, that's an easy one: awareness training. This is probably the cheapest and easiest action an organization can take, but one that will have the most positive effect on its information security posture. The weakest link in any organization is always the human element. You can have all your sophisticated products in place, but if you don't train your users and define proper procedures, they could render all of that moot in a second.

How is it that cybersecurity spending is increasing but breaches are still happening?

Breaches will always happen. That is an immutable fact, and anyone who says the contrary—or says they have a fully secure, unbreakable network—is either idealistic or doesn't know what they're talking about. That being said, there are two main reasons why information security spending is increasing and why breaches are still, and always, happening. First, information security spending is nowhere near the level it should be. Most organizations still see it as a side-spending issue, if they see it at all. On a positive note, global awareness is rising throughout the world (mainly because of all the reported attacks), hence spending will rise as well; but it will still take a while to reach the level it should be at. We still see a lot of organizations that do not invest in information security because they fail to grasp the risk/reward ratio.

Second, in today's digital and ever-evolving complex world, information security is a game of cat and mouse where, unfortunately, the attackers will always have the advantage. Vulnerabilities in existing software or hardware, as well as new attack scenarios, are discovered every day, and you cannot really defend against an attack if you don't know where it's going to come from. That, added to the problem of the human element being the weakest link, is a constant, and this is why breaches will always happen.

Do you need a college degree or certification to be a cybersecurity professional?

Most information security professionals I know do not hold a college degree, or at least not a degree pertaining to InfoSec. As an example, I hold a master's degree in economics and never studied any form of information technology in school or university. So, no, you do not really need a college degree or certification to be an information security professional, and most InfoSec operators will probably tell you the same.

Also, there are no real information security degrees out there currently in most universities' curriculums. That being said, some certifications are useful to show a future employer that one at least knows what they're talking about, and some prospective clients will always feel safer when a company boasts a lot of certifications on their factsheets.

Finally, some certifications are mandatory for delivering certain services, like PCI-DSS certification, which is required when working with credit card processing technologies. So, depending on which spectrum of the information security landscape you decide to service, you might need to get some certification after all.

Most hackers I know could get certified easily, as their own self-taught knowledge far surpasses that which is asked by the certifying bodies.

How did you get started in the cybersecurity field, and what advice would you give to a beginner pursuing a career in cybersecurity?

I was always a hacker at heart. And by hacker, I mean the actual definition of the word, which, in my opinion, is not necessarily related to computers. A *hacker* is someone who has a natural curiosity for things, a thirst for knowledge and details, and someone who doesn't accept things the way they are without always trying to make them better, more efficient. Leonardo Da Vinci was a hacker. Einstein was a hacker. That kid taking his new toy apart and trying to put it back together could become a hacker. I was that kid.

As I grew older, and even though I followed a curriculum not related to IT per se, I remained fascinated by computers and software and would spend most of my time learning, discovering, and delving deeper into that world. With the kind of knowledge you get with time, you come to a crossroads where you decide to use your skills either for bad or for good. I chose the latter and decided to use my experience to help protect others. But I really did not start as a professional in information security (and by professional, I mean someone who makes a living out of it) until I founded my company, Krypton Security, in 2012.

As far as advice for beginners, I would say be passionate. Let your work be your hobby, and vice versa. You can't go wrong when you love what you do, and passion will give you that extra edge that is needed in the information security field. Go to conferences, listen to podcasts, watch videos, and, most importantly, interact with the community. The information security community is not very big, but it is a tight-knit one, and you will probably get your first InfoSec job through someone you met at a hacker gathering.

What is your specialty in cybersecurity, and how can others gain expertise in your specialty?

I consider myself a jack of most information security trades, though a master of none. In the business of information security, there is a gap between the way hackers and corporate management perceive things, so I would say my specialty is bridging the gap between technical operators and corporate management— translating the hacker mind-set to corporate, and vice versa, and what I like to call *conducting*.

I often use the analogy of an orchestra conductor: The conductor does not know how to play all the instruments in his orchestra; and if he does know how to play a few of them, he definitely does not know how to play them as well as his musicians. He chose each musician because they are one of the best at playing that specific instrument, and he knows enough to be able to detect an out-of-tune instrument or a false note. Without the conductor, the orchestra would not play in unison, and without the orchestra, the conductor would not be able to produce a symphony.

This expertise was gained through my formal training in business and economics—as well as my previous working experiences outside of information security—and my dabbling in all things information security, without really focusing or acquiring specialist skills in any one aspect of it.

What is your advice for career success when it comes to getting hired, climbing the corporate ladder, or starting a company in cybersecurity?

Be passionate about what you do; be true to your principles; have the "hacker mind-set" (I talk about this in more detail in the next question); and, most importantly, believe in yourself. If you don't believe in yourself, how can you expect others to believe in you?

What qualities do you believe all highly successful cybersecurity professionals share?

One quality—"the hacker mind-set"—which I would define as passion, curiosity, perseverance, generosity, and modesty.

What is the best book or movie that can be used to illustrate cybersecurity challenges?

This is a tough one, but after some thorough thinking, I'm going to go with *Catch Me If You Can*, released in 2002 by director Steven Spielberg and featuring Leonardo DiCaprio and Tom Hanks. The movie is about the real life of Frank Abagnale—a now-successful security consultant who started out in the '60s as a social engineer, a forger, and a con man—and the FBI agent tasked with catching him. The challenges of information security are illustrated by the ever-evolving landscape that Frank had to deal with to perform his crimes, mainly the financial ones, every time needing to adapt to the new security measures by finding new exploitable vulnerabilities, and so on.

There is also the social engineering part that he mastered, whereas he gained his breach information by impersonating people and abusing the lack of security or verification procedures across many different industries. We finally see a resemblance to the actual InfoSec scene, as, after being caught, he was offered a job with the federal authorities.

So, in the film, we have an ever-evolving landscape where attackers have the advantage over defenders (like red teams versus blue teams), and we have social engineering as the easy but effective method of gaining information (like open source intelligence, phishing, and social-engineering attacks). Then we also have human weakness as the most vulnerable element in any security environment (with law enforcement trying to catch the attackers, and ultimately hiring them after they do, because who better to catch a thief than another thief?). All of those elements in the movie illustrate today's information security challenges.

What is your favorite hacker movie?

My favorite hacker movie is, without a doubt and to this day, *WarGames*, released in 1983, directed by John Badham and featuring Matthew Broderick and John Wood. It was truly a game-changer for me and instilled the passion for all things computer that drove me all my life, and still drives me today.

What are your favorite books for motivation, personal development, or enjoyment?

For motivation, personal development, and/or enjoyment, I like to read white papers, proofs of concept, technical books, and the like. The subjects can be varied; the essential thing I'm looking for is new knowledge. So, you might see me reading a coding manual, an astrophysics book, a quantum theory white paper, or a hacking proof of concept.

One of my favorite books, though, is *A Brief History of Time*, published in 1988 and written by Stephen Hawking. It explains, in non-technical terms, the structure, origin, development, and eventual fate of the universe.

I also recommend *PoC or GTFO* by Manul Laphroaig, published in 2017. It is a collection of proofs of concept revolving around offensive security research, reverse engineering, and file formats that will delight the more technically inclined readers.

What is some practical cybersecurity advice you give to people at home in the age of social media and the Internet of Things?

The main issue with security in the age of smart phones, social media, and the Internet of Things—as well as our all-around connectivity—is that it is not practical. Hence, the problem. Users go for the effortless way of operating, notwithstanding the fact that it will put their personal data and privacy at risk. And yet, there are a few simple steps or actions anyone can take, without having to be versed in information security, that will allow them to at least reduce their exposure to attacks or viruses and to be safer than most users out there.

These are universal and can be applied to any of the social media accounts, applications, or personal devices out there (IoT or otherwise).

- Make sure your operating systems and applications are always updated.
- Make your passwords complex; you can always use a good password manager so you only have to remember one password.
- Don't use the same password for all accounts, especially for important banking or financial applications or connections.
- Don't use the same email address for everything. It's easy to create new addresses that you use just for certain important accounts. That will limit your exposure to spam, phishing, and scam emails.
- Use two-factor authentication (2FA) when available.
- Don't click suspicious links, even if the sender is in your senders list.
- Don't enter personal information on websites or pop-ups without verifying that it is legit. Always check for HTTPS.
- Disable default username and password on all devices.
- Do not leave your Wi-Fi, Bluetooth, or other connection protocols active if you don't need them.

What is a life hack that you'd like to share?

Google it! Or "search engine" it. But let's be real, there's no other game in town (at least not at this time). This is my advice: learn how to properly use search engines. It's not really a life hack, I know, but people sometimes fail to realize just how much information is out there. We live in a day and age when everything about anything is available to us, just a few clicks away. Tutorials, blogs, videos, manuals, and full-fledged courses—all are available online.

Granted, sometimes we get lazy, but how hard is it to just launch a browser and look for the information you need? People will always be more dedicated to helping you out if they see you've made the effort to look for it yourself first.

What is the biggest mistake you've ever made, and how did you recover from it?

The biggest mistake I made was probably thinking I could have a happy and fulfilling life without doing what I loved. I did not have the necessary confidence in myself to believe I could succeed as an information security professional, so I sought the easy way out by just joining the family business. But I wasn't happy, and to make a long story short, I eventually took the leap of faith and started my own company. I was blessed to have family around me—as well as the right friends and partners—to help, support, and accompany me in that adventure.

Today, I am happy with what I do, and I'm part of an amazing community of hackers I call family. I can only wish everyone who reads these lines that kind of success. ■

"For me, regularly thinking through and writing down my top personal commitments helps me not overcommit and make sure I am consistently giving my best to whatever I commit to."

Twitter: @astha_singhal • **Website:** www.linkedin.com/in/singhalastha

Astha Singhal

60

Astha Singhal leads the application security team at Netflix that secures all the applications in Netflix's cloud infrastructure. Prior to this, she managed the AppExchange security review on Salesforce product security. She is a security engineer by qualification who is passionate about proactive security and developer enablement. She is also an active member of the Bay Area security community as an organizer of conferences like AppSec USA and BSidesSF.

If there is one myth that you could debunk in cybersecurity, what would it be?

The biggest myth I think there is in cybersecurity is that it's this unique thing that only a handful of people who have this undefinable skill set can do, but that's really not true. There are so many different roles in security, and we need lots of help.

What is one of the biggest bang-for-the-buck actions that an organization can take to improve its cybersecurity posture?

Knowing what assets you have in your environment is really important to be able to figure out what your risk is and how to prioritize security work.

How is it that cybersecurity spending is increasing but breaches are still happening?

It's really important to prioritize security work appropriately in accordance with your attack surface. Spending more money on generic vendor solutions may not be the right solution in a lot of cases.

Do you need a college degree or certification to be a cybersecurity professional?

I personally got my master's degree in security because I didn't have access to the security market after graduating with my CS undergrad. But today, with a high demand for security talent and a lot of free security resources, it's not necessary to pursue degree programs. That said, degree programs and certifications can definitely help you get your foot in the door.

> "The biggest myth I think there is in cybersecurity is that it's this unique thing that only a handful of people who have this undefinable skill set can do, but that's really not true."

How did you get started in the cybersecurity field, and what advice would you give to a beginner pursuing a career in cybersecurity?

I took a class in undergrad about security protocols and introductory concepts of cryptography. I loved the combination of building and breaking that existed in the security realm. I then decided to pursue further research opportunities in security for my undergrad thesis and apply for grad school in security. In the market today, I would definitely encourage all newcomers to engage with the community and learn from all their work.

What is your specialty in cybersecurity, and how can others gain expertise in your specialty?

I have primarily been focused on product/application security in my career. An understanding of web application security concepts is definitely a good starting point in this field. But it's also important to build communication, collaboration, and customer service skill sets to enable your developers efficiently. In the world today, thinking about ways to scale application security is also important.

> "It's really important to prioritize security work appropriately in accordance with your attack surface."

What is your advice for career success when it comes to getting hired, climbing the corporate ladder, or starting a company in cybersecurity?

Make use of all the free resources out there for self-learning to be able to demonstrate your security skill set.

What qualities do you believe all highly successful cybersecurity professionals share?

Having an enabling mind-set that helps other people (both the business and engineering stakeholders) understand and make security decisions.

What is the best book or movie that can be used to illustrate cybersecurity challenges?

I think for someone new in application security, *The Tangled Web* is a great read to understand how we got here in terms of web security and the internet.

What is your favorite hacker movie?
Hackers is definitely a classic.

What are your favorite books for motivation, personal development, or enjoyment?
- *Multipliers: How the Best Leaders Make Everyone Smarter*
- *The Phoenix Project: A Novel about IT, DevOps, and Helping Your Business Win*

> "Spending more money on generic vendor solutions may not be the right solution in a lot of cases."

What is some practical cybersecurity advice you give to people at home in the age of social media and the Internet of Things?
I think the biggest thing I do for family and friends is to get them to use password managers to minimize password reuse.

What is a life hack that you'd like to share?
For me, regularly thinking through and writing down my top personal commitments helps me not overcommit and make sure I am consistently giving my best to whatever I commit to.

What is the biggest mistake you've ever made, and how did you recover from it?
On one of my first engagements as an associate product security engineer, I ended up taking the hard line on security and preventing a team from shipping their weekly release one Wednesday evening just because I wasn't done finishing security testing and couldn't "sign off." So, I didn't even have concrete evidence of open security issues. The engineering leaders from the team obviously ended up really upset about this. At the time, given my limited exposure to the industry, I thought I was doing the right thing in making sure I could "assure" security of the product before it shipped. The next day, my leadership found out what had happened and was very calm about it. They definitely had my back but gave me critical and direct feedback on what I did wrong. It helped me grow out of the mind-set of "only the technical things matter." It also laid a foundation for understanding risk management, security enablement, and collaboration. ∎

> "An understanding of web application security concepts is definitely a good starting point in this field."

> "A life of meaning is to have an impact and help others. At the end of the day, we're not going to take it with us. No one has ambitions to die rich. What is the legacy that you're going to leave behind?"

Twitter: @dugsong • **Website:** www.dugsong.com

Dug Song

61

Dug Song is the cofounder and CEO of Duo Security, the leading provider of unified access security and multifactor authentication delivered through the cloud. Duo protects more than 12,000 customers globally, including Dresser-Rand, Etsy, Facebook, K-Swiss, Random House, Yelp, Zillow, Paramount Pictures, and more. Founded in Michigan, Duo has offices in Ann Arbor and Detroit, as well as growing hubs in Austin, Texas; San Mateo, California; and London. Prior to launching Duo, Dug spent seven years as founding chief security architect at Arbor Networks, protecting 80 percent of the world's internet service providers and helping to grow the company to $120 million+ annual revenue before its acquisition by Danaher. Dug also built the first commercial network anomaly detection system, acquired by Check Point Software Technologies. Dug's contributions to the security community include popular projects on open source security, distributed file systems, and operating systems, as well as co-founding the USENIX Workshop on Offensive Technologies.

If there is one myth that you could debunk in cybersecurity, what would it be?

That security is so hopelessly complex. Unfortunately, the security industry tends to admire threats and problems as much as actually solving them. You find that folks focus on the wrong things; most security conferences are really sensationalistic with all the stunt hacking and hype. In reality, when you look at how most organizations fail at security, it's always from the same fundamental and basic things that were highly preventable. There are always fancy zero-day attacks, zero-day threats, and super-capable nation-state attackers, but that's not what most security actually is, or where the real problems are. With Duo, we've begun to help change the perception that security is hopelessly complicated.

What is one of the biggest bang-for-the-buck actions that an organization can take to improve its cybersecurity posture?

Hygiene. Since we focus on the wrong things like the "super-sexy attacks," we end up in a situation where we basically fail at the fundamentals. We overlook the most basic things we should be doing, and we end up doing dentistry via root canal. There's been other organizations that have taken a stab at coming up with a very basic security program, for instance, critical point controls. But looking at the organization, do you have a security program? The quality of that stuff is pretty simple.

There's actually a tweet from Alex Stamos (@alexstamos), former CISO of Facebook, where he summarizes pretty well all the things a company should do. It starts with reducing your attack scope by putting everything you need to protect behind single sign-on. Then comes defending that with systems like Duo to understand who your users are, making sure you have a full inventory of all the devices used in your environment and that they're updated and safe, as well as awareness of what's happening in your environment and the ability to audit that activity. Lastly, add some controls to understand what to do when things go wrong.[16]

How is it that cybersecurity spending is increasing but breaches are still happening?

Most security products don't actually protect organizations from the threats they face. In security, a vendor can make money by selling you a box that sits there and does nothing, and the vendor will say, "See? You're more secure; nothing's happening." And the customer will say, "Well, geez, nothing was happening before I bought this dumb box." The reality is, security is a lemon market where people don't or can't understand the effectiveness of the tools and products they buy.

Breaches are definitely still happening, and they're escalating because of the digital transformation of businesses—every organization is bringing their ecosystem into the world. Everybody has a lot more of their customers' data than they ever did. That concentrated risk of data loss is something that's driving it on one side. But on the other side, computing is getting much safer. The consumer IT products we use today are much safer than they ever were and much more capable.

Consider an iPhone. The iPhone is about the safest computing platform out there today. There is no antivirus market for the iPhone, and there never will be; Apple makes sure of that. It's kind of the "Holy Grail" of trusted computing. This exists now today not only for iOS devices, but Android devices and even Chromebooks. It's amazing to me to think that the nation's schoolkids are in safer computing environments than most businesses. Safer options do exist now; we just have to be able to recognize that and make better choices about what we use.

Another aspect is security never kept up with the consumerization of IT. It used to be that almost all great technology was developed first by the government, then it would go to business, and finally it would get to consumers. Today, it's exactly the opposite. My 8-year-old kid has an iPad before anyone at my office does, before the government allows them to be used. This inversion of control means that every user is basically a CIO, and if I don't like your security program—and if I don't want to jump through the corporate firewall and the corporate VPN to get to the corporate file server to share a file with a colleague—I'm just going to use Dropbox. Organizations have very little real ability to tell people what to do anymore. They have to design security IT workflows that people actually want to adopt.

The other piece driving this is that every enterprise today is an ecosystem. The internet has not only hyper-connected all of us individually, but all of our business as well. You look at any modern organization and it's an ecosystem of partners and contractors and vendors, and the degree of third-party risk for all of our organizations in a hyper-connected world is much greater than it used to be, and that's why you see all these breaches happen that way. Someone gets hacked as sort of a second-order effect of another organization getting breached. That exposed attack surface of users and devices—and all the data applications that have left the four walls of your building—that's been a wonderful thing for productivity and users in terms of a better experience, but I think security has just failed to keep up. Security still thinks it can enforce unnatural behaviors on people, and that's just not possible anymore. You used to have to put an agent on an endpoint to keep it from running the wrong software, but now all that stuff is evolving. There are app stores that prevent bad software from getting on my device. There's a natural segmentation within the cloud: salespeople can only go to Salesforce, HR people go to Workday. There's no crossing of streams within a single shared environment anymore.

Computing has gotten much safer, but insecurity today exists at the intersection of people and technology. Hackers have that figured out. Today, they don't go after systems anymore; they go after people.

Do you need a college degree or certification to be a cybersecurity professional?

Hell, no. For instance, at Duo, I would say only 20 percent of our people have prior experience in security, and everybody else comes from a whole bunch of different backgrounds. Even outside of our security team, we have just as large a design team, and our design team also has user research as a function. This team is led by a former journalist, who actually spends their time conducting hundreds of user interviews so we can understand our users' experiences living with security every day. We have to solve for their needs.

How did you get started in the cybersecurity field, and what advice would you give to a beginner pursuing a career in cybersecurity?

I'm not a good example, unfortunately, because I grew up in a very different time and age when we just didn't have access to the things we needed to learn. You learned how to do things in an environment that you didn't have legitimate access to. Today is very different; you have computers everywhere. The barriers are extremely low. In fact, both of my kids, a 12-year-old boy and an 8-year-old daughter, have their own Raspberry Pis. They both have been doing programming since they were very little, and not because I'm pushing them, but because their friends are programming and their schools are teaching them. I'm excited that the joy of creation in technology is becoming much more mainstream. It's not just computers; it's "making" as a culture. I'm happy to see science, technology, engineering, math, and also the arts intersecting much more from an early education perspective than they had before. I have great hope there will be many more folks who will have the skill sets and the mind-sets for this kind of work in the future. Right now there is a labor gap in terms of these skills today.

I got started by just messing around, and I think that's how anybody learns anything, ever. You can sit there and have somebody tell you how to do something, but until you've had the joy and frustration of trying to do it on your own and make that progress yourself, you don't really learn. For example, I love skateboarding as my primary hobby, because, one, you have a super-strong feedback loop, and two, you can't really fool anybody. Either you are able to do something or you aren't, and you figure it out quickly because concrete is pretty unforgiving. It's also the kind of thing where you have no other choice but to maintain a beginner's mind-set, which is what you have to have in security particularly. In other disciplines, you can master something over 20 years and then all of a sudden you know everything you need to know about a discipline. Security is just constantly evolving, and the landscape is shifting, because, again, security is about how things can be made to fail. That's why I think hobbies like hacking and skateboarding are similar, because no matter how much you know or how far you get, you're just one pebble or one zero-day exploit away from falling on your face.

My suggestion to anyone looking to get into security is to find a community to join. For me, security wasn't about just the subject matter alone. It was the socialization of that learning as part of a community and becoming friends. I had to find those friends and network online before the internet with bulletin board systems (BBSs), X.25, etc. In this day and age, there are so many options, and that's what's so wonderful about the democratization of all this knowledge and access via the internet.

One of my favorite articles on this was from my friend Cory Scott, the CISO of LinkedIn. He contributed an interview to *Decipher*, an editorially independent news site of Duo. He talks about the four categories of security minds that he likes to hire and includes folks that he basically describes as being actuaries, like accountants.[17] In a certain respect, a lot of security is about getting the fundamentals right. How do you ensure proper hygiene? Folks who are used to building and reviewing checklists, or building reliable processes, can ensure organizational outcomes. There's a wide variety of things to do in security, so there's many paths into it besides just what I was doing.

What is your specialty in cybersecurity, and how can others gain expertise in your specialty?

I'm not sure I have a specialty, and I think that's one of the fun things about security. No matter how much you learn, there's always something more to get into. I've done everything from authentication and network protocol stuff to operating systems and application security; I've kind of done a little bit of everything. That's the joy in it. I also enjoy being on the people side of it, too. It's not only security design and usability stuff, but thinking about how innovation in security actually happens from open source communities and networks, how security becomes or is introduced as a basic capability on every team, or how you create more successful and diverse security startups.

"I'm not sure I have a specialty, and I think that's one of the fun things about security. No matter how much you learn, there's always something more to get into."

My interests in security persist in ways that are not strictly technical anymore; it's more about trying to contribute to the community that I grew up in that supported me, and now I, in turn, have an obligation to help support and pay it forward. I would like to see more diversity of opinions, thoughts, ideas, experiences, and people in this industry. That's presently what my interest and focus is in.

What is your advice for career success when it comes to getting hired, climbing the corporate ladder, or starting a company in cybersecurity?

I don't think success is linear. Some people are born knowing exactly what they want to be in life, and those people scare me. I have a friend who's a public company CEO, and he said, "I knew I was going to be a public company CEO when I was eight," and that's…scary. I think there are many routes to the top, and it's not just ladder climbing. You can enter a field and find a profession and work your way up the levels; for some people, that works, but that's not me. My interests growing up have been pretty broad—from skateboarding and graffiti to punk rock and hacking—but for me, it's really the exploration. If you're like me, you have the voracious appetite to experience the world from a bunch of different perspectives and incorporate that into your learning.

It is kind of a path of rock climbing, not ladder climbing. You go sideways, you exercise different muscles. There are many paths to the top. We had an office manager who became one of our top-performing inside sales reps who then went on to become one of our top-performing recruiters and now helps us throw corporate parties and DJs them. Explore and try lots of things; there's a very good chance you'll find your way into some opportunity, and you can always pivot from there.

What qualities do you believe all highly successful cybersecurity professionals share?

There are many ways that people achieve success, and not all of them are good. In security, there's probably more opportunity for folks to be successful without actually contributing very much. That's not to say the majority of the industry is bad; I just mean that sometimes incentives aren't really there, and people can get away with a lot. It can be discouraging to see the wrong things happen or people being rewarded for not the best behavior. Likewise, some security companies are creating problems as much as they're solving them.

There's one thing everyone at Duo has in common: we're self-aware. We test this in our behavioral interviews. We're looking for people who can step outside of themselves and not only understand the impact and effect they have on others but also someone else's point of view. That's super important because, in security, you're trying to solve for the ways in which technology fails—often because someone had a different mind-set or didn't have the same understanding.

Second, you have to have a fundamental optimism about technology. In the service of solving these problems, you have to build more technology. The answer is not to get rid of all technology. Cars used to not have seatbelts; now they do. Computers used to not have security; now they do. There's things that you can do to make yourself safe, but you can't give up on the problem.

Lastly, technology is actually a people business and a team sport. Nobody ever accomplishes anything in this industry alone, except offensively. You can be a very successful offensive hacker on your own, but even then, you're standing on the shoulders of giants, leveraging what came before you. The best teams I see out there, and the thing I find that is non-negotiable at Duo, all have this in common: good kindergarten skills. What are the three core values? To engineer the business, learn together, and be kinder than necessary. It's about going out of our way to help each other be successful. At the end of the day, we win as a team or lose as a team, and nothing else matters.

What is the best book or movie that can be used to illustrate cybersecurity challenges?

One is *The Checklist Manifesto* by Atul Gawande. It's basically an explanation of why it's so important to get basics right and why checklists do matter. In our industry, there's a lot of folks saying compliance is just security by accountants, not real security. I think that's wrong. Getting those basics right matters, and how you actually build operationally—the kind of discipline to make sure that the right things happen—is super important.

My second recommendation is also not about security but about the challenge of the hyper-connectedness of our systems and our world and the kind of butterfly effect that arises from that: *A Demon of Our Own Design* by Richard Bookstaber. It's actually about our financial collapse in the last decade, looking at the ways in which complex systems fail. A lot of it is simple. The warning lights, like at Three Mile Island, didn't work, and then there's a cascade of other lack in controls that leads quite literally to a nuclear meltdown. If you're looking for examples of how security fails, it's helpful to look at other disciplines.

What is your favorite hacker movie?

Sneakers. I really like *WarGames*, but *Sneakers* is by far the best hacker movie that ever existed. Everyone likes *Hackers*, but *Sneakers* was great. Duo made an edit of *WarGames* that basically summarized the entire movie in one minute. You can watch it on YouTube.[18]

What are your favorite books for motivation, personal development, or enjoyment?

I actually called this out in *Inc. Magazine*, but I hate business books.[19] I think most are just one idea spread out over 300 pages, super tedious, and not that interesting. One of the more inspiring books, for me, in terms of how I conduct my life and career, is *The Wu-Tang Manual* by The RZA. I wrote about it on LinkedIn (there's an article on my profile that you can check out), but I like the way that The RZA thought about how they created not only a rap dynasty but also a platform of opportunity for everyone involved with the clan, while also considering where they did it—Staten Island (Shaolin). The notion is that being somewhere outside of all the hustle and hype can be a real strategic advantage. Everyone chasing after each other's ideas and dollars sometimes doesn't produce the best results. If you really wanna do

> "Everyone chasing after each other's ideas and dollars sometimes doesn't produce the best results. If you really wanna do something well creatively, you've gotta have the space to stretch out and do that with people you really care about and respect."

something well creatively, you've gotta have the space to stretch out and do that with people you really care about and respect.

What is some practical cybersecurity advice you give to people at home in the age of social media and the Internet of Things?

Make sure you actually have an access point for your house that has a firewall. Some people think all they need is a passthrough bridge, but you should actually have a real access point with a real firewall so you can block things inbound. You can also use that access point to configure things like OpenDNS, which is useful as just a basic preliminary control.

Make safe choices about computing. Use a Chromebook or an iOS device or iPad. Use the cloud. I guarantee you that hundreds of Google's security engineers are going to do a better job of protecting your email and storage in their cloud (Gmail and GDrive) than you ever will.

Pick and choose your battles. Thankfully, most of that is pretty easy to solve in the consumer context.

What is a life hack that you'd like to share?

This isn't so much of a life hack as it is a principle, but it does have quite a bit of bearing on how I conduct myself. My dad was a Buddhist monk, and it's quite a long story of how he got to working at a liquor store. He tells me that reputation takes a lifetime to build, but it can go away in a second. The meaning of life, he said, is to live a life of meaning. What does that mean? A life of meaning is to have an impact and help others. At the end of the day, we're not going to take it with us. No one has ambitions to die rich. What is the legacy that you're going to leave behind? If you're a good person and do right by others, the universe won't let you starve. That's how I conduct my life and career and the models of leadership that I have for myself, my company, and my community.

I started something eight years ago called the Ann Arbor New Tech Meetup. It's a startup showcase of five new companies presenting every month, so we've had hundreds of companies and thousands of founders. What makes this event great is not that you've met a lot of people but that you've introduced a lot of people. Being useful is the greatest hack of all. People think of hacks as shortcuts, but I think of them as strategies. A good hack is an interesting strategy that people overlook, and sometimes the simplest things are standing right before us. I try to be useful and make sure that I'm doing the right things in life.

What is the biggest mistake you've ever made, and how did you recover from it?

This probably isn't a single mistake, but it took a long time to learn: my success isn't entirely my own. It does take a village, not just to raise a family or a child or a company, but even on my personal journey, I would need help along the way, and I'd have to ask for that. I think one of the hardest things to do in life is to know when or how or whom to ask for help. Over time, and also through the course of many relationships, being well-flanked by different perspectives has helped me realize who I can go to, and for what kind of advice, and then actually reach out to them. Sometimes I think people are too proud or don't want to be embarrassed, but the most successful people I know in life (conventionally successful)—who have changed the world and had a huge impact—they're also some of the humblest. They've always kept that beginner's mind-set and never really lost that.

It took time for me to learn how to be vulnerable in a professional context, but it allowed me to reach out and not be afraid or scared or embarrassed to. ■

> "There is no finite point where it's going to be, 'Well, okay, we've now spent enough. We're secure.'"

Twitter: @jaysonstreet • **Website:** jaysonestreet.com

Jayson E. Street

62

Jayson E. Street is a co-author of the Dissecting the Hack series. He is also the DEF CON Groups Global Ambassador and the VP of InfoSec for SphereNY. Jayson has spoken on a variety of information security subjects, including events at DEF CON, DerbyCon, GrrCon, and several other cons and colleges.

If there is one myth that you could debunk in cybersecurity, what would it be?

That humans are a liability. We always want to blame humans: "stupid user clicked on a link," "stupid user had a bad password," "stupid user went to a website," when it was actually "stupid information security who didn't properly train their users." Employees will do everything necessary to stay employed in their jobs and do what they're told. We don't teach them that part of their responsibility is to be security-minded. So, therefore, they don't have to be. It's not up to them to intuitively know about that. It's up to us to teach them that that's expected, and then they'll do that because that's part of their job. We don't need to keep getting technology to protect our users. We need to start getting our users better able to protect the technology.

What is one of the biggest bang-for-the-buck actions that an organization can take to improve its cybersecurity posture?

I think the biggest is investing in security awareness training and training your employees to be an asset instead of a liability. Do that at the beginning of their orientation when they're doing the rest of the training for their job.

How is it that cybersecurity spending is increasing but breaches are still happening?

That's like talking about how "safe technology" is increasing but there's still safe-crackers and bank robberies. There is no finite point where it's going to be, "Well, okay, we've now spent enough. We're secure." It doesn't work that way. Information security is not about eliminating risk. To think that we're eliminating risk is a whole false scenario. What we do is *mitigate* risk. We try to mitigate as much risk as we can with the budget that we have. We then go to upper-level management and tell them we've eliminated this much risk, mitigated it, but now there's this much risk that we can offset by using a cloud service provider or using another company that's got a service level agreement (SLA) and a contract to protect us. At the end of the day, after mitigation, after offsetting, there is still going to be a point where we go, "This is how much risk we have to accept." There will always be risk when dealing with online transactions or anything offline as well. There's always going to be a risk that they have to accept. Our job is to mitigate as much as possible, offset as much as possible, so we can present them with the narrowest amount of risk they have to accept. That requires a budget. It requires constantly evolving technology, and it requires staying ahead of where the attackers are going, what the criminals are doing, and that does cost money.

Do you need a college degree or certification to be a cybersecurity professional?

Well, since I'm a high school dropout who used to live behind a dumpster, I'm going to say "no" on that one. College and certifications and degrees are helpful to give you the methodology and stuff that's already in place so you don't have to learn the hard way like I did. Still, at the end of the day, it doesn't matter what paper you have. You should be judged by what you bring to the table and what knowledge you can succinctly disseminate among your peers and to the executive team. It's up to you to show them the knowledge that you have and to put it into action. The paper may get you in the door, but it's not going to keep you there. It's hard to fake competence in this industry for long, unless you're a thought leader.

How did you get started in the cybersecurity field, and what advice would you give to a beginner pursuing a career in cybersecurity?

I've always been interested in security, and I've always liked helping people. I started more than 30 years ago doing physical security. When I was doing IT help desk back in 2000, I was introduced to the VP of security, Tim Smith. He wanted to hire me to do computer security, and that's when my whole life changed. I never knew you could do computers *and* security and that no one shoots at you, which was amazing. So I was like, "Yes, please." It's really awesome and I never looked back.

A beginner can get into the industry by learning what they want to do for the rest of their lives. This field is so varied—from forensics, malware analysis, IP, TCB inspection, log review, intrusion detection systems, and firewall technology to social engineering, red teaming, pentesting, vulnerability assessment, and code review—there are so many different aspects of the field. Look for the one that makes you happy, that you're interested in, and that you have a passion for, and then find someone to pay you for it. That way, you stop working. I stopped working about five years ago. I still get a paycheck, but now I'm getting paid to do something that I would love to do anyway.

Also, you can go to iR0nin (ir0nin.com) and navigate to the Getting Started page. This is actually a page that I developed for people who are trying to get into information security. It has resources and a couple of videos on how to do that.

What is your specialty in cybersecurity, and how can others gain expertise in your specialty?

I call what I do "being a teachable moment." I do security awareness engagements where people pay me to break into their companies or rob their banks before an actual bad guy does. I don't write reports; I educate every single person on location after I've successfully robbed them. I then go back and talk to them and tell them what I did and how they can do better to detect me next time. So, I have a direct impact on the employees immediately.

There are people who do training for social engineering, like Chris Hadnagy (www.social-engineer.org). He does training on social engineering, and I give training on security awareness and how to engage your users into security awareness. That's my passion now. You also have to have an innate quality (what I call my main attribute) of having no shame and bad impulse control, which is the reason why I'm so successful.

What is your advice for career success when it comes to getting hired, climbing the corporate ladder, or starting a company in cybersecurity?

The best career advice for getting hired is do good work. It's not about playing politics or trying to shine; it's about being consistently good at your job and having a passion for it. In my bio on my web page, I put: "I was the best janitor for two years in a row at McDonald's Southeast Texas region." I was one of the best janitors out there, and I'm proud of that. I did a good job, and I did it very well, and I was recognized for that. Whatever you do, do it well, do it proficiently, have a passion for it, and make sure that you're doing it right. If it's something that you don't want to do forever, then continuously do a good job, but also let everybody know that you want to advance—or find somewhere else where you *can* grow. Never go in and do a half-hearted job because you're not interested or you don't like the position. Make it the position you want it to be, or go somewhere else.

> "Whatever you do, do it well, do it proficiently, have a passion for it, and make sure that you're doing it right."

What qualities do you believe all highly successful cybersecurity professionals share?

Passion and curiosity. You need to have the innate ability and curiosity to want to solve problems and find solutions for things, especially when they're difficult. You also need to have the passion to keep wanting to search and look.

What is the best book or movie that can be used to illustrate cybersecurity challenges?

Apollo 13, because they were in a situation they had never seen before, people's lives were on the line, and they had to create something out of nothing. They took things that were totally contrary to what they needed to do and they did it. This is the very definition of hacking—going around how systems and things are supposed to be to make it work for you.

What is your favorite hacker movie?

Hackers. Everyone wants to say *WarGames* or *Sneakers* to sound sophisticated or refined, but no. *Hackers* is still my favorite. I still stand by the fact that Angelina Jolie got more people into hacking than high-speed modems did. It's approachable and not just a hacker movie—it's also a cool and fun story. I like it for many different reasons.

What are your favorite books for motivation, personal development, or enjoyment?

I like fantasy books. The Dresden Files series by Jim Butcher is about a private eye going after the forces of evil. I like to be devoid of reality as much as possible.

What is some practical cybersecurity advice you give to people at home in the age of social media and the Internet of Things?

When dealing with social media, I make sure everybody understands one important fact: nothing is as private as they want it to be. When you post, know that the person you hate the most is probably going to see it one day. Be careful when you're private messaging because screenshots can happen. People think they're only broadcasting to their five followers or close friends, but when it's on the internet, it's there for everybody to see at some point.

For the internet in general, people need to patch. You can get firewall and antivirus and all of these things to help you, but if you really want to keep yourself protected, keep your systems patched. And not just your operating system, not just the second Tuesday of every month, but everything you own (e.g., Java, Adobe, iTunes). That will protect you more than any antivirus you ever buy.

What is a life hack that you'd like to share?

Showing kindness to others. It's not social engineering if you're genuinely nice and expect nothing. Every once in a while, people can surprise you. You never know what kind of day the person you're talking to is having. Being nice may not help you, but it may help the next person they deal with. There have been a lot of times when I've been upgraded or gotten something different, not because I was social engineering but because I was being nice and they appreciated it, so they ended up doing something nice in return.

Treat every person with respect because you never know when you're going to need their help later on down the line.

What is the biggest mistake you've ever made, and how did you recover from it?

I've never made a mistake that I didn't learn from. Mistakes are valuable. They're not always encouraged, but when they do happen, don't shy away from them, don't try to avoid them—face them head on and learn from them. Those are learning opportunities. There's not one mistake I've made that can be deemed my "worst mistake." I've accidentally robbed the wrong bank before. I've hurt people's feelings before. One time, I took more credit than I should have for an engagement and didn't talk about the full role of others. They called me out on it, I admitted it, and I rectified it. Learning from mistakes is key, and you have to own up to them. ■

"Users are not stupid. They're just not trained or focused on security. Users were hired to do a specific job, which rarely involves security. Users can be educated if they believe security and IT actually matter."

Twitter: @Ben0xA • **Website:** ben0xa.com

Ben Ten

63

Ben has been working in technology and development for more than 20 years. He spent 13 years doing defense in the medical industry before moving over to offense. He uses his knowledge of defense to refine his offensive skills and then uses this knowledge to equip customers with a better understanding of defensive methodologies.

If there is one myth that you could debunk in cybersecurity, what would it be?

That a user is stupid. Users are not stupid. They're just not trained or focused on security. Users were hired to do a specific job, which rarely involves security. Users can be educated if they believe security and IT actually matter. Otherwise, they will do just enough to not get caught or fired.

What is one of the biggest bang-for-the-buck actions that an organization can take to improve its cybersecurity posture?

Build your defense around detections after the initial compromise. Initial vector is not nearly as important as what an attacker does after they are in. When you build your defense with the idea that the attacker is already in, it allows you to detect attacks from rogue devices, rogue employees, or systems that have been compromised remotely. Detection is more important than deflection.

"Build your defense around detections after the initial compromise. Initial vector is not nearly as important as what an attacker does after they are in."

How is it that cybersecurity spending is increasing but breaches are still happening?
The spending is on stopping the attacks. Every time a tool claims to stop an attack, the attackers create new ways to bypass them. When we consistently focus on initial vector, we will always play the catchup game.

Do you need a college degree or certification to be a cybersecurity professional?
I don't have one. I will admit, for some organizations, the degree requirement is nothing more than an HR barrier. It doesn't mean the person knows how to be a cybersecurity professional. I know many people without one, and they are way smarter than some other people I know who have a degree. I don't think it's necessary to do well, but it may be necessary for some organizations.

How did you get started in the cybersecurity field, and what advice would you give to a beginner pursuing a career in cybersecurity?
The company I worked for got broken into. While I had hard drive encryption, I wasn't really into security. This caused me to become more interested, and I began volunteering at conventions like DerbyCon, BSides Chicago, and so on. As I volunteered and listened to more talks, I learned a ton. Then, in 2012, I gave my first talk at DerbyCon. I would always encourage someone to begin by volunteering. In this industry, it's not what you know but who you know.

What is your specialty in cybersecurity, and how can others gain expertise in your specialty?
I have an extensive blue team background. I have developed a comprehensive Adversarial Detection & Countermeasures program for my organization that I have used at several Fortune 500 companies to detect attackers. I've been penetration testing for six years, but I was a defender for more than a decade before. I would say if you want to be a good cybersecurity professional, you should know both the red and the blue. Regardless of your role, knowing both sides makes you better at what you do.

What is your advice for career success when it comes to getting hired, climbing the corporate ladder, or starting a company in cybersecurity?
It is who you know, not what you know. People came to me to hire me. I didn't have to seek anyone out. It was because of my involvement in the community, contribution to projects, volunteering at events, and speaking at conventions. As people know you more, they have a desire to have you on their team and to give you chances to advance within the organization. Keeping up with trainings provided by respected organizations is another way you can continue to advance in this field.

What qualities do you believe all highly successful cybersecurity professionals share?
The desire to learn and to take things apart. Whether it is code or a new widget, I have always wanted to know how or why something works. I think this is at the

core of most of us in the security field. We have the unquenchable desire to know how something works, to see if we can make it do something else, and to see if it can be broken in any way.

What is the best book or movie that can be used to illustrate cybersecurity challenges?

Every Star Trek series out there. They have the most advanced spacecraft out there, yet people can still bypass security controls, get duped into performing a security function for an unauthorized person, get compromised and have their technology work against them, and have personnel who are untrained enough not to spot the obvious villain. Every time I watch an episode, I wonder what control would have prevented the villain from being successful.

What is your favorite hacker movie?

Sneakers...love that movie so much!

What are your favorite books for motivation, personal development, or enjoyment?

I prefer to read survival manuals that detail how to survive with no technology. It gives me a challenge to build something with what is around without using any technology and to survive.

What is some practical cybersecurity advice you give to people at home in the age of social media and the Internet of Things?

Use it! However, there should always be a healthy level of paranoia when it comes to these things. You are allowing something to monitor you in your home. Just as you wouldn't want a guest to watch you at all points, your IoT devices should be able to help you without invading your privacy.

What is a life hack that you'd like to share?

When I travel, I have to stay in hotels. Some of the hotels only have paper cups. When I try to put my toothbrush in one, it tips over. So I poke a hole in the side of the cup near the bottom. Then I slide the end of my toothbrush through the hole so it offsets the center of gravity. The toothbrush stays in the cup and doesn't tip over.

What is the biggest mistake you've ever made, and how did you recover from it?

I tried to get too much too soon when I first went out on my own. I got in way over my head with debt and was evicted from my first apartment. My credit was ruined, and I could barely afford to live as a roommate. It took years of self-discipline and saving, but eventually, I was able to regain control of my finances and have owned two homes since. I learned that it is better to wait for something and not be in debt than to get it immediately and owe something to someone else. I live beneath my means now. ■

> "I learned that it is better to wait for something and not be in debt than to get it immediately and owe something to someone else."

> "Every time someone makes up a new word to make a sale or calls a vulnerability assessment a pentest, they're hurting the whole industry."

Twitter: @viss • **Website:** phobos.io

Dan Tentler

Dan Tentler is the executive founder and offensive security practice director of the Phobos Group. Dan has an established reputation in the industry for his innovative risk surface discovery projects and numerous speaking engagements. Dan and his team have conducted unique targeted attack simulations for companies in sectors including financial, energy, manufacturing and industrials, and various platform service providers. Dan routinely appears in the press to speak on new security risks and security industry development.

64

If there is one myth that you could debunk in cybersecurity, what would it be?

That compliance in any way helps companies be secure. One of the biggest problems we face as community members embedded in the industry is the perpetual stream of bogus information that comes from the news, charlatans, companies with "eager sales and marketing departments," and other sources of information that are patently false, or otherwise purposely skewing information and reports. People misuse technical jargon all the time, and the topic we should really be concerned with is that companies will often do this on purpose to try to make sales, or salaciously solicit the media to get their name in the news. Every time someone makes up a new word to make a sale or calls a vulnerability assessment a pentest, they're hurting the whole industry.

What is one of the biggest bang-for-the-buck actions that an organization can take to improve its cybersecurity posture?

Examining their own perimeter, even with a rudimentary skill set. Many orgs simply ignore security outright and focus almost solely on compliance. It literally translates to "They're putting in zero effort." They do the paperwork dance to keep the auditors away, and they make that circus sideshow of smoke and mirrors so elaborate, so huge, that it takes a whole department of people to produce all of this self-referential documentation to occupy regulators and auditors. If they actually did some kind of security instead of completely ignoring it, it would make staggering, mammoth improvements—even just having an inventory of their equipment and Nmapping it from time to time.

How is it that cybersecurity spending is increasing but breaches are still happening?

Because orgs are happy to spend millions of dollars on "feel good" security, which consists mainly of appliances that wrap open source tools, dramatically increasing the cost for their customers. For example, many "pentest shops" simply run Nessus or Nexpose against the external perimeter of an org, charge several thousand dollars, and call that a "pentest." Oftentimes, the org can simply buy the tool themselves and get far more value. The reason is twofold, the way I see it. First, companies see Equifax and Sony get hacked, and they get nervous and think, "I don't want that to happen to me." Second, these "pentest shops," as mentioned earlier, are happy to slide into that conversation and say, "Oh, we've built something just for that! You should pay us for that!" and companies in many cases are happy to do so. Costs go up for literally no reason other than customer fear. Everyone loses.

Do you need a college degree or certification to be a cybersecurity professional?

No, flat out. I and many other professionals have established careers on their skills alone. Think about it this way: how long does it take for Q1 2018 threat intel and knowledge about bugs and techniques to percolate down to students sitting in chairs? Ten years? How good is that information 10 years later? Maybe parts of it, but certainly not all of it. Certifications tend to be a mixed bag. Many certifications are specific to hardware or equipment. CCNA/CCNP, for example, these are great certs, but only if you're going to be spending a lot of time working with Cisco equipment on switching and routing. You want to do firewalls or wireless? Those are different certs.

There is no "well-rounded security cert," no matter how much people attempt to convince you otherwise. That 400-question, multiple-choice cert that asks you about barbed-wire fences and fire extinguishers? Don't waste your money.

How did you get started in the cybersecurity field, and what advice would you give to a beginner pursuing a career in cybersecurity?

I got started doing freelance work 10 years ago helping people with WordPress blogs and basic network and host-based security posture assessments. I was a sysadmin for 10 years before that, and the knowledge I gained from building systems and networks helped me immensely in determining where security problems were happening.

Arguably, the best thing you can do before getting into security is getting a fundamental understanding of how systems and networks function, even at a basic level. You don't need to be able to recite IP protocol numbers or TCP header and footer offsets or how to construct a Cisco ACL in an ASA off the top of your head, but you have to know what those things are and how they work. If you don't know how MySQL talks to Apache in a LAMP stack for a WordPress blog, you're not going to do very well discovering and abusing SQLi. My advice here is to go be a sysadmin or work in operations for a couple of years before going into security—it will provide immeasurably useful experience. You can't secure a system if you don't know how it works. You can't hack a system effectively if you have no idea what's going on under the hood.

What is your specialty in cybersecurity, and how can others gain expertise in your specialty?

I've landed in a sort of strange spot, where my expertise is a cow-print mask over the corpus of knowable information security knowledge. I'm personally strong in the offensive/attack martial arts, but having gone back and forth between red team and blue team my whole career, I am also aware of the defensive tools, what they are, how they operate, and when to use them. I'm not as strong in defense as I am on offense. Having spent a decade doing systems and networks, I'm a fairly handy sysadmin, and I maintain a surprisingly wide personal network involving several servers, enterprise wireless networking gear, several Cisco ASAs, VPN site-to-site links, and a small VPN service for friends and family to be used at hackercons and shady coffee shops.

For someone else to follow in my footsteps, the best advice I can give is to go be a sysadmin for five to seven years. Learn Linux, Windows, routers, switches, networking, Wi-Fi. Learn what to do when someone is in your lobby being shady. Find out how to spot them using the Cisco WDS heatmap or the Aruba heatmap. Figure out how to examine a pcap that's 2TB in size on consumer equipment with only a 100Mb link to the machine the pcap is on. Get stuck in weird problems, figure them out. Don't just ask the internet. Do it yourself. With your hands. Then attack it, and watch the logs.

What is your advice for career success when it comes to getting hired, climbing the corporate ladder, or starting a company in cybersecurity?

I was never any good at climbing the corporate ladder because, in my experience, that means leaving your scruples and your morals on the road outside the company. Usually, climbing the corporate ladder amounts to "making your management like you enough to promote you."

Getting hired will vary depending on where you're going. Big shops will want something; small shops will want something else. Coming in as a contractor, yet another variation. The best way to grapple with this mentally is to follow these steps:

1. Do cool things and share them with friends. Show your work.
2. No matter what branch of InfoSec you're interested in, you can set up a GitHub account and share your scripts, tooling, code, etc.
3. Having examples of "what you can do now," regardless of what job you're in now, is super helpful.
4. Have a plan. Saying "I wanna go into security" is like saying "I wanna work with animals" or "I wanna work in government." You need to have some idea of where you want to go.
5. If you don't know, say you don't know.
6. Learn to be resourceful. People who can "get stuff done" are the ones who get the job.

As far as starting a company? Ask me again in a year. I'm still working on mine. I can tell you right away, though, don't underprice yourself, and don't charge an arm and a leg without the ability to back up why you're charging so much. This will involve market research. Also, make sure you know how to sell whatever it is you do, services or products. You'll have to learn the ins and outs of basic sales. If you don't like working with people and just want to write code or do hacks, then starting a business is not for you.

What qualities do you believe all highly successful cybersecurity professionals share?

The ability to be malleable. Security rolls forward with technology, and technology is always changing. If you're not prepared to adapt when the new things come rolling in, you'll get left behind—plain and simple. Always be learning; always be interested in what's coming down the road. Some of it is interesting, and some of it is horribly lame. You have to see what's coming and examine whether it's something that you want to be involved with. Your success will depend entirely on the choices you make here.

What is the best book or movie that can be used to illustrate cybersecurity challenges?

This is a toss-up between several different properties. Few movies actually articulate what "security challenges" are, if any. I'm having trouble just thinking of one. There are tons of movies that go over "how to attack stuff," or social engineering specifically, or, at a high level, how to conduct certain types of attacks or operations, but I can't think of any movie that directly mentions or covers "security challenges" from a defensive perspective.

What is your favorite hacker movie?

Toss-up between *Hackers*, *Sneakers*, *Swordfish*, and *Antitrust*.

What are your favorite books for motivation, personal development, or enjoyment?

I spend a lot of time watching conference talks on YouTube and trying out new things from walk-throughs and documentation. I find myself with so little time that I don't spend it on traditional paper books, and my "reading" has turned into fetching audiobooks and listening to them during travel. I've read a lot of Neil Stephenson, I enjoyed *Ready Player One*, and I've been told I'd really like *Daemon*. Also, supposedly, people squint at you if you tell them you haven't read *The Cuckoo's Egg*. I haven't read it yet. I should add that to Audible.

What is some practical cybersecurity advice you give to people at home in the age of social media and the Internet of Things?

Don't let it on the network. I don't care how cool you think it is. It'll get shelled, it'll be part of the next Mirai botnet. Take the time to investigate what it is you're buying and how that will affect an attacker's ability to gain control of your life. If something is super easy, it usually means it's super easy to exploit.

What is a life hack that you'd like to share?

Try the `nload` and `iftop` command-line tools. To install, type `apt-get install nload iftop`. When you see what they do, you'll put them on *every box you touch*.

What is the biggest mistake you've ever made, and how did you recover from it?

I didn't know until 2008 or so that information security was an actual profession. I thought it was just an extension of IT. I haven't recovered from it, and I don't think that I ever will. It arguably set my InfoSec career back something like five years. If I knew that all the hacky stuff I was doing as a sysadmin was "its own job," I'd have been applying for those instead of getting systems architect jobs and trying to convince management that I should be 100 percent focused on security. ■

"There are plenty of highly experienced cybersecurity people in the market right now who would love to be working, and yet employers are completely unable to get out of their own way to get these folks on board."

Twitter: @falconsview • **Website:** www.secureconsulting.net

Ben Tomhave

65

Ben Tomhave is a security industry veteran, progressive thinker, and culture warrior. He holds an MS in engineering management from The George Washington University, has a BA in computer science from Luther College, and is a graduate of the BJ Fogg Behavior Design Boot Camp. Ben is CISSP certified and has previously held positions with Gartner, AOL, Wells Fargo, ICSA Labs, LockPath, and Ernst & Young (EY). He is former co-chair of the American Bar Association Information Security Committee, a senior member of ISSA, former board member of the Society of Information Risk Analysts, and former board member for OWASP NoVA. Ben is a published author and experienced public speaker, including engagements with the RSA Conference, MISTI, ISSA, RMISC, Secure360, RVAsec, and DevOps Connect, as well as Gartner events. He's covered most topics in InfoSec, including application security, DevOps/DevSecOps, security architecture, data security, and encryption and key management.

If there is one myth that you could debunk in cybersecurity, what would it be?

Just one? Today, I think it's the myth of the workforce shortage. In many ways, this is a self-created issue due to a number of deficiencies in vision, strategy, and execution. Automation is not sufficiently wielded. Instead, we see organizations building large SOCs staffed with extremely junior personnel, who stare at screens and push buttons when colors change—changes that are indicative of a threshold being met, meaning an automated trigger all but exists. Instead, we should be focusing our resource development needs elsewhere. Moreover, companies seem unwilling to invest in developing junior resources to help them advance to a journeyman stage in their careers while simultaneously devaluing experienced hires by underpaying them, by not supporting their needs for ongoing career development, and by incredibly short-sighted inflexibility on work arrangements (such as denying remote work). There are plenty of highly experienced cybersecurity people in the market right now who would love to be working, and yet employers are completely unable to get out of their own way to get these folks on board.

What is one of the biggest bang-for-the-buck actions that an organization can take to improve its cybersecurity posture?

Culture change is the overarching "most valuable change" that's needed today. It's also the least common. Culture change impacts behavior, incentive models, accountability, and transparency—and myriad other critical enablers that help to mature and improve cybersecurity programs. Until organizational culture—comprised of values and behaviors—is substantially reformed, cybersecurity failures will continue to abound.

How is it that cybersecurity spending is increasing but breaches are still happening?

Cybersecurity spending is as much an embodiment of "shiny object syndrome" as it is anything else. We have grossly unqualified "leaders" in CISO (or equivalent) roles who simply don't understand the subject, and they're trying to drive change and compliance using a haphazard, vendor-influenced "strategy." Very few organizations are truly taking stock of actual, measurable information risk as it faces the organization, let alone adopting reasonable, agile, quantitative methods for assessing that risk.

Do you need a college degree or certification to be a cybersecurity professional?

No degree or certification is needed, but having a reasonable education doesn't hurt. We need more critical thinkers in our cybersecurity (and IT and development) ranks, and getting a degree can be one means of getting people there. Unfortunately, there are broader issues in society that are decreasing critical-thinking skills among younger generations, such as the weakening of pre-college education programs and institutions.

How did you get started in the cybersecurity field, and what advice would you give to a beginner pursuing a career in cybersecurity?

I came to cybersecurity (or information security, as I still prefer it) quite naturally in the mid '90s when a high school classmate of mine showed me how he was abusing the network and computing resources at the college where my dad was a professor. He showed me how he was making money from "warez" and pirated software, and all without ever having to directly authenticate into the systems he was exploiting. This drove me to explore how he was able to exploit those environments, how to fix the environments to stop those exploits, and so on.

By the time I got to college, I had started to see the promise of the internet as I worked my way through school doing systems and network administration (admin on HP/UX and Novell NetWare systems, as well as literally pulling cables to install network ports, network cards, and TCP/IP software stacks in Windows 3.x systems). I compiled and deployed the first web server on campus and began actively promoting training people on how to create websites, while also promoting the use and development for official purposes by the college. By 1997, we were starting to see early e-commerce sites deployed using SSL, and it was painfully obvious that there was more needed than firewalls. Systems hardening, patching, active testing of software for vulnerabilities, and both user and developer education were all necessary components. My career took off from there.

My advice to people interested in a career in cybersecurity is to not pursue a career in cybersecurity. Instead, we need people with well-rounded backgrounds in systems and network engineering, software development, research, and anything else that inspires the development of critical-thinking skills. Give me a motivated, reasonably experienced technical professional, and I can easily turn them into a "cybersecurity professional" (who will then start suffering from depression and substance abuse—ha-ha...). However, there's actually very little real opportunity for "green," fresh recruits who lack suitable technical and real-world experience. Moreover, there are still far too many "cybersecurity professionals" who simply do not understand how organizations work and who lack the empathy to understand the needs of the organization. We need better thinkers who can apply diverse experience, not pigeon-holed specialists with very limited futures.

What is your specialty in cybersecurity, and how can others gain expertise in your specialty?

I am intentionally a generalist. By trade, I am most often associated with the security architecture role. Security architects generally need to understand nearly all specialties within cybersecurity in order to help formulate a coherent cybersecurity strategy that cuts across all silos and specialties. Gaining expertise as a security architect requires working in a variety of cybersecurity roles in order to understand unique challenges and then parlay that into a broad, strategic vision for the organization.

What is your advice for career success when it comes to getting hired, climbing the corporate ladder, or starting a company in cybersecurity?

Run away! (Ha-ha, just kidding...or am I?)

I have a number of recommendations.

- Have perseverance. This industry is painfully difficult to traverse, and there are more "bad days" than "good days." Stick with it; focus on learning, patience, and perseverance in the face of adversity.

- Early in your career, it will be tempting to hop around a lot to aggressively move up. Be careful doing that, and make sure you're leaving or moving up for the right reasons, which include getting stale in your current role, new opportunities for learning, or moving to a team or organization that is a better culture fit or represents better learning opportunities.

- Be careful about burning bridges, which can be done easily in the current age of social media insanity. Be careful what you say in public forums because you never know when it will come back to haunt you. This industry continues to be very cliquish, which means getting on someone's bad side can have broad and long-lasting negative impacts on your career.

- Find outside interests for your own sanity. Staying too much within your industry and work environment, especially with cybersecurity, can be highly detrimental to your mental and physical health. Jobs in this industry tend to be highly stressful and demoralizing, which greatly increases the need for outside connections and interests. Having a life in meatspace is the best way to stay grounded.

- Be honest and do your research. Whether it's starting a new job, looking for a new job, or starting a new company, it's absolutely imperative that you're honest and that you do considerable research. As a startup, that could be market research to fully understand the competition and what problems your customers are facing. As a job seeker, that could be deep research on prospective employers to determine whether or not it's truly a place you want to work. Or, it could be as simple as building a mentor network to help you grow and mature your career, including identifying seemingly orthogonal or adjacent skill sets that can provide a huge boost to your proficiency and overall expertise.

What qualities do you believe all highly successful cybersecurity professionals share?

The two most prevalent skills found in successful cybersecurity professionals are curiosity and critical thinking. They have the willingness to ask "why?" and then pursue finding an answer, while also being able to suss out truths by reading between the lines. A third important skill, though one that's still in short supply, is empathy: the ability to understand and identify with our customers, whether they're internal or external, and provide reasonable, rational, and kind support to them.

What is the best book or movie that can be used to illustrate cybersecurity challenges?

My strongest recommendation for reading today is *Reinventing Organizations* by Frederic Laloux. The book is about organizational culture and makes extensive use of case studies. What's fascinating about the book is that, unknown to the author, it closely aligns to the DevOps movement, which leads to my second recommendation, *The Phoenix Project*. Neither book is about cybersecurity, but they nonetheless perfectly highlight the key challenges facing cybersecurity teams today. Lastly, I recommend reading *Surveillance* by Aaron Pogue because it's a near-future, semi-dystopian crime drama that, in many ways, accurately represents what could soon become our modern reality.

What is your favorite hacker movie?

I don't tend to watch "hacker" movies because I find most of them ridiculous. If forced to answer, I suppose I'd suggest *Sneakers* as an okay example since it demonstrates some (albeit ridiculous) problem-solving and critical-thinking skills with a remarkably diverse cast for the time. One could also point to *WarGames* as the cult classic, but it's a bit too dated for many people today.

What are your favorite books for motivation, personal development, or enjoyment?

I've done a fair amount of reading over the past couple of years around the topic of "generative culture," which is a culture that develops strong, positive benefits while thinking about impact on future generations. There are a number of interesting books that one can read, ranging from Senge's *The Fifth Discipline* to Scharmer's *Theory U* to Kotre's *Make It Count*, and so on. Further, Westrum's seminal NIH research paper, "A typology of organisational cultures," is interesting reading, as is anything and everything one can find from BJ Fogg on

Behavior Design. One's time is also well spent reading Cialdini's books *Influence* and *Pre-Suasion* to understand how people can be influenced and preempted. *Nudge* by Thaler and Sunstein is also very interesting, as it holds similar notions to the so-called "butterfly effect," as does Cialdini's *Pre-Suasion* as well as Fogg's "Tiny Habits" theories, in terms of how seemingly small things can greatly influence decisions and change.

In terms of reading for enjoyment, I almost exclusively read lightweight sci-fi and fantasy fiction. I'm a big fan of Michael G. Manning (Mageborn series and all related works), as well as John Conroe's Demon Accords series (and related works), Kel Kade's Dark Tidings series, the dystopian Silo series by Hugh Howey (*Wool*, *Shift*, and *Dust*), and Steve McHugh (Hellequin Chronicles and Avalon Chronicles).

What is some practical cybersecurity advice you give to people at home in the age of social media and the Internet of Things?

Honestly, I'm generally so overwhelmed and inundated by cybersecurity in my work life that I tend not to be proactive about cybersecurity advice to friends and family. I focus more on teaching my kids to be skeptical and aware of their surroundings. My oldest (a girl) has reached an age where kids are starting to be mean, and I have already had a couple conversations with her to set expectations that this sort of nonsense will continue. I will actively oppose her involvement with social media for the foreseeable future, instead emphasizing real-world friendships and activities.

What is a life hack that you'd like to share?

I enjoy cooking (the process), but life often conspires against me. Eating out gets tiring, not to mention expensive. Many a day, I forget to thaw meats from the freezer, and that used to leave me scrambling to figure something out—until I found the Instant Pot. You won't be mistaken for a gourmet chef, but there's something magical about being able to throw meat (thawed or frozen) into a pot with some water or broth, push some buttons and magically have cooked food a little while later (up to 90 minutes sometimes, but that's okay if you're not in a rush). Eating a home-cooked meal with minimal manual effort frees me to do other things (like going for a walk!), which is so important to surviving.

What is the biggest mistake you've ever made, and how did you recover from it?

The biggest mistake I've ever made, professionally, was not taking a chance and going for a front-line manager position more than a decade ago. The person who ended up in the position became my boss, and my job went from enjoyable to miserable in less than two weeks. I subsequently left the company a month or two later out of sheer frustration, which began a decade-plus of trying to find a new, lasting position somewhere else. While I've definitely learned a ton of interesting and useful things over the past decade, I also lost a lot of progress in career development. Today, as I write this response, I'm miserable! All because I didn't take a chance at a pivotal point in my career. So, the lesson here is to take chances and push yourself, even if it feels uncomfortable at the time. Otherwise, you may not only be left with regrets, but it may also set your career back. Recovery from such setbacks are difficult, lengthy, and—for me—not yet concluded. Ask me in another decade how things have turned out. ∎

"Certifications do not make people more qualified. Some of the best people in the industry don't have any certifications."

Twitter: @TProphet • **Website:** www.seat31b.com

Robert "TProphet" Walker

66 TProphet began writing for *2600: The Hacker Quarterly* while still in high school and authors the Telecom Informer column. He is one of a handful of individuals to have attended every DEF CON and is a cofounder of Queercon (the forefront LGBTQ organization in the InfoSec community) and the founder of the famous TeleChallenge phone-based puzzle challenge. Robert works as an information security architect.

If there is one myth that you could debunk in cybersecurity, what would it be?

"Certifications are a necessary qualification." Certifications do not make people more qualified. Some of the best people in the industry don't have any certifications. Certifications tend to be pursued by people who are pure InfoSec rather than where InfoSec is just part of the job. Also, most certifications issued today didn't even exist when the most senior people in the industry entered it.

What is one of the biggest bang-for-the-buck actions that an organization can take to improve its cybersecurity posture?

Getting the basics right. Most people are compromised, even still, by malicious email attachments, phishing, and clicking dodgy things in browsers. There is also a lack of multifactor authentication and failure to patch systems. That's actually probably one of the top things. A lot of problems can just be prevented in the first place by staying on top of patches. So many enterprises that run Windows don't take Microsoft patches the day they're pushed because they're afraid there's going to be a bad patch. In 13 years at a large Fortune 500 company, there were only two bad patches that I deployed in internal environments. And only one of those caused any disruption—once in 13 years. But, in that same time period, there were a large

> "Most people are compromised, even still, by malicious email attachments, phishing, and clicking dodgy things in browsers."

number of attacks that could have been prevented by patching on time.

How is it that cybersecurity spending is increasing but breaches are still happening?

Spending is *not* really up, actually. In most organizations, it's flat or even down. And this is speaking as somebody who was trying to build a startup in the information security area and sell a product; budgets are down across the board. It's largely because security is constrained to IT budgets, which have to do more with less every year.

But, at the same time as budgets are staying flat or even going down, at least in my view of the industry, the number of attack surfaces has dramatically increased with movement to the cloud. The number of information systems and tools is much larger than it's been in the past because we rely on technology a lot more. And the number of devices that are being used to access information has gone up because we're all running around with a couple of phones and a tablet in addition to a laptop or three. So, when you increase the attack surface by an exponent of 5 or 6 and you don't spend any more on security—or even less—and you don't change any of your existing information security practices (such as not patching on time), then it just makes your organization as a whole a lot more vulnerable.

Not only is there way more stuff to attack than there has been in the past, there are a lot more people doing it because criminals have figured out that they can steal a lot of money by compromising information systems.

Do you need a college degree or certification to be a cybersecurity professional?

It depends. Do you need a certification? Well, to actually do the job, probably not. But, increasingly, it's become a requirement for no particular reason, even though certifications usually don't prove anything other than you spent several hundred dollars on a certification. HR departments all around the world have blindly started adding this as a checklist requirement to the point where I can't get certain gigs because I don't have a certification, even though I've been doing the work since before the related certifications even existed. So, do you need it? Probably not. Do you need it *in practical terms*? Maybe.

I think college degrees are good at exposing you to a whole bunch of different ideas that are outside of the realm of experience you're normally in. You learn a lot of stuff that's not what your degree is in by going to college, and, more importantly, you prove that you can stick with something for four years or longer and come out on the other end of it. So, if you want to go into any kind of management role, it's not a hard requirement, but I think that it is helpful to have in many environments.

Also, you need to be relatable in the role that you're in to the people you're working with. If you're working in an organization that is relatively well educated and you aren't, then that's going to be a problem for you potentially. On the other hand, if you're on the technical side and not managing anybody, you can learn how to do that stuff in high school. You can go straight out of high school (or even drop out of high school) and do this professionally. But, you might hit a wall where your limitation in educational experience is one you can't get beyond. That's not true in every organization nor in every city, but certainly here in Seattle we value education highly.

How did you get started in the cybersecurity field, and what advice would you give to a beginner pursuing a career in cybersecurity?

I got started in high school when I started phreaking. So, I actually started on the black-hat side of things as a juvenile before I was 18. Over time, as I got more education and experience and started working on things professionally, information security became part of my job. By the time I got to a large Fortune 500 company (and was running a fairly substantial IT enterprise for them), security was a pretty big part.

I've never in my career held a pure information security role. Actually, most information security workers do not hold an information security title. That's something that's really important to call out. It's a relatively new thing to have a title of "cyber engineer" or "engineering security something." It's typically been part of an IT job, and, even now, it's still part of an IT job in most places.

What is your specialty in cybersecurity, and how can others gain expertise in your specialty?

I am in a fairly unique position because I've worked across a large variety of disciplines in IT and software development, including research. In addition to that, I have startup experience and an MBA that I got later in my career. Where I sit is at the intersection between business and technology. I can really see technology problems through the lens of being a business problem, but not through a *stupid* lens because I do have technology experience. That's one of the things that happens commonly in our industries. You have businesspeople making decisions and they don't really understand technology at all, or the security implications of the decisions they've made. I'm really, really good at being able to see it across a broad spectrum.

And my last pure information security thing was a startup where we were doing the intersection of physical and digital security, which is another area where there's not a whole lot of overlap.

What is your advice for career success when it comes to getting hired, climbing the corporate ladder, or starting a company in cybersecurity?

That's going to depend on where you're getting hired. If you want to get hired at the Pentagon, then go do cyber-something for the Army and then get hired by a defense contractor on the back end of that to do cyber-something. Work on a cyber-y thing that is very cyber that you can't tell anybody about. You're going to live in a world that's completely different from the commercial space, and you'll probably never really have a lot of success in the commercial space because the thinking and the work are very different.

If you want to be on the commercial side, where do you want to be? There's also a difference between governments, I should point out. There's civilian government, and there's the military side of government. Those are two entirely different sets of roles. If you want to get into the civilian side of government, it's pretty simple. They have a checklist of things you *must* be in order to be able to apply for that job because they have to evaluate everybody equally and score them on a scale. That'll also be the case in pretty much any kind of public hiring, like a university, for example. They'll have some boxes to check, and if you check enough boxes, then you qualify to be interviewed, and then they'll pick somebody who is the most qualified based on some neutral criteria so they don't get sued.

In the commercial space, if you want to work in a company that isn't a software or information security company, familiarity with the industry is helpful. For example, if you want to work in the oil industry, it's great if you know oil field stuff, like the systems and processes they use. A lot of people grow into an information security role inside of the company from some work that they're already doing there. That's a very common thing. You can be in IT for something, then you just start doing more and more security stuff, and they create a security position for you because they realize they need that.

If you want to get into consulting, it's helpful if you have some consulting experience in general. A lot of IT security people work as consultants. The first rule of consulting is that you have to be a good consultant and also know how to do the thing you're consulting on. It kind of goes in that order.

Just like any other job that you're going to find, a lot of the opportunities that are available to you come informally. Most jobs aren't posted someplace; they're positions that are created for someone. You'll want to actually go out and meet the people who you'd potentially want to work with and impress them.

And then there is starting a company. I actually teach a class at The Evergreen State College on how to start your own company, so I'd encourage people to come take that. It's called "Startups and Entrepreneurship." The first rule of starting your own company is figuring out who's going to pay you to do the thing you want to do. Figure out your market. That is job #1 of an entrepreneur. We use a series of techniques called "Lean Startup," where we do rapid iteration in what we call a "build, measure, and learn" loop. Basically, go find people who you think might pay for something, and try to get some validation that they're actually going to pay you to do that. You do enough of those loops, and you'll figure out how many people are buying what you're selling and whether you can build a business around it.

The only other thing that I would say is this: don't rely on being able to raise outside capital. That's what sank my last company. We needed to raise venture capital to be able to do it, and that is exceedingly difficult to do in this space. If you're going to start a company, you might choose something that you can make money with right away, where you don't need any outside investment.

It gets back to these declining budgets that I talked about before. It's a shrinking market in terms of money. It's not a shrinking market in terms of problems, but it is in terms of money being invested. That gives venture capitalists a lot of pause in putting money into this space. It's also more expensive than average to build an information security company because you have to hire people who are very much in demand and have very high salaries. Your costs are higher, but the amount of money being spent is lower; it's just very tough.

What qualities do you believe all highly successful cybersecurity professionals share?

Intellectual curiosity. And another thing: being nice. Most jerks in this business, people who are not nice, may be really brilliant in technology, but they'll never gain a lot of traction. There's only so far you can go. The best people in this industry are nice people who really share and engage a lot with the community and maintain the respect of their peers.

> "Most jerks in this business, people who are not nice, may be really brilliant in technology, but they'll never gain a lot of traction."

Communication skills also matter. You can point to people who are really out in front, and the common thread they all hold is that not only are they really smart technically, but they can explain what they're doing and make things understandable. They're just genuinely nice and they share a lot.

Finally, they're doing this kind of work because it's what they love. If you come into this and you're not intrinsically motivated, you're not the right kind of person to be in this field.

What is the best book or movie that can be used to illustrate cybersecurity challenges?

Sneakers.

What is your favorite hacker movie?

Sneakers, although *Hackers* has better music.

What are your favorite books for motivation, personal development, or enjoyment?

I am a real fan of *The Lean Startup* by Eric Ries. If you're entrepreneurially minded, that is probably the best book to read if you're thinking of starting your own company.

What is some practical cybersecurity advice you give to people at home in the age of social media and the Internet of Things?

Be careful what you click because antivirus won't always protect you and firewalls don't always work. Know that's not the state of things as they should be, but that's the state of how they are today.

What is a life hack that you'd like to share?

I have visited all seven continents without paying any airfare. I am very good at using miles and points to do it. You can read more about some of the hacks and tricks that I like in the travel space at www.seat31b.com.

What is the biggest mistake you've ever made, and how did you recover from it?

I thought my boyfriend loved me and moved to another continent to follow him, but he ended up dumping me. Recovering from it, I got an MBA, started two companies, and learned a lot. ∎

"I'd like to put to rest the idea that preventative security alone can solve all your security problems."

Twitter: @georgiaweidman • **Website:** www.georgiaweidman.com

Georgia Weidman

Georgia Weidman is a serial entrepreneur, penetration tester, security researcher, speaker, trainer, and author. Her work in the field of smartphone exploitation has been featured internationally in print and on television. Georgia has presented or conducted training around the world, including venues such as the NSA, West Point, and Black Hat. She was awarded a DARPA Cyber Fast Track grant to continue her work in mobile device security and is a Cybersecurity Policy Fellow at New America. Georgia is also the author of *Penetration Testing: A Hands-On Introduction to Hacking* from No Starch Press.

67

If there is one myth that you could debunk in cybersecurity, what would it be?

I'd like to put to rest the idea that preventative security alone can solve all your security problems. This may sound strange since that's how most preventative security products are marketed. "Buy our panacea solution and you will never have to worry about security again!" And yet, all these enterprises with their giant security budgets are still getting breached. What's missing? Penetration testing, vulnerability assessment, impact analysis, call it what you want; the missing piece is simply confirming that your security solutions hold up under a simulated attack and then finding the weaknesses and limiting the impact of a successful breach as much as possible. No preventative solution alone can stop sophisticated attacks.

What is one of the biggest bang-for-the-buck actions that an organization can take to improve its cybersecurity posture?

Just do testing! It's all too common to go to Gartner and buy all the things in the top right of all the magic quadrants, turn them on, and consider security taken care of. The security needs of each organization are unique; the risks they have are unique. You cannot fix security with preventative products alone. Testing is a necessary and often-overlooked part of security. How will a real attacker break into your organization? Will they be able to bypass your preventative solutions? (Hint: yes.)

How is it that cybersecurity spending is increasing but breaches are still happening?

Perhaps we are just spending our money on the wrong things. And, don't get me wrong, I get it. As someone who runs a product-oriented startup in the security-testing business, I am constantly up against companies that claim their product fixes everything. "Put our Silver Bullet 3000™ on your network, and mobile and IoT will never be a problem again! BYOD? No Problem!" How can I compete with that when our message is "Install our product and understand what your risks around mobile and IoT are, how to fix them, and the effectiveness of the preventative security controls you have deployed in detecting and stopping attacks?" If I were the (nonsecurity expert) signer of checks, I'd buy Silver Bullet 3000 too. But Silver Bullet 3000 isn't getting the job done.

Do you need a college degree or certification to be a cybersecurity professional?

Well, you might need to be certifiable, but no, you don't need a degree to get started. It certainly helps with getting your foot in the door, though. I have a master's degree in computer science, and all the big contractors just showed up at my school begging for people. I didn't actually have to prove I knew anything about anything to get my first job.

How did you get started in the cybersecurity field, and what advice would you give to a beginner pursuing a career in cybersecurity?

I went to college at 14 and finished in four years, so you might say that in graduate school I kind of treated it like undergrad. I joined a lot of department activities, but it was the Cyber Defense Club that really rang my bell. We played in the Mid-Atlantic Collegiate Cyber Defense Competition (MACCDC), which is basically legal torture. The students were the recently hired security staff of an organization under active attack. We had to keep our systems alive, keep the attackers out, do business injects like installing new services, and periodically get yelled at by a CEO who was really mad about these security breaches. The real goal of the red team (volunteer real hackers) was not so much to breach and destroy our systems but to make us cry and vomit. Naturally, MACCDC was a very stressful and tiring experience. But that first time I saw a popup box (it said "I like turtles") on one of my game machines, I knew it was the red team, and I was hooked. How had they done that from another room? I knew I wanted to do that to people's machines for the rest of my life.

What is your specialty in cybersecurity, and how can others gain expertise in your specialty?

My two areas of concentration are penetration testing and mobile and IoT security. But as an independent researcher and startup founder, I find that, really, I specialize in everything. When I was starting out, it seemed like most of the material available was geared toward experts. I ended up writing the book

I wished I'd had available to me, *Penetration Testing: A Hands-On Introduction to Hacking*. It assumes no prior knowledge and has helped many people breach into the industry.

What is your advice for career success when it comes to getting hired, climbing the corporate ladder, or starting a company in cybersecurity?

Recognize that no one knows everything, and everyone is constantly learning. Everyone feels like a moron sometimes. Don't be like me and beat yourself up about it. There are plenty of people in this industry to do it for you. Never stop learning.

What qualities do you believe all highly successful cybersecurity professionals share?

Perseverance, resilience, and arrogance. In penetration testing, in particular, you are always wrong until you are right. But once you land the shell, it's hard to stop gloating.

What is the best book or movie that can be used to illustrate cybersecurity challenges?

I'll have to go with mine: *Penetration Testing: A Hands-On Introduction to Hacking*.

What is your favorite hacker movie?

You think I have time to watch television? Okay, sometimes I do watch, but I often wonder if doctors come home to watch *House MD*. I assume not, for the same reasons I don't watch movies or TV shows about cybersecurity. So, I'll have to go with the PBS documentary I was in, *Roadtrip Nation: Life Hackers*.

What are your favorite books for motivation, personal development, or enjoyment?

Wuthering Heights, Autobiography of Red, The Secret History, Infinite Jest, A Confederacy of Dunces.

What is some practical cybersecurity advice you give to people at home in the age of social media and the Internet of Things?

The only completely secure system is smashed, melted down, and buried. And even then, I'm not so sure. There is no silver bullet that will make things secure. People have to understand the risk and impact to make informed decisions about how they choose to use technology in our connected world.

What is a life hack that you'd like to share?

I used to work so hard and so single-mindedly that I would routinely burn myself out. After a few rounds of that, I realized something had to give. I re-engaged in my childhood sport of horseback riding. I'm still a super-driven, competitive person, so instead of a relaxing hobby, I compete for equestrian titles. Taking the time to put work aside for a few hours, focus on my riding, and bond with my horse, Tempo, allows me to focus single-mindedly on work the rest of the time.

What is the biggest mistake you've ever made, and how did you recover from it?

It is really hard to A/B test reality. Many things that seemed like big mistakes in the immediate aftermath have come to seem like some of the best decisions of my life so far in hindsight. ■

> "Actively acknowledge the things you won't be proficient in and seek out experts you can call on when you need solid advice on a topic."

Twitter: @MalwareJake • **Website:** www.renditioninfosec.com

Jake Williams

68

InfoSec professional. Breaker of poorly written software. Incident responder. Digital defender. Business bilingual. Jake Williams treats InfoSec like the Hippocratic Oath: first do no harm. By addressing realistic risks, Jake helps businesses create secure environments that actually function. He penetration tests organizations so they can find the weak spots before an attacker does. When an attacker does find a weak spot first, Jake works with the organization to remove the attacker, assess the damage, and remediate the vulnerabilities that allowed the attacker access in the first place. Jake is also a prolific conference speaker, an instructor, and an InfoSec mentor.

If there is one myth that you could debunk in cybersecurity, what would it be?

That everyone who is a cybersecurity expert in one discipline is an expert in all disciplines. Cybersecurity is a broad topic. Nobody knows it all. For instance, I'm an expert in offensive cyber operations, forensics, and incident response. I consider my knowledge base fairly broad, but I'm not a virtualization security expert. When you're starting out, decide what you want to specialize in and focus your studies there. Actively acknowledge the things you won't be proficient in and seek out experts you can call on when you need solid advice on a topic.

What is one of the biggest bang-for-the-buck actions that an organization can take to improve its cybersecurity posture?

Get users out of the local administrators group, and use a solution like LAPS to ensure that local admin passwords aren't shared across workstations. So few organizations do this today that attackers just don't expect it. They'll make lots of noise trying to determine why their normal tricks aren't working.

How is it that cybersecurity spending is increasing but breaches are still happening?

This "conventional wisdom" irks me. The question is asked consistently, but completely ignores the fact that 1) more organizations are digitizing data (increasing the opportunities for breaches), and 2) attackers are getting better at their craft. We should expect more breaches to occur as attackers see more blood in the water. Also, don't expect cybersecurity spending to eliminate breaches. That's not how any of this works. Spending (smart spending, anyway) just makes it *harder* to compromise your network.

Do you need a college degree or certification to be a cybersecurity professional?

This is a contentious topic. I'll tell you that I seek out college graduates for my business because writing and communication are key. Analysts who aren't college educated regularly tell me that they write just as well as college-educated analysts. That may be true in some cases, but it's not true on average. My largest costs are acquiring and training personnel. Even if you're the exception, I'm playing the odds. Also, don't just pay for a college degree. Every employer has universities they avoid like the plague. I won't list them here, but you can probably guess them. As for certifications, meh. Certifications get you an interview; they won't get you the job in most cases. Certifications are useful tools for HR to select candidates. People regularly complain that certs don't indicate knowledge, but I ask how should HR at a Fortune 500 filter the thousands of résumés they receive?

How did you get started in the cybersecurity field, and what advice would you give to a beginner pursuing a career in cybersecurity?

I came through the military and intelligence fields. Go serve your country and get your education paid for by them. But don't assume that by itself will do it. Every year, there are hundreds and perhaps thousands of others taking the same training program you've taken. Do something, anything, to distinguish yourself. This goes double for anyone getting a degree in cybersecurity.

What is your specialty in cybersecurity, and how can others gain expertise in your specialty?

I specialize in offensive cyber operations, forensics, and incident response. These fields are all tied together with a fundamental understanding of how operating systems and applications work (and don't work).

What is your advice for career success when it comes to getting hired, climbing the corporate ladder, or starting a company in cybersecurity?

Show a passion for your craft. Passion is infectious. I've worked in a few industries over the years (and my consulting work has taken me to many more). One thing I've noted consistently is that those who are involved in InfoSec tend to be more passionate about their jobs than those in other fields. I'm not knocking other fields here, just making a point. While you may have gotten away with a humdrum, 9-to-5 attitude somewhere else, that is less likely to fly in InfoSec. If it flies at all, it won't make you successful.

What qualities do you believe all highly successful cybersecurity professionals share?

Passion (as I mentioned earlier) and curiosity. There are so many passionate people in this field, it's hard to stand out (in a good way) if you're not one of them. As for curiosity, this is another critical area. Some of the best research I've ever done came from asking "I wonder what would happen if?" questions. Most people I know who are successful are wildly curious. Finally, I would note that without outside-of-the-box thinking, you're unlikely to be asking the right questions, so I would focus on that as well.

What is the best book or movie that can be used to illustrate cybersecurity challenges?

It's the movie that hasn't been made yet about the Equifax breach(es). I think that movie/book will detail the fact that running a vulnerability management program is *way* harder than people like to give credit for. I'm not excusing Equifax for failing at it, but I think the story will be one we use to illustrate the issues inherent in vulnerability management programs for a long time.

What are your favorite books for motivation, personal development, or enjoyment?

If I can give one recommendation here, it's to read *Good to Great*. This book is critical if you run your own business. If you coordinate with businesspeople (MBAs), assume they've read the book—they almost certainly have. It will give you an immediate common talking point and make you less of an outsider. In other words, read this and you'll have infinite social engineering opportunities. (Also, it's a great book.)

What is some practical cybersecurity advice you give to people at home in the age of social media and the Internet of Things?

Everything you put on the internet is out there forever. Nuance gets lost in character limits. Be careful what you post. We do social media searches for every candidate we look at hiring. The stuff you post today will be with you forever. IoT is a place we're not seeing as much in the way of long-term privacy impacts yet, but given time, it's coming. Be smart about how you use IoT, and always assume someone will sell (or steal) your "private" data later.

What is the biggest mistake you've ever made, and how did you recover from it?

I stayed too long in a job. Constantly re-evaluate whether the job you are in is the right one for you. Just because it was when you took the job doesn't mean that it still is now. Be smart about identifying the right time to move. Complacency will make you a rat on a sinking ship. Once I realized I had stayed too long at a job, I immediately started looking to move and took steps to find another job where I could grow professionally. Surround yourself with people you can learn from. If everyone is coming to you for knowledge and you aren't learning from those around you, it's probably time to make a move. ∎

> "I think the biggest myth surrounding cybersecurity is that someone has to be very technical to get into a system."

Twitter: @rej_ex • **Website:** www.redteam.it

Robert Willis

Robert Willis is a security consultant at 1337 Inc. with a BS in management and certifications in IT and security from Stanford University, USAF, DHS, CompTIA, EC-Council, ELS, and various other organizations. He began his journey into programming and hacking in the late 90s on AOL. Robert is also currently enlisted in the TXSG, working in cybersecurity at Camp Mabry in Austin, Texas.

69

If there is one myth that you could debunk in cybersecurity, what would it be?
I think the biggest myth surrounding cybersecurity is that someone has to be very technical to get into a system. There have been studies showing that most attacks begin with a simple phishing campaign, which doesn't require much skill.

What is one of the biggest bang-for-the-buck actions that an organization can take to improve its cybersecurity posture?
Stay updated on patches; they're free. While working on projects, double-check everything you do. Also, make sure your organization's employees are properly trained to handle social engineering attempts. Humans are the weakest link.

How is it that cybersecurity spending is increasing but breaches are still happening?
Many companies (including very large organizations) don't want to invest in protecting themselves until their lack of security becomes a financial burden

they can measure after their first breach—or if it becomes so bad that even the biggest skeptic would be horrified. Companies look to meet regulatory compliance to continue doing business and avoid fines, but being compliant doesn't make you secure.

Organizations that do take measures to secure themselves rarely have ways to verify that their security is continuously working between penetration tests and vulnerability assessments. I highly recommend breach and attack simulations for this reason.

Do you need a college degree or certification to be a cybersecurity professional?

A degree isn't required for many IT-sector jobs. A degree or certification will get you past HR and get your foot in the door at a lot of places. I know people who don't have a degree or a single certification who are incredible at what they do, but unless someone has a solid network of professionals who know them and their quality of work, they could lose a job opportunity to an entry-level person. Is a degree or certification needed? No. Can it help the nontechnical HR person who knows nothing about security offer you a job? Yes.

How did you get started in the cybersecurity field, and what advice would you give to a beginner pursuing a career in cybersecurity?

I knew at a young age that I wanted to be in cybersecurity after spending countless hours on my old, zombified PC learning everything I could about hacking, programming, and computers in general. I had my first paid cybersecurity job through the military and worked hard to be a security researcher after many years in IT-related roles.

My advice to someone pursuing a career in cybersecurity would be to meet the right people and to surround themselves with other like-minded individuals. Everyone started at square one—learn as much as you can and never give up. Don't jump into advanced topics without laying a solid foundation to understand them fully. Don't have an ego or overlook small details; you'll only hurt yourself.

What is your specialty in cybersecurity, and how can others gain expertise in your specialty?

My specialty is building security programs for organizations seeking to map to compliance for regulatory or business-enablement purposes. I also do many red team/blue team activities for clients, ranging from vulnerability assessments and penetration tests to threat modeling.

What is your advice for career success when it comes to getting hired, climbing the corporate ladder, or starting a company in cybersecurity?

Be humble, and make friends who believe in you (and make sure they are also worth believing in). Know when to ask for help, and know when to offer help to others. I've found that the overlap of my job also being my hobby outside of work greatly helps expand my knowledge; the more you know (and can do) plays a large part in how your employer assesses your value.

What qualities do you believe all highly successful cybersecurity professionals share?

I think the most successful people I've met don't see giving up as an option. Understand that, in many cases, you can achieve what you want; you just have to find the answer. Be willing to be driven crazy while still being able to execute constructive thoughts and actions. Hardworking people can accomplish great things; accomplishing something great usually requires overcoming many difficult tasks.

What is the best book or movie that can be used to illustrate cybersecurity challenges?

Apollo 13. Many things can go wrong, but you have to keep faith and take it home by trying harder.

What is your favorite hacker movie?

I am a big fan of *The Matrix* and *Hackers*. I first saw *Hackers* at a young age and was excited that there was a technical "alternative" culture. I had a love for tech prior to seeing the movie, so this really helped me identify what I wanted to pursue within the field based on my personality and interests. *The Matrix* was released almost 20 years ago and is still one of the best movies ever made.

What are your favorite books for motivation, personal development, or enjoyment?

The Four Agreements is a book that I learned about at work, and it literally changed my life. It's hard to be social when you're on a computer all day; not having deep relationships with other humans can cause self-questioning like, "I hope *X* didn't take what I said the wrong way." As long as you follow the Four Agreements, you have nothing to worry about.

What is some practical cybersecurity advice you give to people at home in the age of social media and the Internet of Things?

Nothing is secure. If you don't want naked pictures of yourself available to individuals unknown to you, don't take them. Also, whenever you create an account, assume that the password is going to end up in a dump somewhere after the company gets pwned. I've known individuals who had very embarrassing passwords that got leaked, and it horrified them. It's just a matter of time before your credentials are out there.

> "Nothing is secure. If you don't want naked pictures of yourself available to individuals unknown to you, don't take them."

What is a life hack that you'd like to share?

It takes less time to do something the right way than it does to do it the wrong way.

What is the biggest mistake you've ever made, and how did you recover from it?

The biggest mistake I made was going to college. I have been on my own since a very young age, so I had to put myself through school. Because of this, it took many years of struggling to get a degree. If I could do it all over again, I would have dropped out of high school, quickly earned a GED, and studied hard for certifications to get an InfoSec job much earlier in life. ■

"Security is a wide subject area and needs everyone from policy writers to exploit developers."

Twitter: @digininja • **Website:** digi.ninja

Robin Wood

70

Hacker, coder, climber, runner. Robin is the co-founder of the UK conference SteelCon, as well as a freelance security tester. He is the author of many tools and is always trying to learn new things.

If there is one myth that you could debunk in cybersecurity, what would it be?

That you have to be a hardcore techie to get into security. Security is a wide subject area and needs everyone from policy writers to exploit developers. Most people don't know that much about their chosen area when they're starting out, but as long as they're prepared to learn on the job and put in the hours, they'll soon develop the skills.

What is one of the biggest bang-for-the-buck actions that an organization can take to improve its cybersecurity posture?

Training their people—and not just the security team; teach all staff at least basic security skills. For example, if product QA knows that something really bad happens if they put a single quote in an input field and get a SQL error message, then you've got a whole department who can now pick up low-hanging fruit. Similarly, explain to normal office users what phishing is and why it's bad, and then give them incentives to look out for it and report it. You now have your frontline acting as an intrusion detection system (IDS).

How is it that cybersecurity spending is increasing but breaches are still happening?

There are more people in the industry, all wanting a piece of the pie and all offering differing services that claim to solve all your problems. Good salespeople sell these as must-haves, and companies buy into the sales pitches without first addressing the fundamentals. Having perfect threat intelligence isn't much use if you're running a 12-month-old WordPress installation. An amazing perimeter firewall isn't much use if the disgruntled receptionist walks out with all your sales data on a memory stick.

Do you need a college degree or certification to be a cybersecurity professional?

No. But depending on the type of company you're looking to work for, it may help you get past HR. If I'm interviewing, then I'll weigh a degree or certificate alongside other things, such as experience and general life skills, so it definitely puts some points on the scorecard, but those points can also be gained through other channels.

How did you get started in the cybersecurity field, and what advice would you give to a beginner pursuing a career in cybersecurity?

The company I was working for had a web server hacked, and I spent 12 hours sitting with the boss going over every line of code in a complex app to try to find the vulnerability. That got me hooked, and from then on, I slowly moved sideways from development into security testing.

The bit of advice I give to everyone is to get yourself a reputation in the community. Create a blog, be active on forums, ask questions on email lists, and go to conferences. The more active you are, the more chance you have of meeting the person who will give you your big break. None of these interactions has to be at a super-elite technical level. For the blog, write stuff up at your level, and don't worry whether anyone will ever read it. Even if they don't, when I interview you, I'll read it, and it will show me that you are prepared to put the time in to learn, understand, and give back.

On mailing lists and forums, don't just ask questions; show your workings to get to the point of asking the question. Say what you've tried, what worked, what failed, and what you are trying to achieve, and, really important, feed back into any answers given. Don't just take an answer, use it, and then drop the thread. If the answer fixed the problem, say so; same if it didn't. And most important, say thanks. Most people who offer help will be doing it on their own time. That "thank you" shows them that their efforts were appreciated.

What is your specialty in cybersecurity, and how can others gain expertise in your specialty?

I mostly test web applications, and I'd recommend doing some development work before learning to test, or at least doing dev alongside it. Understanding how an application works from the inside, and being able to put yourself in the mind of the person who wrote the app, makes a big difference. You'll know the different ways the feature could have been written, what mistakes you made when you developed something similar, and the problems you have to work around.

Having a background in development also helps you talk to the developers during and after the test to explain your findings. You don't just hand off a bland report and leave them to get on with the fixes; you can talk to them and explain (in terms they will understand) what each issue means.

What is your advice for career success when it comes to getting hired, climbing the corporate ladder, or starting a company in cybersecurity?

Something really important for me when I started freelancing was to have cash in the bank before I quit full-time work. It wasn't easy, but I put enough cash aside so I could go six months without getting any work in; this way, there was no initial panic on day one. I've seen a few friends fail, as they didn't have reserves. They didn't get as much work in the first month as they expected and then ran out of cash and had to quit their dreams within three months.

I also had a second job as a climbing instructor, where I worked evenings and weekends to bring in extra cash. It didn't interfere with the 9-to-5(ish) client work, but it did mean that my mortgage was covered each month.

What qualities do you believe all highly successful cybersecurity professionals share?

The ability to get on with things when they can, learn when they need to, and ask questions when they get stuck. You have to be motivated; otherwise, you won't progress. It's important to learn rather than being spoon-fed everything. But realize when you get stuck or don't have time for research. It's okay to ask for help.

What is the best book or movie that can be used to illustrate cybersecurity challenges?

Kevin Mitnick has done some good books. *Kingpin* by Kevin Poulsen and *We Are Anonymous* by Parmy Olson are also good reads.

What is your favorite hacker movie?

Hackers followed by *Sneakers* and *WarGames*.

What are your favorite books for motivation, personal development, or enjoyment?

I don't read much about IT stuff; I prefer biographies and stories from adventure-sports people. I've read some good books by people who have gone from not being able to run a mile or swim a length—but have put in the time and effort—and are now really enjoying their chosen sports. A lot of it mirrors good hackers; they put in their training around their normal 9-to-5 lives—squeezing in a run in the evening, a swim before work, a capture the flag (CTF) after the kids have gone to bed, or reading blog posts over breakfast.

What is some practical cybersecurity advice you give to people at home in the age of social media and the Internet of Things?

Think before you act. Is something too good to be true? If so, then it probably is. Have you spent money with Company X recently? If not, then the refund or invoice is probably a fake.

What is a life hack that you'd like to share?

Have hobbies outside of IT so you spend time away from the screen. I run, climb, and swim; without those, I'd be stuck in front of a screen 24/7, which really isn't good for anyone.

What is the biggest mistake you've ever made, and how did you recover from it?

Being too reliant on one client, who then went bust, owing me quite a bit of cash. I recovered, as I had cash in the bank, but I've made sure to try to spread out my work much more widely since. ■

Epilogue

One of the mind-blowing things that Dug Song talked about was how the meaning of life is to live a meaningful life. For me, this encapsulated a lot of the things I've felt but couldn't fully express. Throughout life, we kind of feel a certain way about stuff, and then, every once in a while, someone comes along and articulates something that really resonates, condensing everything you felt into a few concise words: *the meaning of life is to live a meaningful life.*

Anybody who knows me knows that I quote books all the time. There aren't a lot of books that are actually written from a cybersecurity perspective, and I wanted to create a book where the perspective is from people who have worked in the field. I'm surrounded by a lot of really smart people, and I wanted to share some of my conversations with them. I learn a lot by networking and communicating with the people in this space.

One of the things I hope readers will understand is that some of the folks in this book are very well known, successful, and considered in high regard. I wanted to humanize them because sometimes we think our heroes aren't human. One of the questions I asked was about mistakes, which gave us the opportunity to share how we've messed up and, ultimately, reveal that we're all human.

On Running a Company

There are a lot of cybersecurity companies out there, and it can be hard to differentiate yourself in this field. Cybersecurity is still a relatively new area. Amazon launched EC2 in 2008, and as of the writing of this book, it's been less than 10 years since cloud infrastructure emerged. In some regards, it's a really young industry, and people are rushing to adopt the technologies without really understanding the security ramifications. There are actually a lot of products that don't work, and there are legacy concepts that no longer work. Selling cybersecurity products is a new field and a fast-paced, moving creature. So how do you keep up? How do you differentiate? I don't like to perpetuate myths; I'm a myth-buster. I like to find out what *actually* works, and what doesn't work, and then deliver that to customers.

However, just like anything, some customers and industries are stuck in the past. They're trying to do stuff that was "hot" 15 or 20 years ago. Many of these things have been proven ineffective, but they somehow end up in books or taught in schools. Some companies have cybersecurity lobbyists who manage to get things to become federal regulation or standard. There are a million ways that these bad things get in, and some of them just don't work.

It's like the medical field. Every time they come out with a new medical study, they then figure out, "Oh, snap, we were kind of wrong about that." Every year, the cholesterol story seems to change. Same thing with whole milk versus skim milk. Cybersecurity is somewhat like this, except it's slower. So, whose advice do you trust? How do we become that trusted advisor from a business perspective? For example, people have been told for years to run an antivirus, and now there are folks saying that antivirus is dead. What do you believe? Do you believe antivirus isn't that important because there are people out there saying it isn't? Should you not run an intrusion detection system (IDS) because some people are saying IDSs are dead? That's the struggle in being a security company, right there.

On the Future of Cybersecurity

Back in the 1970s, mainframes were the common thing when you talked about computers. In the '80s, big companies and government agencies were starting to use client-servers in their organizations. Then in the '90s, there was the dot-com boom, where technology became more of a commercial thing. Before that, the client-server side was mostly businesses. However, the dot-com era enabled the creation of B2C, or business to consumer. In the 2000s, cloud computing came into prominence, and companies like Salesforce.com were selling enterprise apps directly to companies (B2B, or business to business).

Then, in 2008, Amazon came out with EC2. This allowed anyone to harness the power of an infrastructure like Amazon. Now any regular person can deploy things. From a security perspective, it totally changed the way businesses operate. Back in the day, security was like digging a moat around an old-school castle to protect it. Now we can all work from home because everything is in the cloud. The next generation of cybersecurity people are going to have to understand how the cloud works. There's a funny saying that goes, "There's no such thing as the cloud; you're just using other people's computers."

A part of going forward is understanding the limitations of this. For instance, if I use Amazon or Microsoft Azure, I have to understand where their security stops and where mine begins. People are going to have to understand how to operate in this kind of environment—where you don't really control everything, but you have to essentially supplement what other people are doing with your data and applications—and then learn how to secure that. You have to understand that going forward.

In the future of cybersecurity, everything is decentralized; you don't own the infrastructure, you may not own the platform, but you still have to defend your data from an internal perspective (your "secret sauce"), and you have to protect your customers' data. The new question is, how do you still ensure that all your corporate secrets are safe and your customers' data is safe?

Staying in Touch

For my last piece of advice, get on Twitter. It's the best way to break into this field. For some reason, all of the cybersecurity people are on it, and they're usually interacting and sharing information. Twitter will be around for a long time, and it's super similar to some of the old-school chat programs, like IRC. So, if you're trying to get into this field, get on Twitter and follow some of the people in this book. We look forward to seeing you there!

Endnotes

1. You can take the test here: https://www.gallupstrengthscenter.com.
2. Peiter Zatko, better known as Mudge, is a prominent hacker and network security expert.
3. Kelly Jackson Higgins, "Top US Undergraduate Computer Science Programs Skip Cybersecurity Classes," *Dark Reading*, July 4, 2016, accessed April 2018, https://www.darkreading.com/vulnerabilities—threats/top-us-undergraduate-computer-science-programs-skip- cybersecurity-classes/d/d-id/1325024.
4. You can read the interview here: https://clutch.co/it-services/failings-cybersecurity-education-interview-professor-ming-chow.
5. Eric Capuano, "Fortune 100 Infosec on a State Government Budget," 2017, accessed April 2018, https://cdn.shopify.com/s/files/1/0177/9886/files/phv2017-ecapuano.pdf.
6. Josh Abraham, "How to Dramatically Improve Corporate IT Security Without Spending Millions," *Praetorian*, accessed April 2018, https://p16.praetorian.com/downloads/report/How%20to%20Dramatically%20Improve%20Corporate%20IT%20Security%20Without%20Spending%20Millions%20-%20Praetorian.pdf.
7. Gary McGraw, "Software Security: The Trinity of Trouble," *Freedom to Tinker*, February 15, 2006, accessed April 2018, https://freedom-to-tinker.com/2006/02/15/software-security-trinity-trouble/.
8. Ming Chow, "How I Hire," *LinkedIn Pulse*, July 15, 2015, accessed April 2018, https://www.linkedin.com/pulse/how-i-hire-ming-chow.
9. You can read the proposal here: https://mchow01.github.io/docs/proposal.pdf.
10. YouTube, "Springfield Nuclear Power Plant—*The Simpsons*," Video, January 19, 2015, accessed April 2018, https://www.youtube.com/watch?v=eU2Or5rCN_Y.
11. Minimalist Mantra: Stop buying the unnecessary. Toss half your stuff, learn contentedness. (Minimalist Mantra, n.d.)
12. https://www.sfs.opm.gov/.
13. Matthew Syed, *Black Box Thinking: Why Most People Never Learn from Their Mistakes—But Some Do*, ebook (New York: Penguin, 2015), accessed May 2018, https://books.google.com/books?id=d-VJBgAAQBAJ.
14. Adobe, "2018 Adobe Cybersecurity Survey," *Slideshare.net*, January 12, 2018, accessed May 2018, https://www.slideshare.net/adobe/2018-adobe-cybersecurity-survey.
15. L. David Mech, "Alpha Status, Dominance, and Division of Labor in Wolf Packs," *Canadian Journal of Zoology* no. 77: 1196-1203, Jamestown, ND: Northern Prairie Wildlife Research Center Online, http://www.npwrc.usgs.gov/resource/2000/alstat/alstat.htm. (Version 16 May 2000).

16. Alex Stamos (@alexstamos), "1) Unify behind cloud SSO (Okta, OneLogin); 2) Two-factor (Duo, Yubikey); 3) Push IT to ditch Exchange for GSuite or O365," *Twitter*, May 3, 2018, https://twitter.com/alexstamos/status/992206933418430465.

17. Fahmida Y. Rashid, "LinkedIn CISO: How We Bring Diversity into Security with the Stories We Tell," *Decipher*, April 13, 2018, accessed May 2018, https://duo.com/decipher/linkedin-ciso- bringing-diversity-into-security-with-the-stories-we-tell.

18. YouTube, "WarGames: The Two-Factor Edit," Video, June 5, 2014, accessed May 2018, https://www.youtube.com/watch?v=WH_KuCCf0c0.

19. Christina DesMarais, "25 of the Most Inspiring Books Everyone Should Read," *Inc.com*, February 16, 2017, accessed May 2018, https://www.inc.com/christina-desmarais/25-of-the-most- inspiring-books-everyone-should-read.html.

Bibliography

Abraham, Josh. "How to Dramatically Improve Corporate IT Security without Spending Millions." *Praetorian*. Accessed April 2018. https://p16.praetorian.com/downloads/report/How%20to%20Dramatically%20Improve%20Corporate%20IT%20Security%20Without%20Spending%20Millions%20-%20Praetorian.pdf.

Adobe. "2018 Adobe Cybersecurity Survey." *Slideshare.net*. January 12, 2018. Accessed May 2018. https://www.slideshare.net/adobe/2018-adobe-cybersecurity- survey.

Capuano, Eric. "Fortune 100 Infosec on a State Government Budget." 2017. Accessed April 2018. https://cdn.shopify.com/s/files/1/0177/9886/files/phv2017- ecapuano.pdf.

Chow, Ming. "How I Hire." *LinkedIn Pulse*. July 15, 2015. Accessed April 2018. https://www.linkedin.com/pulse/how-i-hire-ming-chow.

DesMarais, Christina. "25 of the Most Inspiring Books Everyone Should Read." *Inc.com*. February 16, 2017. Accessed May 2018. https://www.inc.com/christina- desmarais/25-of-the-most-inspiring-books-everyone-should-read.html.

Flora, Matteo. 2015. Claudio Guarnieri

Jackson Higgins, Kelly. "Top US Undergraduate Computer Science Programs Skip Cybersecurity Classes." *Dark Reading*. July 4, 2016. Accessed April 2018. https://www.darkreading.com/vulnerabilities—threats/top-us-undergraduate-computer- science-programs-skip-cybersecurity-classes/d/d-id/1325024.

McGraw, Gary. "Software Security: The Trinity of Trouble." *Freedom to Tinker*. February 15, 2006. Accessed April 2018. https://freedom-to-tinker.com/2006/02/15/software-security-trinity-trouble/.

Mech, L. David. "Alpha Status, Dominance, and Division of Labor in Wolf Packs." *Canadian Journal of Zoology* no. 77: 1196-1203. Jamestown, ND: Northern Prairie Wildlife Research Center Online. http://www.npwrc.usgs.gov/resource/2000/alstat/alstat.htm. (Version May 16, 2000).

Minimalist Mantra: Stop buying the unnecessary. Toss half your stuff, learn contentedness. Minimalist Mantra, n.d.

Rashid, Fahmida Y. "LinkedIn CISO: How We Bring Diversity into Security with the Stories We Tell." *Decipher*. April 13, 2018. Accessed May 2018. https://duo.com/decipher/linkedin-ciso-bringing-diversity-into-security-with-the-stories-we-tell.

Stamos, Alex (@alexstamos). "1) Unify behind cloud SSO (Okta, OneLogin); 2) Two- factor (Duo, Yubikey); 3) Push IT to ditch Exchange for GSuite or O365." *Twitter*. May 3, 2018. https://twitter.com/alexstamos/status/992206933418430465.

Syed, Matthew. *Black Box Thinking: Why Most People Never Learn from Their Mistakes—But Some Do*. Ebook. New York: Penguin, 2015. Accessed May 2018. https://books.google.com/books?id=d-VJBgAAQBAJ.

YouTube. "Springfield Nuclear Power Plant—The Simpsons." *Video*, January 19, 2015. Accessed April 2018. https://www.youtube.com/watch?v=eU2Or5rCN_Y.

YouTube. "WarGames: The Two-Factor Edit." *Video*. June 5, 2014. Accessed May 2018. https://www.youtube.com/watch?v=WH_KuCCf0c0.